'OMG, what an amazing story. This book really takes you into the heart of South America, but what makes it such a great read is not just the gripping travel story, it's the love story between a young woman on her first trip abroad and a Peruvian artisan. And beneath that is the compelling tale of a woman searching for and ultimately finding, self-love and self-acceptance.'

– Lisa Messenger,
Collective Hub

'This book is fucking fantastic. It made me feel young again. These are the adventures that we only ever dream of, that are reserved for the truly free. Leigh, you love hard and let your soul take the wheel. The minute I closed it, I wanted to buy a one-way ticket to anywhere. Thank you for sharing and for waking me up. I couldn't put this book down. My husband stole it off me, he is a book snob, has read everything and absolutely fell in love with you and your story. Someone has to make it into a movie!! Love love love and gratitude and fire.'

– Constance Hall,
author of *Like a Queen* and *Still a Queen*

This is a book that will sweep you along in its narrative. Extremely personal, raw and honest, Leigh doesn't hesitate to question her decisions, expose her choices for what they sometimes were, and plumb the depths of her own psyche as she takes the reader on this passionate, wild adventure — of love, of culture and of people. I thoroughly enjoyed this, and am looking forward to the sequel. What a ride! What a life.

– Karen Brooks,
author of *The Locksmith's Daughter* &
The Chocolate Maker's Wife

A compelling memoir that beautifully captures the emotional intensity that its author discovers in South America, just as the wave of the 1990s self-help culture was on the rise. But this memoirist never paints herself as a saint amongst sinners, she looks back to this emotive odyssey with great courage, recreating her naivety but also her explorer's heart at a distance. The manner in which Robshaw captures every setting and encounter is more than journalism or travelogue, it's a soul journey. The result is full of pathos, wrong turns, u-turns, and the hope of a creative's heart. Go on the journey with Leigh Robshaw, if you're of the same generation (as I am), it's a great reminder of the period when we all faced a few demons abroad and learned more about home in the process.

– Michael Burge,
author, journalist and founder of the
High Country Writers Festival

You Had Me at Hola

In search of love and truth
in South America

A memoir

LEIGH ROBSHAW

MORPHO
BOOKS

A catalogue record for this book is available from the National Library of Australia

First published in 2019

Paperback ISBN: 978-0-6485626-0-3

Ebook ISBN: 978-0-6485626-1-0

Published in Australia by Morpho Books, 2019
PO Box 56
Maleny, Queensland 4552
Australia

All inquiries should be made to the author.
Email: leighrobshaw@gmail.com
Website: leighrobshaw.net

Cover design: Nolito Fortaliza Jr.

For Herrin

AUTHOR'S NOTE

In writing this book, I referred to personal journals and letters, conducted research and consulted several of the people who appear in the story. I also relied on my memory of events and the places I visited. Some names have been changed or identifying details modified in order to preserve anonymity. All characters in this book are people I know or have known and where possible, I have consulted with them before going to print.

CHAPTER ONE

IN A MARKET in San Telmo, I meet an artisan. It's my third day in Buenos Aires and I am besotted with the place; with the way music inhabits every part of the city, seeps out of crevices in buildings both crumbling and new, as if it's the force that holds everything together. The people speak Spanish in a whispery tone and their beauty scares me. I am a wild, unkempt creature on the loose. I have a vicious desire for adventure, a voracious need for love so intense, I will not return home until my bones bend me into a different shape. Until my veins run with fresh blood; dark blood, from this strange and beautiful and better place. I am so sick of living with my own blood.

As I stroll through the market on this slow Sunday afternoon, the scent of barbecued flesh sticks to my nostrils. Music and laughter, my eyes flicking from one strong face to the next, sunlight beaming off a dancing girl's bangles. A man with brown biceps thumps out a Latin rhythm on a *cajón* and sweat beads bounce off his skin. I hide behind cheap plastic sunglasses and smile. I am here. I am finally here and I am free. It's mine, this whole continent is mine to explore and it might take forever.

I smile again at that thought and this time, my smile is returned. The artisan thinks I am smiling at him and comes over. Love has eluded me at home, but today, it comes quickly and effortlessly. If you don't count me flying halfway around the world in search of it, you could say I fall in love without even trying.

I see the Andes in his high cheekbones and thick black hair curling around his collar. I'm sure he's from Peru. He's not tall, but he's tall enough. In high heels I'd be taller, but I never wear high heels. He's not muscular like the guy playing the *cajón*. He's a gentler soul, boyish but with something streetwise about him.

'Hola,' he says. A roll of wire hangs in the crook of his arm and he's holding a pair of pliers. I glance at his hands; not the rugged hands of a labourer or a fighter or a farmer, but not feminine either. Somewhere in between.

'Hola,' I answer. 'Hablas Ingles?'

'No,' he smiles. 'You speak Spanish?'

'Un poquito.' *A little bit.* That's stretching it.

He looks at me for a moment.

'No importa.'

In a swift gesture, he grabs my hand and leads me away from the market, tossing a request of some sort over his shoulder to one of the market vendors. He walks in a jaunty way that excites me and I fall into step with him.

'Vamos a tomar una cerveza.'

Cerveza means beer. Every traveller knows that.

'Me llamo Gabriel,' he says. *My name is Gabriel.* This name takes me by surprise. I am expecting a Javier, a Julio, an Enrique. He looks too playful, too mischievous, to be a Gabriel.

We walk in silence to the corner of the park and out into the street, holding hands, smiling the goofy smiles of children caught in a current that feels fun and exciting, before they realise there's danger ahead.

We stop at a corner kiosk that sells cigarettes, chewing gum and beer. Gabriel jams his hand down the front pocket of his jeans, pulls a few coins out and says something to the man behind the counter, who looks me up and down. He's standing on a platform, which gives him a good view of my cleavage. He nods his approval, then reaches behind the counter and hands Gabriel a condom.

Gabriel laughs and shakes his head, says a few words I don't understand and looks at me, smiling. I have no idea what's being said, what words of knowing are passing between the two men and I could walk away, but I don't. The vendor hands over a large bottle of Quilmes beer and I'm relieved when we head back to the relative obscurity of the park.

We sit on a soft patch of grass in the sun and Gabriel opens the bottle, splashes a few drops of beer on the ground and says, *para la Pacha*—for Pachamama. She is the Andean earth goddess, sacred to Peruvians and Bolivians, and I am charmed by this simple way of honouring nature. It seems to come naturally to him, like a prayer of thanks before eating a meal.

We sit close, sip cold beer out of the same bottle and attempt to understand each other. We weave together the words we know in Spanish and English into a tapestry that slowly comes to life. We cling to the words that sound the same in both languages and laugh at our attempts at sign language as the flow of cars, trucks, buses and taxis in the surrounding streets slows and the happy market sounds fade.

I am twenty-three. He is twenty-six. I believe in the wisdom of the heart, ripe for a chance meeting that could pull me into the shape of an entirely new person. I have no love for logic and reason, no wish to consider consequences. Supernatural forces are at work, guiding me towards something transcendent.

'Soy artesano,' he says. *I am an artisan.* I know it's not just his job; it's who he is. It sounds ancient and artistic, the occupation of a man driven by creativity and beauty rather than money. I don't trust people who are driven by money alone. I have little respect for it and how it corrupts people, so I have scraped together just enough to get myself to South America and travel rough.

He says my hair is like noodles of gold. He likes my green eyes, my pink mouth, my nose. *Ojos, boca, nariz.* As he says each new word in Spanish, I am able to understand it. Something about his clear accent and the way he forms words, floats them into my brain in a form I can comprehend.

Dusk folds into the fading afternoon and darkens the city sky. I think I've been gone for a long time; how long, I don't know. I don't wear a watch.

'I have to go.' I point in the direction of the hostel.

'No,' he says, grabbing my hand. 'No te vayas.' *Do not go.*

A peck on the cheek to say goodbye, which is the local custom, becomes a full kiss on the lips. Much later, when we know each other well, he'll say it was me who kissed him first, but I will remember it being the other way around.

The lanterns of San Telmo cast a ghostly glow through its old streets and I sense stories coming to life around me in the summer night air, in the muscle and breast and seduction of this place. I feel lifetimes of stories, I hear them suspended in the melodies that waft through cobblestone alleyways.

I have entered a culture with deep roots; deeper than my own, which feel barely deeper than the topsoil. Fragile roots that could be pulled out and snapped in two. Lost stories of broken people. I want these deep, old roots to entangle me now. Here I can become someone special, someone extraordinary. Someone worthy of love.

'Ven conmigo,' he whispers. *Come with me.* His face is smooth and free of stubble and I trust that smooth skin. He leads me into a secluded grove and we lie together beneath a giant tree, hidden from the moonlight in its shadows. A bright spot of torchlight shines from a car passing through the park and we freeze. It's the police, checking the park for vagabonds, like us. We cover each other's mouths to mute our laughter.

'No te muevas,' he says. *Don't move.* He is lying on top of me and our faces are so close they're almost touching. We are perfectly still, his black eyes, my green eyes and the moon. Before I'd left Australia, I had eagerly listened to many warnings about South American men and how they weren't to be trusted, then promptly ignored them all.

He calls me *loca* and he's right: I am crazy. One day I will learn his language so fluently I will begin dreaming in it and I will know love has rewired my brain. When I can finally talk to him with ease, I'll ask him everything I want to know about him, find out who he really is. But some certain part of me already senses he is a good person. A man who would never hurt me. And so on our first night together, in a grand old park in San Telmo, I take the kind of risk only a naïve young girl in desperate need of love would take.

CHAPTER TWO

MY FRIEND EMILY doesn't have a thing for Latinos, the way I do, but she does have a thing for travel. She would have been happy with India or Southeast Asia when we'd met a year earlier, but I'd said let's go further and she'd readily agreed. We worked in the same office building in Surry Hills and bonded over vegetarianism, grunge music and a mutual desperation to embark on our first big overseas adventure.

Fresh out of university, I was working at a New Age newspaper called *The Planet*. Every new self-help book would land on my desk for review, from *The Celestine Prophecy* to *The Alchemist*, feeding my desire to pursue spiritual experiences in mystical places. South America wasn't just a dream—it was an obsession bordering on a mental health disorder.

Emily was a graphic designer for a promotions company in the same building and we'd spent all of 1994 planning our trip over tofu salads and soy lattes. We'd bought identical blue backpacks, one copy of the brick-like *Footprint South American Handbook* to share so we didn't have to lug two around and on February 3, 1995, said an eager adios to Australia. We planned to start in Argentina and spend three months backpacking through Brazil, Bolivia and Peru, then fly to London to work and replenish our savings.

Once settled on the plane, I had taken out my journal. On its cover was a picture of a little pig gleefully flying through space, orbiting the Earth just above South America. I opened it to the first page and wrote: 'I am flying to freedom'.

My first glimpse of South America was of the mountains of Patagonia with a frosting of snow on their brown peaks. It was a formidable landscape that made the Blue Mountains look like mere hills. Pools of bright blue water dotted the arid valleys and I didn't think my little Instamatic camera could capture even a fraction of that beauty, but my forehead stayed stuck to the plane window and my finger kept clicking as we flew towards Buenos Aires.

We arrived to a frenzy of cab drivers shouting across the airport, seemingly desperate to nab customers, and quickly attached ourselves to a driver with a trustworthy face, asking him to take us straight to our hostel in San Telmo. The faded grandeur of the city's oldest *barrio* had moved me in a way no shiny new neighbourhood could. It had an old soul, with narrow streets and colonial buildings adorned with lanterns and intricate cast iron verandahs. A place where wrinkled old men, with the colour and smell of tobacco seared into their skin, lingered in dimly lit bars, drinking strong drinks and talking strong politics with angry hands cutting through smoky air. It was where tourists and backpackers mixed with performers, artisans, musicians and antiques vendors.

The backpackers at the hostel—mostly German, Canadian, North American and English—were more Emily's speed than mine. She chatted like she'd known them for years. I admired her instant familiarity with people. Tall and slim with sparkling blue eyes, bee-stung lips and strawberry blonde hair she wore in a choppy bob, she was a bubbly girl and always up for some fun.

Armed with the guidebook, we'd spent our first two days visiting the landmarks of Buenos Aires: the Casa Rosada and the Plaza de Mayo, the Botanical Gardens, the Obelisk and El Teatro Colon. The swarthy young city dwellers wore skintight jeans and rock band T-shirts and were exceptionally good-looking, with long dark hair, serious eyes and strong chins. Emily and I chose comfort and convenience over sex appeal, in chunky brown leather hiking boots and not a scrap of makeup. We did not turn any handsome heads in this glamorous place, which had the elegance and style of a European city. Every new street sign, or doorway or storefront captured my interest, but it was the gritty guts of the continent I craved.

We returned to San Telmo that afternoon with aching, sweaty feet, showered at the hostel and wandered down the alleyway to hang out at Plaza Dorrego, buzzing with a mix of tourists and locals. The moody melody of a *bandoneón*, a billowy sounding concertina, washed over the square. A slim woman with short black hair, a slinky black dress and a red feather boa wrapped a spindly, fish-netted leg around a man in a suit and a black fedora. They danced the tango like two spiders performing a mating ritual and tourists photographed the famous dance in its home town and tossed coins into a guitar case. I snapped a couple of photos and turned my attention to the people on the periphery. The little old lady in black shuffling past, buckling under the weight of grocery bags. The old men in hats, smoking cigarettes. I focused my attention on the people who didn't know they were being watched.

We danced our own dorky version of salsa and drank beer with backpackers in the bars around Plaza Dorrego all night. We did the same the next night and by day three, I was eager for more. Day three was the day I left Emily in the hostel sleeping off jetlag mixed with a hangover. Day three was the day I set off strolling around San Telmo without the heavy guidebook, hoping fate would guide me towards something extraordinary. Not hoping—willing.

As I walked alone along Calle Defensa, black taxis sharked past me and leering men hissed and whistled. I saw a park up ahead, a haven away from the sleaze. Parque Lezama. In the northwest corner of the park, I found the market and entered a new world.

CHAPTER THREE

I AM ONLY half-right about Gabriel being Peruvian. He does have a Peruvian father, but his mother is Argentinian. He looks more like his darker-skinned father and while he was born in the Andean northwest region of Argentina, he grew up in Lima. His family aren't wealthy, but neither are they poor, not by South American standards. His father owns a truck and delivers industrial salt to factories around Lima, a business Gabriel and his brother Jorge are expected to take over one day.

But Gabriel is a creative soul with dreams of his own, so he has left home to travel South America selling earrings, bracelets and necklaces he makes by hand in the style of Peruvian wire jewellery. With a roll of alloy wire and three pliers, he can transform semi-precious stones into treasures to adorn the wrists, necks and earlobes of ladies without the money or inclination for diamonds and pearls.

He tells me about his family and his travels as we stroll through the dark corners of Parque Lezama hand-in-hand, walking in sync. How his father had been hurt when he left. But he knows there is more for him and he will return to Lima one day a success. He'll make his father proud.

A group of young locals with guitars, smoking weed and playing the folk songs of León Gieco, Argentina's Bob Dylan, have gathered on the stairs of the amphitheatre. Gabriel bellows the words as he passes me the joint, and no one asks me where I'm from. I have a few tokes and pass it on. It's strong stuff and within minutes, I'm floating.

'I like to play with balls,' I hear myself say to the group. I'd been given juggling balls by a Sydney friend as a farewell gift and have been teaching myself to juggle. I have chosen this moment to announce my juggling skills to the group, but in my limited Spanish, it sounds like I enjoy tickling testicles.

They fall silent and stare at me; then Gabriel breaks the silence.

'Buenisimo! Let's go, baby,' he says, and they fall about laughing.

I sound like an idiot, but I don't care. With Gabriel by my side, I belong.

He walks me back to the hostel in the early hours of the morning and I invite him into the women's dormitory to write down his phone number and address. It's against the rules to bring him inside, but so what? Rules are boring. We are invincible.

We tip-toe into the dark room of seven sleeping women and sit on my bottom bunk. We giggle a little too much and kiss a little too long and the hostel manager, Antonio, bursts into the room. He switches on the lights, waking the dorm and sparking a cascade of complaints in at least three different languages. He shouts something at Gabriel, and Emily blinks awake, shaking her head at me in disbelief.

Antonio is furious at me for bringing 'Peruvian scum' into the hostel, warning the women to check their belongings for missing passports and money. I don't even consider checking mine. He grabs Gabriel by the arm and drags him outside into the street. He's unperturbed as he falls onto the footpath, laughing and calling out to me. I pick up the words *mi casa* and *mañana*, which I know mean my house and morning. Before Antonio slams the heavy timber door and locks it, I catch one last glimpse of Gabriel, laughing like a mischievous boy. He's so unfazed, it's like this sort of thing happens to him all the time. I wonder why Antonio was so angry and if he's right about Peruvians. Gabriel just doesn't strike me as a thief.

I can't sleep. I lie in my sleeping bag on my narrow bunk running over and over the previous day as I wait for dawn. The other girls are still asleep as I creep out of the hostel, somehow get on the right buses and make my way to Gabriel's apartment.

He makes me a potato tortilla for breakfast and tells me in a mix of Spanish and sign language that he has come to Buenos Aires from Lima to stay with his sister Elsa, who has a good job in a bank. She's putting him up for a while so he can make some money selling jewellery in comparatively affluent Buenos Aires, before returning to the dirty slog of Lima to help his parents. His heart isn't in it, but he's obliged to go back.

Elsa has already left for work, so we have the place to ourselves. He excuses himself to have a shower and I look around. It's a bright, comfortable apartment with two bedrooms. Family photos in silver frames are displayed on a timber sideboard. Gabriel with Jorge, his older brother, and their parents: his father is obese and balding with dark skin and a friendly smile; the mother is tiny with greying hair pulled into a bun and chubby cheeks. Elsa has her mother's lighter complexion, while Gabriel and Jorge are dark.

Wearing only a towel, he runs his hands over my white skin and asks me about my scars. The biggest one is a grotesque gash about twenty centimetres long on my lower right leg.

'Que pasó?' he asks, running his finger along it. *What happened?*

'I stood on a glass coffee table to feed our pet bird when I was about eleven and fell through it. It severed my artery and blood was spurting everywhere, like a fountain. All the fat was hanging out and I could see my shin bone.'

'Dios mio!' he says and leans down to kiss it.

I'm taken aback. I've always hated that scar. I remember how embarrassed I was to go to school after they removed the forty-five stitches and I was left with an angry red reminder of my own stupidity. I have always worried men would find it repulsive.

'What happened here?' he asks, rubbing his fingers across my upper back.

My tattoo. I was so desperate to get a tattoo the second I turned eighteen, I had my appointment booked in well before my birthday. It was an act of rebellion and an attempt to feel special. I saw a picture I liked on a set of French fortune telling cards and impulsively decided on it, putting little thought into finding a meaningful design that would mark my skin for the rest of my life. It was a red heart with purple, white and blue roses sitting above it and green vines winding down and around it. To me, it symbolised love, and that was reason enough to get it inked into my skin forever. But the tattoo artist drew the heart a bit wonky and it ended up looking like an apple.

'It's a love heart with roses,' I say, matter-of-factly.

'It looks like an apple,' he says.

'No it doesn't!'

'Sí, it does. You must really love apples!'

We roll around on the bed while he teases me about my apple tattoo and I laugh and am completely comfortable with him. My hands explore all of his smooth brown skin that day and we have no need for words.

In the late afternoon, he takes me to catch the bus back to San Telmo. Emily and I have flights to Iguazu Falls the next morning and from there, we will embark on our three-month trip around the continent. We have planned to return to Buenos Aires before going to London, but only for one day. My mind is scrambling to come up with a way to spend more time with Gabriel. This chance encounter has unsettled me. I wanted something like this to happen, just not so soon. If it weren't for Emily, I'd change my plans and stay with him. I don't care what people say about Peruvian men, about South American men. How they can't be trusted.

'Un regalo para ti,' he says. *A gift for you.* As we wait for the bus, he pulls a wire contraption threaded with small beads from his satchel. He pushes and pulls the wires, transforming it into a globe, a cup and a flower. He says it's a mandala and asks me to carry it on my journey, and to think of him. He also gives me a simple pair of hematite earrings. I study the metallic-grey stone, cut at angles to reflect the light. Not a pretty stone, but it's a piece of him, so I put the earrings straight into my earlobes and tuck the mandala into a small brown suede bag I wear across my body.

We ask a passerby to take a photo of us and we sit close on a bench, his arm around my shoulder. Then he snaps one of me sitting on my own, hands me the camera and gives me one last kiss before I get on the bus. It feels wrong to be leaving him.

The next morning, Emily and I eat the hostel's free breakfast of white bread rolls with *dulce de leche*, a caramel spread so sweet it's a heart attack in a jar, and strong coffee. Emily fills me in on her day without me. She'd visited Cementerio de la Recoleta and the grave of Eva Perón and I feel terrible for leaving her. And Evita's final resting place. How have I missed seeing such an iconic monument?

I'm six again. I'm playing *Don't Cry for Me Argentina* on my grandparents' pianola over and over again, shaking my head when Grandma asks through her wheezing asthma voice if I want to speak to my father on the phone. I don't know where he lives, but it's not with me and Mum and my brother. Sometimes I do talk to him, just so Grandma doesn't look so sad. But I don't know him, don't know what to say to him. I go back to the pianola and pedal hard, watching the scroll's tiny holes roll around faster and faster: *I had to let it happen, I had to change. Couldn't stay all my life down at heel, looking out of the window, staying out of the sun. So I chose freedom. Running around trying everything new…* A ghost is playing the piano keys and I have no idea who Evita is, but she sounds sadder than Grandma.

Emily says it's okay I'd left her alone in Buenos Aires so I could spend the day with Gabriel, but I know it isn't. I've ditched her twice now and she also copped a serve from Antonio, the hostel manager, for my irresponsible behaviour. She's come all this way to travel with me, and I'm being a selfish bitch.

She's not talking much over breakfast, which is unusual for her. I sense her irritation. This is not a good start to our epic adventure. It pains me to admit it, but I can't abandon our plans and stay in Buenos Aires with Gabriel. I have to stick to the program, but then I will come back and be with him. If he still wants me after three months. She will have to go to London alone, I decide. She'll be okay, she has family and friends there.

We've booked a taxi to take us to the airport, but I need to speak to him before we leave. I pick up the wall phone in the hostel, unlace my boot and take out my passport. Bum bags are a target for thieves, so I travel with my passport in the sole of my boot. It's uncomfortable to walk on, but the passport gradually moulds to the shape of my foot, like the sole of a Birkenstock sandal. The navy blue cover is already beginning to stink. I find the piece of paper Gabriel has scribbled his number on, wedged inside my passport.

I dial his number and hear a strange ring tone, different to the short *bleep bleep* of an Australian ring tone. How can I explain over the phone, in a language I don't know, that I think I've fallen in love with him? Maybe I should keep that ridiculous thought to myself.

He answers quickly and as I hold my English-Spanish dictionary, the receiver sandwiched between my shoulder and my ear, I cherry-pick words.

'I will write to you,' I plead into the phone. 'Write letter! Um… escribir carta.' I kick the wall with my boot. I try to say I'll see him in three months, tres meses. Tres meses, okay?

'Sí, sí, sí,' he says quickly, like he's going to lose me. 'Tres meses. Por favour, please, escribame una carta… write me the letter.'

He pauses. 'Te quiero,' he says.

I love you.

Chapter four

RESIDENCIA EL TUCÁN looks more like a home for stray cats and dogs than a hostel. It is definitely not a residence for toucans, the only creature I can't see living here. Doña Irma's rambling old cottage is home to at least twenty cats, ten mangy dogs chewing fleas off their legs, and an unpleasant number of geese.

We arrive at Doña Irma's place after a two-hour flight from Buenos Aires to Puerto Igauzú. A room in her rustic animal palace is only $US3 a night, so it's a popular hangout for travellers, roving musicians and artisans with no money.

A tiny woman with a mop of grey hair, Doña Irma is a cuddly ragdoll who welcomes us with open arms and chamomile tea. She's so busy looking after the animals, she says she only sleeps three hours a night and complains about the dogs spreading shit-stained toilet paper around the house. The sewage systems of South America can't cope with flushed toilet paper, so it gets placed in a bin beside the toilet, which may or may not have a lid. Doña Irma's doesn't.

She's complaining about those bloody dogs as she shows us to our small, dusty rooms. My bed is covered in cats and they looked pissed off at having to move.

'Fuera!' She shouts at the cats to get off the bed and clouds of dust and hair float into the air. I picture the bony cats riddled with fleas and worms, which may have laid eggs on my pillow. I let my backpack thump to the wooden floor, glad to release its weight from my back and shoulders, and flop onto the bed.

Images of Gabriel's boyish smile immediately fill my mind. His chocolatey lips. The playful twinkle in his dark eyes. I jump off the bed and silver filaments of cat hair float through the air and dance around a confetti of dust, illuminated in the afternoon light streaming through a cracked window. I rifle through my backpack, flinging undies and T-shirts onto the floor, pull out my Spanish-English dictionary and sit on the bed to write Gabriel a letter.

It's a passionate outpouring of emotion I'm sure makes absolutely no sense. I pluck words from the dictionary like grapes and string them into fruity sentences that showcase my complete ignorance of Spanish grammar. I leave Emily, who is attempting to chat to Doña Irma in the kitchen, and walk into town to post it, unsure of how or where I will get a reply.

The only way we can stay in touch with people is to find a phone box, which may or may not work, or send postcards and letters. We tell our families and friends to write to us at the post restante equivalent, the *lista de correos*, at the main post offices of Rio, Salvador or Lima, but really, who knows where we're going to end up?

Back in Buenos Aires, I'd told Gabriel we were going to travel from Iguazu Falls by bus to Rio de Janeiro, then up the east coast of Brazil to Salvador in the north, then along the Amazon River by boat to Manaus. From there we could take another boat to Peru, or fly to Bolivia. Maybe even go to Venezuela. We could change our plans on a whim.

'But I definitely want to see Machu Picchu, the Nazca Lines and Lake Titicaca,' I'd told him, as he stroked my back that day in Elsa's apartment.

'Lago Titicaca… titi por Peru y caca por Bolivia,' he had joked about the lake that straddles both countries. Tits for Peru and shit for Bolivia. I'd laughed at his irreverence and thought, there is no man on this earth I would rather be with. I barely know him, but my heart knows him and strangely, I feel at peace with him. When you're that sure about something, critical thinking only gets in the way.

I post the letter and find a one-hour photo shop. My first roll of film will have the photo of us together on it and I'm desperate to see it. I wait on a plastic chair out of the heat until it's ready, jump up, thank the attendant with a bunch of pesos and stand there, flipping through the stack of thirty-six photos.

The shots I'd taken of Patagonia from the plane have turned out well. There's a photo of Emily and me with beaming faces in front of an Italian restaurant, opposite the hostel on our first night in Buenos Aires. A series of touristy shots of us in front of city landmarks and at the lollipop-coloured shacks of La Boca, and then there it is: the photo of Gabriel and me sitting together on a park bench near Elsa's apartment. He has his arm around my shoulder. Long strands of my hair, lit up in the afternoon sun, fall across his brown hand.

But something is wrong. The film hasn't wound on properly, and the other photo he took of me sitting alone has been transposed sideways onto the same print. I am a ghostly image, eyes cast down, with a quizzical half-smile, like the Mona Lisa. I sit back down on the plastic chair and look closely. The photo lab attendant blatantly stares at me as I stare at the photo, trying to work out what it means. If it's a sign from the universe I will be with Gabriel for a time, but ultimately, I will end up alone. Unworthy of the love of a man so beautiful. It is unthinkable he could be unworthy of me.

The roar of Iguazu Falls is so loud you can't hear anything else but the torrent of water when you stand close and even if you try and shout over it, the sound is swallowed up. The fresh smell of gushing water mixed with earth, rocks and jungle fills my being and bathes my soul, beating my anxiety into submission. It is the closest thing to God I have ever experienced. I stand near the places where it falls most powerfully, let it spray me in the face, purify me. Like Nature's baptism. The raging water calms my incessant mind in the same way blaring rock music at bedtime drowns my thoughts and allows me to sleep.

I'd first seen Iguazu Falls as a teenager in the film *The Mission*. Spellbound by their beauty and magnitude, I began to search for novels set in South America. I discovered Isabelle Allende and Gabriel García Márquez and allowed those tales of magical realism to swallow me like quicksand. I loved the lawless towns of fiery people, the slippery jungles pulsating with life, far from the cold, dry Blue Mountains, where I spent my teen years. I felt no affinity with the Australian bush, where there might be snakes and kangaroos, but no anacondas or jaguars. No excitement, no humid nights, nothing unknown.

But it was much earlier, when I was a dreamy child playing *Evita* on my grandparents' pianola, that Latin America first entered my psyche. I sat with the *Encyclopaedia Brittanica* weighing heavily on my skinny lap, fascinated by the ruins of Machu Picchu, a puzzle of smooth stones and boulders fitting perfectly together to make a hidden city high in the jagged jade-coloured mountains. I turned the pages slowly and stared at natives in the Amazon jungle, their saggy boobs hanging out, and bowl haircuts like the ones Grandpa gave my brother and me to save Mum money. I stared at deep blue waterholes in Central America where the bones of women and children were found.

I took the book with me when we moved to Katoomba. Mum remarried and my stepdad was posted to a new job, out of the city, up in the fresh mountain air. I missed the city lights and sounds and smells, the sweltering Western Sydney nights when you'd sweat in your sleep. The old flat we moved to in Katoomba had ice on its concrete walls and a railway line outside my bedroom window that shunted long coal trains from Lithgow to Sydney at all hours of the night.

Katoomba was cold, wet, windy and miserable. I wasn't suited to the climate and came down with pneumonia every winter. One misty Sunday, to relieve the melancholy we all felt, Mum took us out.

'Let's go and have a look at the Inca gallery,' she said. 'It'll fill in an hour.'

Mum said she'd driven past it many times and wondered how a gallery of artefacts from South America had found a home alongside the potpourri and Devonshire Tea shops of the Blue Mountains. It was a spontaneous adventure and I loved spontaneous adventures. It would help break the Sunday despair that crept up on me once Mass was out and there were no boys around.

The gallery occupied two rooms in a cottage in Wentworth Falls. A small collection of Inca pottery, jewellery, masks and tools were displayed in glass cabinets along the walls. We wandered around, taking our time, not talking much. A turquoise necklace caught my eye. It was a vibrant blue-green that felt like the sea. It was an opaque stone that seemed to glow from within. It was the colour of summer; of happiness.

The Inca Gallery was unlike anything else in the 1980s Blue Mountains. A spark from those treasures had flicked into my soul and stayed there, waiting to ignite. By the time I finally made it to South America, it had the force of a volcano.

Emily and I follow a series of timber walkways around the Argentinian side of the falls. We follow strange creatures with our cameras—fat capybaras that look like dog-sized guinea pigs—and meet other travellers equally awed by the falls. After taking an entire roll of photos of gushing white water, we spend a couple of hours cooling off in the surrounding rock pools with a group of Brazilians. They wail with envy when we tell them of our plans to go to Carnival in Salvador da Bahia in the north of Brazil.

'Carnival in Salvador is so much better than Rio,' they cry. 'People will be dancing in every street of the city. It will be the biggest party of your lives.'

Emily and I exchange a smile as we paddle in the shallow water and balance our pale bodies on the rocks. We are pleased with ourselves for choosing to go to Carnival in Salvador instead of Rio, a tip from a South American friend in Sydney. Things have been tense between us since Buenos Aires—I can't blame her for being pissed off at me—but the water has washed it all away. We're hyped and ready to begin our journey on the right foot.

We leave the falls late in the afternoon and a very blonde German couple, she voluptuous and giggly, he shirtless and chatty, offers us a ride back to town in their van. Emily chats with them as they tell her how they like to 'make love in zee back of zee van', and I retreat into my own head and watch the thick roadside vegetation pass by in a green blur. Visiting the falls has given me a reprieve from the anguish I've felt since leaving Gabriel.

But the high is beginning to fade. I have an urge to run back to him before he forgets about me, or worse—finds someone else. Buenos Aires is only one short flight away. I could fly back and see him the next day. I could cancel the trip with Emily, use my travel money to support myself until I could find work. I want Gabriel to teach me how to be an artisan. I want to live with him, marry him. Argentina is a civilised nation, Buenos Aires a fine city. I look at the three of them, laughing and joking. I don't want to be just another tourist. Emily will understand if I go back—she'll make new travel companions. Look at her.

Or, maybe she won't. As besotted as I am with Gabriel, I can't abandon my friend. I know what abandonment is like—it leaves a hole inside you that can never be filled.

No, we have spent a year planning our trip, sitting huddled in cafes underlining passages in the guidebook, getting our arms jabbed, taking self-defence classes, applying for visas. I can't let her down.

And I can't turn my back on Brazil, Bolivia and Peru. I want to dance at Carnival in Brazil. I want to stand barefoot on the jungle floor and hear its strange and terrifying sounds and be bitten and stung by its creatures. I want to feel the Andes under my own two feet. If I stay with Gabriel, I might never get the chance. Who knows how poor we'd be? I could get pregnant and be stuck in Elsa's tiny apartment looking after a baby while Gabriel tries to support us. From some place deep in my gut, a force emerges, telling me to keep going.

The next morning, we rise early and pack up to leave. We hug Doña Irma and take a few photos together outside her ramshackle home, then take a bus to the Brazilian border. A sixteen-hour bus trip from Foz do Iguaçu to Sao Paulo, South America's most populated city, is the first of many long, overnight bus trips. We are on edge from the moment we arrive at the city's cavernous bus station, the *rodoviaria,* early the next morning. Throngs of people surge through the corridors, sit on the floor in groups, and push their way to get to wherever they're going. Even though we are just passing through for the day on our way to Paraty, it becomes apparent just how much attention two fair-haired, fair-skinned young foreign girls in South America can attract. It isn't the kind of attention we want—big-bellied men having a good old gawk.

We're due to catch a bus out of the city to Paraty at 7pm and we're at a loss as to how to spend the day. We don't want to sit around the *rodoviaria* all day, nor do we want to lug our backpacks around the city. We find a baggage check-in and tentatively hand our bags over to a group of black guys who appear ecstatic to see us. We can't understand a word they're saying in between their shouts and hollers, but their facial expressions and lewd body language get the message across.

'Oh shit, I forgot to get my water bottle out of my pack,' I say to Emily as we walk off to look for the subway, carrying only our small day-packs. 'Sorry, I'm so vague. Hang on, I'm going to run back and get it.'

I'm always forgetting something or losing something. It drives Emily nuts. She's always so organised. We weave our way back through the swirling pile of people and when the baggage guys see us again, they're all smiles and giggles and nudges. I don't know how to say I've left my water bottle in my bag in Portuguese, so I resort to sign language. I curl my fingers and hand around as if gripping something cylindrical, and hold it to my mouth. I slowly move it back and forth in front of my mouth with my lips open, as if I'm drinking from an imaginary water bottle.

A cheer of jubilation erupts and the men nod frantically. A group of five or six motion for me to go behind the counter. I follow them through the labyrinth of shelves stacked to the roof with luggage, further and further towards the dark back corners of the building. I'm scanning the shelves, trying to find my backpack. Where is it? A hot prickle in my gut. Something's not right.

We come to a dead end and they surround me. One mimics the action I'd made with my hand earlier. Then, he unzips his pants.

'No! I shout. 'No, no, no, I didn't mean *that*. I just need my water bottle. Oh fuck, I didn't mean THAT!'

The men move closer, touching their crotches and grinning, calling me baby and other things I can't understand. A wave of panic shoots through my body and then the adrenaline rush hits. I push past the group and bolt back down the aisles to the front door, leaving them in fits of laughter. They could have done anything they wanted—but they didn't.

'What's wrong with *you*?' Emily cries, looking worried as I run out the door, my face ablaze.

'Those baggage guys thought I'd kindly offered to give them all blow jobs! They didn't even take me to my bag, they just took me to a secluded corner and pointed at their dicks.'

She laughs harder than they had and once I'm safe, I burst into hysterics too. Days of pent-up emotion pours out until our stomachs ache, and we can barely stand upright as we walk out of the bus terminal, not giving a damn who's staring at us.

We spend most of the day in Sao Paulo savouring the air-conditioning in a fancy café in Avenida Paulista, drinking coffee and writing postcards. A respite from sightseeing, from being seen, and from the heat. Rejuvenated, we return to the *rodoviaria* in the late afternoon, grab our backpacks and have one last laugh with the baggage handlers, who haven't forgotten me, and find the bus to Paraty. It's a seven-hour bus trip and after the long trip from Foz, we're dreading it.

Fatigue is setting in and we've only been in South America for a week. I'm having reservations about going to Rio after Paraty. Everyone we meet warns us about Rio. They say it's too dangerous for young women like us who don't speak the language. I need to meditate more, to visualise myself covered in white light, and to ask for help from my guardian angels. Think positive thoughts. It's the best way to protect myself.

The bus is empty, except for two long-haired Argentinians sitting up the back. About ten minutes into the trip, they move to the seat in front of us and introduce themselves as Fernando and Julio. It takes hours to convince them we don't want to be their girlfriends and finally, they relax. We arrive in Paraty at 2.30am in the rain. We have nowhere to stay, so they invite us to their pousada. We don't have much choice, other than to sit in the rain until sunrise. We trudge through the town's 300-year-old streets in the dead of night, stumbling under the weight of our backpacks as we try to find our footing on the slippery cobblestones, with the two Argentine Lotharios leading the way. Fernando hasn't quite given up his seduction and entertains us with a rolling commentary of pickup lines: 'I am zee chalk, you are zee blackboard. I am zee orange, you are zee apple.' It's more comical than sexy, but he continues all the way to the pousada.

Once inside, he instructs us to dump our bags and go out partying with them. It's almost 3am, as good a time as any to go dancing when you're in Brazil. We meet up with six of their overly affectionate, drunk Argentinian friends at a bar a few streets away, who kiss us like old friends. Slippery brown bodies gyrate on the dance floor and it's our first taste of dancing with Brazilians. Intense eyes scan us up and down, before the music pulls us into its current and one dripping wet man after another swings us around by our hips and hands. We drink our first *caipirinhas*— Brazil's national cocktail, made with cachaça, sugar and lime—and grin at each other, high on the music, the humidity, the men, the women and Brazilian cocktails.

When we finally collapse at the pousada a few hours later, the only place to sleep is on the floor, underneath the bed. Eight very intoxicated men are crammed into the tiny room and a fleeting concern they might want sexual favours vanishes when I look across the floor and see their hands down each other's pants.

We pass out for a few hours then wake at lunchtime, leaving the brown-chested lovers slumbering with their arms around each other and their luscious hair fanning across their pillows. We go in search of our own pousada and check in to the cheapest one we can find. Our room is bare with two single beds, a table and two chairs. We dump our bags on the tiled floor and immediately set off to explore the town. Calm bays curve around Portuguese colonial buildings set along the waterfront and steep mountains wrapped in lush jungle form a stunning backdrop.

The air in Paraty is a sultry soup that keeps us damp, even when it isn't raining. Torrential downpours quickly turn the uneven cobblestone streets, with their poor drainage, into streams, then rivers. Hesitant to hang around the town in the rain, we spend days holed up in our room, writing in our journals, our drenched clothes draped all over the place. I grab the guidebook and read to Emily.

'Before the Portuguese arrived, this area belonged to the Guaianás people, who named it Paraty (Para-chee): *river of fish*. When the Portuguese colonised it in 1667 it became a port for transporting gold from the mineral-rich interior of Brazil to Rio. So its waters ran with rich supplies of fish and gold.'

'Mmmm,' she says, drawing in her journal. She's a good artist—better than me, which isn't hard because I'm not an artist at all.

'Fish and gold,' I repeat.

'Mmmm.'

'Have you been thinking about home?' I ask her.

'A bit—not much really,' she says. 'Mum's probably missing me. Have you?'

'Nup. Not at all.'

I'm not thinking about home, I'm thinking about him. I lie on my bed and fondle the mandala as the rain pelts against our windows—is he thinking about me? He is so far away now. I take out my journal and flip through its pages until I find the photos of us in Buenos Aires. I study Gabriel's face, looking for warning signs, anything that might indicate a red flag. I see only good in those beautiful eyes; not a hint of danger. I'm right about him. I am convinced I have nothing to fear.

'I'm hungry,' Emily says, tossing her journal onto the bed. 'Let's go and find some food that isn't pizza and spaghetti.'

Being vegetarian in South America is so far proving frustrating—and bad for the bowels. We're living off whatever you can make with white flour, plus coffee, beer and cheese. There's plenty of fruit though, and avocados galore.

We pull our emergency plastic ponchos over light singlets and cotton skirts—our standard uniform in the relentless humidity—push our money into our bras, tuck our passports, safe and dry, into the soles of our boots, and brave the torrential streets in search of dinner. The only vegetarian food we can find is cheese pizza with a token olive on each slice. It's a total rip-off, but we need a good feed.

With nothing else to do, we head to a bar and drink beer, which never disappoints. We chat to travellers from around the globe, all of whom have had enough of Paraty's endless rain. I spot a Brazilian woman with black curls cascading down her back and an ample cleavage spilling out of a tight black dress. She's sitting on her own, smiling at me. Her name is Regina and she welcomes me to her table with great enthusiasm. She's like an affectionate cat with no boundaries. She's also totally off her face. She strokes my hair and rubs my back as she tells me in pretty good English that she works at the tourist information centre. Then she asks:

'You like cocaine, darling?'

'Um… I've never had it.'

'Oh my love, you must have some. You want to buy from me?'

'No thanks, I don't have much money on me.'

'Is very cheap darling, this is Brazil!'

'No thanks, Regina. I don't touch that stuff.'

It's the first time I hear the c-word. Cocaine. It won't be the last.

Regina looks deeply hurt, then shrugs it off. She tells me it has been raining for ten days straight in Paraty and it isn't about to let up, so the next morning we cram our sopping wet clothes into our backpacks, lug them to the bus station, and set off for Rio.

CHAPTER FIVE

AS THE BUS curls around the misty mountains south of Rio, a slow burn rises in my belly. I am fulfilling a dream and I should be ecstatic, but I'm torn between a man I hope is waiting for me in Buenos Aires—a man I hardly know and can't stop thinking about—and the unknown road ahead of me. If I find a letter from him waiting for me in Rio, it will ease my conflicted mind.

We stop for a lunch break at a roadside café. Here, it seems fashionable for the local men to roll their singlets up at the front to expose their fat bellies, which they rub tenderly, the way pregnant women do. A small boy with huge, glassy black eyes and a swollen, malnourished stomach appears and says something I don't understand. But I do understand—how could I not? Against all advice, I start to reach inside my bra for some money, turning away from his sad little eyes. Before I can hand him the money, a burly shopkeeper runs out of his store shouting at the boy, which sends him peddling away on his rusty bicycle.

As the bus continues towards Rio, my spirits begin to lift. It's a spectacular journey, skirting the southeast coast, passing fishing villages and mountains cloaked in tropical jungle, glowing green treetops poking through low-hanging clouds. Brazil's natural beauty calms my nerves and I mentally prepare myself to face whatever comes our way when we arrive in Rio. I can handle fear. All I have to do is say some affirmations and visualise white light surrounding me.

I am safe, I am strong, I am protected, I whisper to myself as I gaze out the bus window.

'What?' Emily looks bewildered.

'Oh nothing, I'm just doing some affirmations. Surrounding us both in white light. Asking my spirit guides to protect us in Rio.'

She shakes her head and goes back to reading her book.

Then she looks up again.

'You and your hippie shit. You really think that New Age crap works, do you?'

'I know it does. I've been doing it the whole time since we arrived in South America and nothing bad has happened yet, has it?'

'That's debatable.'

I ignore her dig at Gabriel. She pisses me off sometimes. Why is she so bloody cynical? She puts her headphones on and blocks me out. The incessant rain and expense of Paraty has put us both on edge.

I look up at the television mounted on the front windscreen of the bus. It's playing a melodramatic telenovela and the driver's eyes are flicking between the screen and the road. At one stop, a filthy boy selling chewing gum on a wooden tray gets on, asks us at least ten times in rapid succession if we want to buy some, then plonks himself on the armrest of Emily's seat to watch the show. She looks at me for help and I laugh. He's not doing any harm, until he stands up and starts moving his bum around, trying to scratch his itchy anus on the corner of her armrest.

'Ew! Get off! That's gross,' Emily shouts, wiping the armrest with her shirt. The boy is mesmerised by the TV and takes his time to stand up and shuffle down the aisle, before the bus driver kicks him off.

The vendors who board the bus at every stop are equally absorbed by the telenovela. They sell whatever they want, it seems, on any bus, at any time of the day or night—everything from boiled corn on a stick to cigarettes to fluffy toys to chocolate, popcorn and chewing gum. When they're not allowed inside the bus, they stand outside with their wares on the end of long sticks and poke them through the windows at the passengers, who toss coins at them.

As we near Rio, the bus rounds a corner and reveals not another tropical vista, but a Coca-Cola billboard. After so much natural beauty, it's a stain on the landscape. Homes built out of cardboard with tin roofs become more frequent until that's all we can see on either side of the road. Raggedy children play in mud as life swirls around them. Rio's shanty towns, or *favelas*, are home to one-and-a-half million people. Not since leaving Sao Paulo a few days before have we seen such poverty.

We arrive at the Rio bus terminal and roam around in stifling heat looking for the bus to Copacabana, sweating under the weight of our backpacks, our feet burning in our boots. We quickly discover Rio's buses are not designed for backpackers. Every bus has a narrow turnstile to pass through after paying your fare, and squeezing through it wearing a large backpack is near impossible. We hold up the queue trying to push through, our faces flushed with embarrassment. The passengers laugh and a couple of guys give us a big heave from behind, until we are spat out like a pair of clumsy tortoises on the other side, our legs and arms protruding from the huge shells of our backpacks. We're relieved to find two seats together at the back of the bus and the standing passengers hang on for dear life as the driver tears around corners, sending everyone swaying from side to side.

The trip through the centre of Rio to Copacabana is sticky, speedy, scintillating. At one stop, a man with no arms gets on and the other passengers don't flinch. His hands jut out from his shoulders at right angles and he robotically recites what sounds like a speech he's used a thousand times as he walks up the aisle, begging. A few passengers hold out coins and he leans over and picks them up with a deformed hand. We shoot each other a brief look and hurry to find some coins in our pockets without revealing where our notes are stashed.

Our hostel in Copacabana looks like a plain apartment building from the outside, with no international flags or signs to alert would-be thieves. Inside, it's clean and minimally furnished, with cool white tiles. Best of all, there's a vegetarian café just around the corner, with actual vegetarian food. We stuff ourselves with soy steaks, bean salads and vegetable frittatas. Our plates are full to the brim and while we can't speak to the two guys who serve us, we give them the thumbs up as they continue to plonk vegetarian morsels onto our plates. At the end of the meal, the owner, a softly spoken man with kind eyes, seems to just pluck a figure out of his head and it's half of what we expect.

Rio feeds our bodies and souls with freshly made juices and healthy food, a city full of beautiful people with beautiful bodies—and a dark underbelly. As we sit at a café in the city centre that afternoon, kids with swollen bellies hold their tiny hands out for money and offer to clean our boots. Some look as young as four or five and hold babies with hungry, hopeful eyes, who seem to have given up crying. We hand over some money and are immediately inundated with more children. I feel like a rich bitch, reclining back with my glass of beer, watching Rio's struggles from the comfort of my restaurant table. Emily looks equally dismayed. We leave without finishing our beers.

It's only been two weeks since we waved goodbye to our friends and family at Sydney Airport, but they seem so far away. We need to hear the familiar voices of home, but Rio's sticky streets are hectic and we can't find a phone. We give up and return to the hostel, change into our swimmers and head to the beach. Walking along Copacabana's back streets, we pass families living on the footpath with their belongings in piles of plastic shopping bags. They bathe their babies in ice-cream buckets of dirty water and feed them Coke straight out of the bottle. They live at the foot of high-rise buildings that house the super-wealthy.

Copacabana Beach is exactly as I'd always imagined it, a buzzing, dynamic scene of sun-worshippers with glistening boobs and buttocks, and fit people rollerblading along the black and white swirling pattern that decorates its famous esplanade. Stocky men with machetes scalp coconuts, stick a straw in the hole and sell it as chilled coconut water. The real deal, straight from the nut, sweet and natural. Hawkers try to flog us ice-cream, peanuts, number plates, watches, lottery tickets, balloons, batteries and trick beer glasses, all dangling from their bodies in colourful, clanking bunches as they trudge up and down the scorching sand, fully clothed, sweat pouring off their faces. Glorious physical specimens saunter past us and oiled muscle men whistle and hiss the word *shoosha* at us.

'What the hell is a shoosha?' Emily asks.

'I have no idea. I'll look it up in the dictionary later. Probably means hot babe.'

'Yeah, you wish,' she smiles.

We're wearing one-piece swimmers. We may as well be Amish women next to the bronzed goddesses of Rio, in their dental-floss bikinis that only just cover the nipples and crotch. They are incredible, all flowing dark hair and ridiculously round, tight bums. No amount of exercise, prayer, white light or witchery will ever make my flabby white bum look like that.

Sunburnt and salty after our afternoon at the beach, we return to the hostel, shower and settle in to the lounge area to watch a bit of Brazilian TV, none of which we can understand. We attempt to chat with a group of guys in their early twenties who are lazing around the room in tight shorts and no shirts. One of them, a chubby guy with a friendly face, speaks English and becomes the translator of the group. He says they're from a regional part of Brazil and are staying at the hostel for Carnival.

'My friend wants to ask you something,' he says, motioning to a brooding stallion with gleaming biceps and long black hair that frames a face straight from *Vogue*. He's been pretending to watch TV while eyeing us off.

'Sure, what does he want to know?' My cheeks flush.

'He wants to know if you like Brazilian meat,' he says, stifling a shy giggle. The other guys crack up and the stallion moves his hand down to his crotch and rubs himself slowly, his smouldering eyes shifting from the TV screen to me.

Emily scoffs in disgust, then looks at me, eyebrows furrowed. I think she's worried I might actually say yes. He's hot and he knows it. I must admit, I briefly entertain the notion; what red-blooded woman wouldn't? But thoughts of Gabriel sweep through my mind. He's not sleazy, like this guy. He's not up himself, though to me, he's equally beautiful. The stallion would no doubt be a fine horse to ride, but his ego is repulsive.

'Olá,' I respond, looking directly at him. He sits up, looking hopeful, hand still on his crotch. 'I'm vegetarian. *Vegetariana*. No like Brazilian meat.'

The room erupts in laughter. The stallion removes his hand from his genitals ever so slowly, turning his eyes back to the TV as if it makes no difference to him whether he's watching a game show or attempting to seduce a woman.

At that moment, all the men in the room turn to the screen and shout, 'Shoosha! Shoosha! Shoosha!' That word again.

A tall, attractive woman with short blonde hair and an angular face dances across the screen with young children, singing to the camera and smiling a dazzling smile. The English-speaking guy, seeing the puzzled looks on our faces, explains the mystery.

'That is Xuxa,' he says. 'Xuxa is one of Brazil's most beautiful women, all Brazilian men, we love her. You look like Xuxa to us because you have the same hair colour and light skin. Very beautiful.'

Ah, so that explains it. Apparently, we are total babes in Brazil.

That night, we slip on light summer dresses, borrow some makeup from the Brazilian girls in our dorm and launch ourselves at Rio like rock-stars, lapping up the attention as groups of men call out, 'Xuxa!', clapping and cheering as we saunter past with newfound confidence.

Every corner of the city is buzzing with excitement for the impending Carnival. We will be in Salvador da Bahia by the time Carnival kicks off, but we want a taste of Rio nightlife. We look for clubs and bars recommended in the guidebook and the bus drivers either try to chat us up or shake their heads in disbelief at two foreign girls scampering around the city at night, all alone. One bus driver tells us it's the second time that night we've been on his bus, so we must be going in circles. At first, he was worried we'd get robbed, he says, but on second thoughts, we don't look like girls with money.

We think we're on the right track but by the time we reach the beach-side suburb of Botafogo, the famous club Oba Oba is closed. Undeterred, we catch another bus to Leblon, Rio's most affluent neighbourhood, hoping to find some action. A fresh-faced young guy with short dark hair, sitting on the back seat of the bus and strumming a guitar, is on his way to a samba club and invites us to join him. Feeling brave, we get off at his stop and follow him a few blocks to a sprawling old building heaving with pulsating samba beats. Dolled up young women and men loiter out the front in the balmy night air, drinking, chatting, smoking and kissing, while our guitarist friend goes inside looking for his friend, the star of the samba show.

A miniature Sammy Davis Junior by the name of Bibi emerges, a petite man in a red satin shirt, gold chains draped across his chest, and tight black pants. He links his arms in ours, and takes us inside without a word. The club is heaving with hundreds of Brazilians dancing to infectious rhythms, music that possesses the power to creep into your body through the floor, snake its way up your legs and settle into your hips, where it shakes you from the inside.

The top of Bibi's head is directly in line with our breasts, and he smiles widely as he parades us around the club on each arm. We are no match for the Brazilian women in their skintight dresses, short flouncy skirts and towering heels, but we've become instant celebrities.

'What the hell is going on here?' Emily shouts to me over the music. 'Are we like, this guy's handbags for the night or what?'

'Just go with it,' I laugh. 'At least he got us in for free. Hey, where's the guitar guy?'

'Hopefully, he's waiting out the front. I don't want to spend the whole night stuck to this weird Bibi guy. Is he gay or what?'

'Camp as a row of tents! At least we'll be safe with him.'

When he's sure everyone has seen him parade around the club with us, Bibi leads us out the front and says something to the guitar guy, who is still waiting.

'Bibi asks if you girls want to come to a better club, other side of Rio,' he says.

We know it's a bad idea, we know we should be cautious, we know we should refuse. It's close to midnight and we have no idea where we are, who these men are or where they want to take us.

'Sure, let's go,' I say, linking arms with Emily, who tonight is happy to abandon all common sense in the name of fun. I quickly pop us into a white-light bubble before we jump into Bibi's car, a beaten up bomb with one of the side windows missing. We speed through the streets and surrender to Rio's spell, the breeze blowing through the broken window and messing up our hair. We arrive at a smaller club where Bibi once again glides in with Emily and me on each side, our arms linked with his. A cheer goes up—we're not sure if it's for Bibi or for us—and a hoard of lecherous old men descend upon us.

They're not much to look at, but man can they move. One expert dancer after another holds us firmly and confidently, twirling and toss-ing us around, our legs parted by their legs, their crotches grinding into our crotches, pushing us back into dips and pulling us up abruptly to meet their penetrating eyes. I'm relieved when two sexy young black guys wearing tight black and white striped T-shirts whisk us away from the old timers and swing us around without trying to shove their knees into our genitals, then go back to dancing with each other.

I don't know what kind of dance we're doing, but it's more lambada than samba, more sleazy than sexy. And hot as hell. Gabriel fades from my mind as I lose myself in a haze of cigarette smoke and a blur of caipirinhas and R-rated dance moves with short, beady-eyed men. Emily leaves me to it and heads to the bar, where I see her chatting with a tall, muscular guy. She introduces him as Paulo and when the club closes, he joins Bibi and us for a trip down the world-famous sambadrome in his rusty little car. Bibi, it turns out, is one of Rio's star samba instructors and has VIP access to the sambadrome. The samba schools are practising their routines under the floodlights in the early hours of the morning and we smile and wave as we cruise past. It isn't a dress rehearsal, so there are no extravagant feathers or sequins, but by God there is dancing.

Afterwards, Bibi takes us to a clifftop overlooking Ipanema beach to watch the sunrise. A makeshift bar is set up on the grass and a few plastic tables and chairs are scattered perilously close to the edge of the cliff. Health and safety rules take a back seat to the pure enjoyment of life in Rio, in Brazil—and in all of South America. This is what I love about it. This freedom. Few rules, few restrictions. Endless fun.

We order more drinks and attempt to have sign language conversations with Paulo. Emily says she wants to go home with him and now it's my turn to worry, although he seems like a good guy. She's been trying to give him a hint, but he's not getting it, so she asks me to tell him in Spanish.

'Paulo, mi amiga quiere ir contigo,' I say. *My friend wants to go with you.*

He looks confused.

'Mi amiga te quiere,' I say. *My friend wants you.*

A slight smile. I'll have to spell it out.

'Mi amiga quiere tener sexo contigo.' *My friend wants to have sex with you.*

My theory that most Portuguese speakers understand Spanish is incorrect. Either that, or he can't believe what he's hearing. He sits there smiling, eyes darting between Emily and me. Emily is smiling at him, awaiting his response.

I give up talking and resort to sign language. I make a circle with my left thumb and forefinger, then stab my right forefinger through the middle in the universal gesture for sex. Then I point to Emily. Finally, the penny drops. His face lights up, then he asks me to tell her he lives with his parents and they'll have to go to a hotel. Emily agrees and I tell her to stay safe as they wander off, arm in arm. I'm delighted she has found a companion for the night. I don't sense any danger from him; he's a gentle giant without a mean bone in his body. After kissing my hand, Bibi disappears without a word, his slim hips slinking off into the pink glow of dawn.

A new day in Rio. A city that is as shocking as it is seductive; as beautiful as it is ugly. Extremes of wealth and poverty, beauty and deformity. After a few hours' sleep at the hostel, we take a bus through the city to Corcovado Mountain. The city's pre-Carnival buzz is becoming more infectious each day. I love how the city wraps itself around mountains cloaked in tropical forest, how high-density concrete is encircled by the sea, winding its way in and out of a dense urban landscape.

High on Corcovado Mountain, overlooking it all, is the statue of Christ the Redeemer, Brazil's most recognisable icon and one of the images that has beckoned me since childhood. He towers over the sinful city with his arms outstretched, watching in silence as people live and love and rob and rape and laugh and die. This thirty-metre soapstone Christ gives the impression that a holy man is watching from on high, protecting the people. But the more I discover about Rio's crime rate and its many injustices, the more I suspect no one is.

To reach the top of Corcovado Mountain, we take a little two-carriage train painted bright red that contrasts starkly with the vibrant green of the Tijuca Forest. It's almost four kilometres and it takes twenty minutes to reach the summit. Emily leans her head back on the seat and closes her eyes. I rest my head against the window. The forest casts cool shadows across my face and I feel myself drifting away.

I'm four years old, and a brick has smashed through our lounge room window. Mum screams and I vomit. He's shouting, the dark man with scars on his face. He has followed her home from her job at the pub and he's drunk. He wants to kill Mummy. Why isn't my daddy here to protect us? Why don't we ever see him? The police lights flash in red and blue and someone tells me to go to sleep but I can't. The flashing lights are too bright and I'm too scared.

A camera flash startles me awake. A clean cut man wearing a white T-shirt and jeans with a camera hanging around his neck says something in Portuguese and disappears into the next train carriage.

'That was weird,' Emily says, brushing her hair out of her eyes. 'What did he say?'

'Wouldn't have a clue,' I shrug.

'Well, I guess he's just a weirdo who wanted a photo of us. I shudder to think what he's going to do with it.'

'Maybe he thinks we're American celebrities.'

'Yeah. Or maybe it's the Xuxa thing.'

'I bags being Xuxa!' I say.

'No, I bags being Xuxa!'

We're getting on well now. She'd returned to the hostel that morning with hilarious tales of the hotel room Paulo had taken her to the night before. The walls and ceiling were covered in mirrors and all she could see were dozens of images of their naked bodies everywhere she looked. She tells the story like only she can and has me in stitches. She's an excellent travel companion. The earlier tension of Buenos Aires is far behind us. She knows nothing of my hope to stay in Buenos Aires instead of going to London and there's no point saying anything until I know whether Gabriel has sent me a letter to the poste restante in Rio. I might hear nothing from him. He's probably already forgotten about me. So why can't I forget about him?

We stay quiet for the rest of the trip to the summit of the mountain, where finally, we get to stand at the feet of Jesus. Christ the Redeemer is massive up close, but it's the view of the city from the mountain that is the real attraction. There she is, Rio de Janeiro, where mountains meet the bluest sea and a mass of humanity scrambles for crumbs and riches and the river spits out dead bodies and still, people dance.

'Excuse me, photo please?' Emily asks a friendly-looking Brazilian woman to take our photo with the statue. It's usually me doing all the talking, all the asking—for prices, directions and schedules. We stand together on the stairs, Jesus at our backs and a panorama of the city scalloped by a sparkling ocean below. Another of my South American dreams fulfilled. I'm so light and happy, I could flit across the sky and land softly on Sugarloaf Mountain, way off in the distance.

On the way back down Corcovado Mountain in the red train, Emily and I chat about our plans for the next day.

'I want to find the central post office,' I say. 'We might have mail from our families.'

'Don't get too excited, I don't trust the postal service in this place,' she says. 'We should probably try to call them. Let's just find a phone.'

We've agreed to take turns calling our mums once a fortnight. Our mums then call each other with news of our whereabouts. Of all the people following our wild adventures in South America, no one would be thinking about us as much as these two women.

'I found the address of the post office in the guidebook, it doesn't look hard to find,' I say, trying not to sound too eager.

'Holy crap!' she shouts.

I turn to find the young guy who'd taken our photo on the train on the way up the mountain, standing in front of us. He's holding two dinner plates, our contorted faces printed in full colour in the centre with 'Rio de Janeiro, Brazil' plastered across our foreheads.

'No!' we cry in unison. Had we known our photos would end up as tacky souvenirs we might at least have smiled. We politely decline this kitsch purchase. One, the photos are ugly. Two, we don't want to be carrying fragile plates around in our backpacks, which are thrown on top of buses, crammed into cargo holds, sat on and slept on.

On our last morning in Rio, I find my way to the central post office. I line up at the lista de correos desk, palms sweating, tummy twisted tight. I hand my passport to the desk clerk, who flicks through a box of letters looking for my name. She shakes her head and my heart sinks.

He hasn't written to me, even though he knew I was going to check at this post office. I arrived in Rio full of hope and fear—hope that I would hear from him, fear something terrible would happen to me. But despite the risks we've taken, Rio has put on a sparkling show of hospitality, while the person I most wanted to rely on, the one I'd felt safe enough to spend the night with in a city park on the same day I met him, has let me down.

I try to hide my disappointment from Emily. She thinks I'm upset about not receiving any letters from home.

'Don't worry, it's probably too soon for them to write to us yet. C'mon, let's call home reverse charges.'

We call our mums and blurt out a barrage of details about Buenos Aires, Iguazu Falls, Paraty, Rio, Christ the Redeemer, Copacabana and Xuxa—leaving out our wild night speeding through the streets of Rio in a beaten up car and dancing with strange, possibly gay men.

Hearing Mum's voice makes me miss home for the first time, but it also feels good to be so far away, soaking up Latin American culture, becoming more and more comfortable with its quirky customs, its warm people and its streets that stink of piss.

As we prepare to leave that afternoon, I regret not buying the plate. It would have been a funny reminder of Rio, with its tenacity and all its charming and not so charming surprises. Despite all the sad things about Rio—the poverty, the homelessness, the deformities, the crime—it's a wonderfully visceral, upbeat, optimistic place.

We've become regulars at the vego takeaway and when it's time to leave, we walk past with our full arsenal on our backs to say goodbye. The man with the kind eyes packs us two boxes of vegetarian snacks for the bus trip and refuses to let us pay. The city I was so fearful of before I arrived has embraced us like daughters.

The excitement of Carnival will continue to build for days in Rio and then explode into a week of dancing, drinking, drugs, sex, sequins and feathers that will end at noon on Ash Wednesday, marking the beginning of Lent and the resumption of moral behaviour. But we're ready for a new adventure: Salvador da Bahia, 1629 kilometres north of Rio.

CHAPTER SIX

I CAN'T SLEEP on the overnight bus to Salvador. I fish around in my daypack and take out my journal with the flying pig on the cover, flipping through its pages until I find the photo of Gabriel and me in Buenos Aires. I stare at it for a long time, trying to convince myself what I felt was real. Then I write. For what seems like hours, I pour my utter despair onto page after page. Every now and then I glance over at Emily, asleep beside me, her long legs stretched out into the aisle. I look around at the other passengers, all apparently sleeping soundly, their limp bodies jiggling slightly. I look towards the front of the bus and see the driver's eyes in the rear-view mirror, thankfully alert and focused on a straight road that seems to stretch into infinite darkness. His whistling cheers my bruised heart.

Why hasn't Gabriel written to me? Did the letter get lost? Did it go to another post office in Rio? Did it arrive after we left? Maybe he would send one to Salvador. After all, it had only been a couple of weeks since we left Buenos Aires.

I pack the journal away and pull out the mandala he gave me from my brown suede bag. I clutch it to my chest and lean my head against the window. I'm yearning for him and I feel stupid, but during that long, sleepless night I'm elevated by moments of pure pleasure, where the full impact of what I am doing hits me and I smile at how far I've come.

We arrive in Salvador late in the afternoon, the day before Carnival begins, and catch a bus straight to a hostel in the beachside village of Ondina. All the beds are taken, so the manager gives us mattresses on the floor in separate rooms. It's against fire safety regulations, but breaking the rules is what South America is all about. My room has eight bunk beds scattered with clothing, makeup and bags. All the women are young Brazilians and they smile as I settle in.

'Estados Unidos?' asks one girl with liquid brown eyes and tight brown curls. *United States?*

'No, Australia,' I reply.

'Crocodilo Dundeeeee!' she exclaims.

'Sí, sí, Crocodilo Dundee.'

'Kangooroos!'

'Sí, kangaroos!'

Wherever we go, Crocodile Dundee and kangaroos are the two things everyone seems to know—and love—about Australia.

Emily is put in a room down the hall, and after the long bus trip it's a relief to spend the night relaxing in the hostel drinking beer, swaying in hammocks and watching the preparations for Carnival in Rio on the TV in the common area.

That night I sleep heavily, dreaming of a tumultuous ocean and desert roads. I wake with a start. How did I get on the floor? Where am I? Where's Emily?

'Emily! Emily! Mi amiga, mi amiga, where is Emily?' I'm screaming, almost hyperventilating with panic.

'Ssshhh, it's okay, it's okay.' The girl with the liquid brown eyes is kneeling on the ground next to me, patting my leg through my sleeping bag, trying to comfort me. She's a vision in her white nightie, her gentle eyes filled with concern.

'Amiga is other room. Okay?' She runs down the hall and wakes Emily up, who staggers in and tells me in a weary, parental voice to go back to sleep.

The girl, a total stranger, puts her arms around me and hugs me.

Carnival in Salvador is all about the party trucks. The sixty-foot-long *trios eléctricos* are semi-trailers fitted with stages and high-powered sound systems, that transport Carnival bands around the city. Festivalgoers pay to walk in front or behind each truck, inside a roped barrier held up by a line of security guards. This is the safest place to experience Carnival, so we avoid it altogether and throw ourselves into the fray of thousands of humans high on life and everything else you can be high on.

We spend our first night of Carnival in Barra and Ondina. The rules are clear: dance or be crushed. The only way to avoid being squashed by the surge of bodies is to go with the flow, which means dancing as you walk in front or behind the trucks. We drink beer, eat coconut cakes smothered in condensed milk and dance to blaring Brazilian party anthems that everyone knows every word of and we understand nothing of. The atmosphere is electrifying and we're swept up by the unbridled ecstasy of it all.

Trying to get to the side of the road for water or food is like swimming out of a rip in the ocean. No point trying to fight the current, you have to go with it and edge yourself sideways until you're free. Lines of military and civil police march through the crowds in single file and we jump on the end of the police conga line with other people who want to break free of the crowd.

Our first two nights of Carnival are wilder than we'd ever imagined. The *Guinness Book of Records* describes it as the biggest party on the planet, with four million people celebrating throughout twenty-five kilometres of streets, avenues and squares. By the third day, we're exhausted. We have three more days of Carnival to get through, so that afternoon we laze around in the hammocks at the hostel and toss up having an early night, just to pace ourselves for the remainder of the week. The Brazilians are horrified.

'Are you serious?' asks one wide-eyed girl. 'No es possible, this is CARNIVAL!'

'It is pretty lame of us,' Emily says, as she swings in her hammock. 'How about we just go for an hour or two?'

'Okay, let's do it. We came all this way, may as well throw ourselves back into the chaos. But I want to find a really cool percussion group to dance to. It would be amazing to find where Olodum are playing. Some of those Brazilian rock bands are highly dodgy.'

'Yeah, they're a far cry from Nirvana, eh?' Emily laughs.

As we make our way towards the city from Ondina at dusk, I spot a couple of black guys dressed in African print costumes. Straining to understand their Portuguese, we work out they're headed to Pelourinho, the historic centre of Salvador to see Olodum. They introduce themselves as Roberto and Marzu and invite us to share a cab, which takes us up winding, increasingly narrow, steep streets connecting the lower part of the city to the upper part. Somewhere up the side of a mountain, we stop in a sprawling favela of tin and concrete homes. We follow them further into the favela, where naked kids run through dirt streets trickling with sewage, women hang out of small windows chatting and men sit smoking and drinking, eyeing us off suspiciously. We move swiftly, staying close to our companions and people look at us like we are apparitions; lost souls in the wrong place.

But Roberto and Marzu know exactly where they're going and we emerge from the favela right into the heart of Pelourinho. Named for the whipping post in its central plaza where African slaves were punished, it was the original city centre of Salvador, which was founded by Portuguese settlers in 1549—the first slave market on the continent. Pastel-hued buildings in blue, yellow, pink and green stand proudly above narrow, cobblestone streets. It is an area rich in historical monuments from the seventeenth to the nineteenth centuries, alive with art and music. An outdoor elevator, the Elevador Lacerda, connects the upper historic part of the city to the administrative area that lies at sea level, seventy-two metres below. This imposing Art Deco construction is the most recognisable icon of the city and not only offers passengers sweeping views of the surrounding bay, but is a distinctive landmark that enables us to get our bearings.

A group of fit, bare-chested men in white pants gather in the main square, playing capoeira to the music of the *berimbau*, a single-stringed percussion instrument with a gourd on the end that acts as a resonator. The part-dance, part-acrobatics, part-martial arts performance is spectacular to watch even on Bondi Beach, but seeing it here in Salvador gives me goosebumps. The men jump and spin and kick and twist with impossible speed and precision, and then their eyes scan the crowd to see who's watching.

The population of Salvador is predominantly multiracial and black, with less than twenty percent white. Snappy old timers with cigarettes hanging out of their mouths play percussion on samba drums and tambourines and tiny kids carrying skinny babies rush up to ask us for money.

Other kids walk past selling cigarettes and beer, their streetwise little faces older than their years.

Roberto and Marzu take us to an outdoor bar in Pelourinho where we shout them beers and plonk ourselves down on white plastic chairs, as Roberto lights a joint in plain view. We smoke together and our smiles grow wider as euphoria washes over us; we want to dance! They motion for us to follow them down the street and around a corner into a narrow laneway. And there they are: five-hundred drummers lined up, dressed in T-shirts printed with the word Olodum, carrying drums painted in black, red, yellow and green stripes. One drummer at the front begins playing a loud samba rhythm I'm not quite ready for and it sends a jolt of power through my body. At his signal, all five-hundred drummers beat out a deafening party anthem with impeccable timing as they move off in formation. The beat takes on a life of its own and rises like a beast to echo through the streets.

We follow along, surrounded by a moving, jumping, gyrating mass of humanity. Caught up in the wave of emotion, we dance for hours like two women possessed, swimming through a sea of white smiles and bobbing black heads and ear-splitting whistles. In the crush of bodies, dark hands brush against my breasts and hair and I have to resign myself to having random dicks pressed against my bum. I don't know if it's accidental, but there's no escaping it.

In between being pushed and shoved, it becomes harder to dance. The crowd is growing wilder and I want to be part of this primal ritual, to swim with the tide, but I can't handle it. I'm suffocating, on the verge of panic. I don't mind the groping at first, but then it all becomes too invasive and claustrophobic.

Dripping with sweat, grazed and bruised and desperately thirsty, we eventually break free of the human current, buy some water at a roadside stall, and guzzle it. There's no point carrying a bag during Carnival because it would simply vanish. We can't carry our guidebook either, and have to find our way back to the hostel by asking directions. It's a long walk, and we have no idea which bus to catch.

The trios eléctricos slide around the city like musical monsters, and we begin to run the other way when we see a truck, for fear of being swept up again. Men hiss at us and call out Xuxa—and strangely, laugh at our boots. We can only assume they're not used to the sight of girls wearing short skirts and boots.

A shiny coach pulls up next to us, stopping in the middle of the road. The driver opens the door and tells us to get in. He's an older man in a respectable bus driver's uniform, and he says it's dangerous for two foreign girls to be walking around the city alone at this time of night. There are no other passengers onboard, but it seems safer than trying to find our way home in the increasingly lawless streets. We sit at the front of the bus, trying to make conversation with what little Portuguese we have picked up. The old man immediately adjusts his rear-view mirror downwards to get a good view of our legs, rather than the road. Emily and I roll our eyes at each other, but we're both so grateful for the ride home in our own private coach, we don't mind giving the old guy a bit of a perve.

The hard-partying days of Salvador, while being everything we'd hoped, are also exhausting and a little depressing. The streets stink like a urinal and people toss rubbish out of car and bus windows without a care. It's not hard to say goodbye and brace ourselves for the fifteen-hour bus trip to Fortaleza, then a further twenty-hours north to Belém.

Just before we leave, we hunt for the post office in the lower part of the city. We take the Elevador Lacerda to the bottom and pause to get our bearings. Voluptuous black women dressed in white cotton dresses with white headscarves and colourful strings of beads are selling hot food at street stalls. Their speciality is *acarajé*, deep fried bananas stuffed with prawn paste, spices and cashews. It smells intoxicating and the women beckon us to try it, but we're suspicious of street food. Street vendors tend to adamantly nod their heads when we ask if their food is vegetarian, when we know it isn't. A man in a business suit overhears us asking for directions to the post office and goes out of his way to walk us there.

I stand at the *lista de correos* desk, telling myself not to be disappointed if there's nothing for me. My heart pounds when I see my name on the list; I know it's a letter from him. There are letters from home for both Emily and me, but when I see the airmail envelope scrawled in Spanish with an Argentinian stamp on it, I immediately tuck it into my bra. I don't want

Emily to know he's written to me, or to know I'm still thinking about him. I want to wait for a private moment to tear it open.

We're about an hour out of Salvador and Emily has her eyes closed and her headphones on, when I finally open the letter. Two sides of the airmail envelope are covered in neat Spanish. I move my eyes over the two pages, trying to pick out words I can understand. Then I reef out my English-Spanish dictionary and painstakingly translate Gabriel's words.

Hola mi amor,

I was so happy to receive your letter after the brief (but very intense) time we had together. I felt very content knowing you had thought about me a little. Here, I haven't stopped thinking about you and remembering that Sunday in Lezama Park. I haven't been able to contain my sadness, but that's life, no?

This week I'm going to see Los Rolling Stones and I'm going to get drunk, very drunk. How great you met Doña Irma and all the cats and dogs, how crazy no?

I hope you return to Buenos Aires soon, I will always be waiting for you. You are very special and you will always be in my heart. Perhaps one day we can travel together, the world is small and people can find each other if they want to. It's an unalterable law.

I hope that you tell me everything you do on your trip. I want to know everything, and I also hope the cord between us never breaks, that it is there forever, to close the distance between us, strong, firm, soft.

I can't find the words to express how I feel.

When you get to Lima, Peru, contact my brother, but behave yourself please, because he's very handsome and he will treat you very nicely.

With respect to your letter, I loved your Spanish, it was very funny and charming. When I'm sad I read your letter and because I'm so enchanted, my face changes. You are very lovely, and I'm so happy

I was able to meet someone like you. Seriously, I've never experienced anything so, I mean SO crazy. The words between you and I were not important, it was the moment, wasn't it? The present, and nothing else.

I'm working to replenish my bag of artesania. Last weekend I sold well and I'm buying more material to make more pretty things, little by little, slowly but surely, do you understand?

I warn you, in Peru don't smoke marijuana or take any drugs. Peruvians are very dangerous—remember how I almost kidnapped you? Ha ha ha.

Well, I hope that when you read these lines you are enjoying your journey and it might help you to know you left a little heart amazed at your charms. It would be wonderful if you could return to Buenos Aires and stay with me a while.

Well, I finish this letter with all my love and I hope I will see you again soon.

Note: send me a photo so I can remember you.

Kisses, hugs and everything else,

Gabriel.

His words are balm for my heart.

CHAPTER SEVEN

IT'S REAL. THE letter is proof of our connection, something solid to hold onto. I want to run and dance and scream, but I have two long bus trips ahead of me. We are going to Belém, where the mouth of the Amazon River meets the sea, and I am as restless as a starving piranha. I'm still wearing the hematite earrings he gave me and I take out the mandala. I twist and turn it into the world, the cup, the flower, hold it to my cheek. Maybe it's symbolic of all the things he would give me, if only he could.

I have another gift from him, apart from the mandala and the earrings. I've been keeping it in my suede pouch, saving it for the right time.

The bus pulls into a roadhouse alongside six identical buses. The Brazilians file off the bus to go and eat—which they seem eager to do at any time of the day or night—and Emily stretches awake.

'Hey, let's wander down the road a bit and smoke this,' I whisper, showing her a joint in my palm. 'It will help pass the time. We can spin out at the scenery.'

'Where did you get that?' She's not really a smoker, but I think she'll make an exception in this case. These long bus trips can get boring.

'Gabriel gave it to me for the trip and I've been saving it.'

'Okay, but we'd better not wander too far away. We're stuffed if the bus leaves without us.'

Always so sensible.

Standing on the side of a dusty road that stretches towards an empty, flat, dry horizon, we take turns in smoking what turns out to be pretty strong stuff. The landscape begins to look mystical, the sky grows bigger, bluer. Lone birds fly in the distance but feel closer and closer and we giggle at nothing, forgetting time, just being in the moment, infused with beauty and light.

'Holy shit! The buses are leaving!' Emily shouts, breaking the spell and bringing us crashing back to reality.

'Which bus is ours?' I shout as we run back up the road.

'I don't know—they all look the same!'

We run from bus to bus, trying to find a familiar face among the passengers jostling to get back on. Buses begin to pull out as we dash around frantically until one of the drivers whistles and motions for us to get on. He looks no different to the other drivers—chubby, dark hair, sunglasses. But when we get on the bus and see the passengers laughing at our panicked expressions, we begin to relax.

I grab the window seat.

'That was scary,' Emily says, settling into the aisle seat.

'I know, imagine if we missed the bus and were stuck in the middle of Brazilian woop woop,' I say, and we burst into laughter. It wasn't that funny, but we're clearly stoned.

I lean my head against the window and slip into a semi-dream state, imagining all sorts of new lives that could unfold for me were I to find myself stuck in the middle of Brazil with no money, no possessions and no Portuguese.

Emily must be pretty out of it. She's leaning further and further into the aisle, her eyes fixed up the long aisle of the bus and out the front windscreen, her fingers nervously tugging the ends of her hair. I sense she's on edge, but then, she's often on edge. She likes to be organised, planned, in control. Qualities that get you nowhere in South America, where the best-laid plans disintegrate in a second and the only way to survive is to let go of any need for control or security and just accept that things rarely turn out as planned.

'Did you see that?' she says, panic growing in her voice. 'The bus driver is drunk or on drugs or something.'

'What do you mean?'

'He's swerving all over the road! Look, he did it again. I've been watching him swerving left, then right. He's not driving in a straight line. He's going to fucking kill us all.'

I lean towards the aisle and look out the front windscreen at the bus swerving, then at the other passengers who are completely relaxed. Why isn't anyone else worried? Emily can't take it any more. She jumps out of her seat, stands in the middle of the aisle and shouts at full volume: 'WOULD SOMEBODY STOP THE FUCKING BUS?!'

Forty heads swivel to stare at Emily, and then the entire busload of passengers bursts into fits of laughter. A well-dressed lady calmly walks down the aisle and pats Emily on the arm.

'Miss! Bus okay. No crash. This driver, he does not want to hit holes in the road.'

She points out the window as we swerve around a large pothole, then another. He isn't driving dangerously; he's driving carefully, doing his best to keep us safe on the dilapidated road.

'Obrigada!' I say, pulling Emily back down onto her seat. Thank you is one of the few Portuguese words we've both managed to learn.

After having a hearty laugh at Emily's expense, the passengers settle down and she shrivels into her seat.

'Well, we'll be laughing about that one for years to come,' I say.

'Shut up. This pot is way too strong.'

'Hey, wanna draw each other?'

'Yeah okay.'

We pass the time by sketching each other in our journals, and while Emily is the arty one, my portrait isn't too bad. It captures something of her girlishness. Next, we have a cutthroat game of Animal, Vegetable, Mineral and get into a heated argument about the differences between fur, hair, wool and skin, which ends in our refusal to speak to each other for over an hour. Eventually we agree to disagree and settle in to try and sleep. It's going to be a long night.

'Do you want the window?' I ask, trying to make peace. I prefer the window so I can lean my head against it, while Emily prefers to stretch her legs into the aisle, but I feel I should be more accommodating.

'No, I'll stay here. You can have the window seat. But keep your bum over your side of the line.'

'Yes boss!' I say, bringing my hand to my forehead in a salute. 'Buenas noches.'

'Buenas noches,' she says, shifting her body around to get comfortable, legs outstretched, back turned away from me.

I go over and over Gabriel's letter in my mind, watching a desolate landscape pass by. I think about his beautiful, smooth skin. Skin that both turns me on and puts me at ease, because it's not the tough skin of a man I should fear, it's the skin of someone sweet and gentle. I feel right with him, excited and comfortable at the same time. Shouldn't love be exactly like this?

My body is worn out, sore and seedy. My face has broken out in pimples from too much alcohol and bad food. A pair of black tyre sandals I bought in Rio are cutting into my feet and leaving black stains on my skin, my eyes are sore and bloodshot and I am more tired than I have ever been. I feel bloated and fat. I've been living on beer, pasta, cheese, ice-cream and chocolate. I am also horribly premenstrual.

But—I'm doing it. I'm travelling through South America with all my belongings on my back and this feeling of unrestrained freedom has given me an unquenchable thirst, like a drug I can't get enough of. I also know without a doubt I'm in love. I'm not sure which of the two feelings is more intoxicating. But then, every addiction begins with pleasure, before it becomes unbearable pain.

As we swerve our way north towards the state of Pará, I begin to relax. It's a relief not to have to go anywhere or do anything, to find directions, haggle over room prices, check beds for bugs or worry about our stuff getting stolen. I love the time on long bus trips from sunset onwards, when I can pull out my Walkman and listen to music from home as the sky slowly darkens.

As I stare at the vast open spaces I feel weightless, lulled by moments of sheer bliss. We pass over a mountain range during the night and it reminds me of the Blue Mountains, but a tropical version. The air is crisp and clean, unlike the sultry air of the Brazilian coast. Verdant vegetation lines the road, interrupted occasionally by huge rocks painted with ads. Brazil seems to be living in the dark ages when it comes to respect for the environment.

We arrive in Belém to torrential rain, exhausted and looking forward to a break from long bus trips. A relaxing five-day boat trip up the Amazon River is just what the doctor ordered. We haul our backpacks out of the storage compartment underneath the bus, hoist them on our backs, hang our daypacks across our chests and set off for the port in the downpour.

Along the way we pass the usual beggars in the street. We try to ignore them and keep walking. I always feel heartless doing that, but the second we stop to give one person money, we will be besieged, and it's not smart while we're carrying all of our belongings.

But one beggar shocks us into immobility. He is just a head and a torso, with tiny stumps where his arms and legs should be. He is sitting on the side of the road, bent over in the middle, leaning forward with a pencil in his mouth, drawing pictures on a piece of paper on the ground. He smiles at us. I reach into my daypack, take out my wallet and toss some *reales* into his upturned hat on the ground. Emily does the same and silently, we walk away.

The port is a frenzy of activity. It's Friday afternoon and the last of the week's riverboats are being loaded up with sacks of food and boxes of supplies, ready for the long trip upstream. In our haste to get tickets on the last boat leaving for the day, the reality of where we are doesn't hit us at first. The murky brown expanse of water stretching before us and widening into the distance isn't just any river: it is the Amazon. The longest river in the world, swimming and crawling and slithering with deadly creatures.

It will take five days on a three-deck riverboat to navigate 1317 kilometres upstream to Manaus, the city in the heart of the jungle. The boat is scheduled to leave at 7pm and if we miss it, there won't be another boat until Monday. We race back into Belém to cash some traveller's cheques and buy essential supplies—toilet paper and chocolate—and make it back to the boat by 6.30pm. We should know by now not to rush because the boat doesn't leave anywhere near on time. Time is an arbitrary thing in Brazil, as it seems to be everywhere else in South America.

'Do you serve vegetarian food? *Comida vegetariana?*' Emily asks the ticket collector.

'Sim, sim, sim, 150 reales,' he says without looking up.

He says it way too emphatically. By now we know Brazilians will say yes, take our money then serve us meat anyway. In fact, they say yes to just about any question we ask, whether they know the answer or not. Sometimes they know the answer is no, but they say yes anyway, for reasons we can never fathom.

We book ourselves a hammock space and climb aboard the weathered old white riverboat, keen to find a place where we can drop our heavy backpacks. There are only a few cabins on the top deck and they're fully booked and beyond our price range. Most people travel on the middle and lower decks, sleeping in a tightly strung web of colourful hammocks. The scene resembles a life-size piece of 1970s string art. Every inch of space is crammed with hammocks and people. No one mentions the need for life vests and it doesn't occur to us to ask.

Naked babies and kids run around, pooing and weeing straight onto the deck. We weave our way through the crowd of people, struggling to squeeze through with our backpacks, until we reach three long dining tables at the back of the boat, directly outside two toilets. The toilets are in tiny compartments that also house the 'showers', which are merely holes in the side of the boat where murky river water gushes in and back out through a drain. Both toilets smell putrid. There is nowhere left to string up a hammock.

A German hippie chick with matted, long brown hair and Rasta clothing is stringing her hammock up above one of the communal dining tables.

'Zis is zee only place left to put your hammock,' she says, shaking her head. 'They charge us a fortune for zis shit boat.'

'Have you ever done this before?' I ask her.

'No! And I will never do it again,' she moans.

There's an awkward silence. We're all in the same boat—literally. Emily breaks the silence with her usual friendliness.

'Hi, I'm Emily,' she says, and begins to string up her hammock above the table.

'Hello, I'm Connie and zis is my lover, Franky.' German travellers seem so quick to introduce people as their lovers and talk about their sex lives. He's a tall, lanky man with a friendly face and frizzy grey hair that falls to his shoulders, balding on top.

'I can't believe we have to spend four nights and five days like this,' I whine.

I am despondent. It wasn't how I'd pictured myself experiencing the Amazon.

'Don't worry, it will be fun,' Emily says, seeing my despair. 'We're going to see the Amazon jungle up close. It'll be cool.'

She begins to chat with Connie and Franky like they're old buddies. I start to string up my hammock directly above the dining tables, the last bit of space that isn't inside a toilet bowl.

While we wait for the boat to leave Belém, we join the other foreigners on the top deck: a conservative looking English couple, Chas and Lisa and a feral German girl called Nina with a smattering of freckles, the sides of her heads shaved and piercings in her nose, ears and bottom lip. There are two Israeli guys with long ponytails and a quiet Swedish girl called Ana. Then there's Silvia from Spain, who has dark hair that falls past her waist. She plays percussion and juggles, and says she's been travelling for eight years, making jewellery to earn an income. She has the air of an untameable woman revelling in her freedom and I am in awe of her, the way primary school girls are in awe of high school girls.

A kiosk on the top deck of the boat sells beer, water, chips and biscuits—at least we won't starve if there's no vegetarian food. We settle in with a few cold beers to take the edge off the afternoon humidity. It's five hours after the scheduled departure time and as the hazy light fades and evening descends over the river, we chat about all the places we've seen and are yet to see.

Around midnight, we turn in. Brazilian hammocks are made of tightly woven, striped cloth in rainbow colours and are surprisingly comfortable to sleep in once you learn how. If you lie diagonally so it flattens out, instead of curling up with your back in the shape of a crescent moon, it's almost like a bed. I sleep well on that first night, but am woken at 6am by a loud horn blaring. Breakfast. Sickly sweet coffee and white bread rolls with nothing but margarine. A meal of sugar, caffeine and carbs, not unlike the breakfasts back in the hostel in San Telmo. The hungry hoards storm the dining area and fling us out of our hammocks while we're still yawning awake.

After cruising all night, we're now deep into the jungle with no sign of civilisation. Finally, I can allow the impact of where I am to hit me with full force. I grab my daypack and skip to the top deck, fishing inside for my journal and pen. I pull a plastic chair to one side of the deck and put my bare feet up on the railing. Emily is drinking coffee and chatting with Connie and Franky near the kiosk. Good, I don't want to be disturbed. I just want to be left in peace as I take it all in, leaf by leaf, cloud by cloud, current by current.

The river's size astounds me; it is as wide as a sea in parts, so wide we can't see the opposite side. The boat hugs the riverbank on our right as we chug upstream, keeping out of the strong currents, dangerous whirlpools and god knows what else lurking in the centre of the river.

I sit there for the whole day, listening to a symphony of birdsong and watching the unfolding of the jungle, so close I can almost touch it. An impenetrable tangle of vegetation rises like a fortress, higher and higher into the distance, glowing with every shade of green invented by nature. It is a pulsating labyrinth of life and I want to explore it, to jump overboard and swim to shore, get sucked into its hidden parts. What is out there, watching us from the depths of that other world? I'm jolted back to reality by a Brazilian boy of about ten, nudging me to watch him turn his eyelids inside out. It makes me smile; my brother used to do that.

My brother is a year older than me and as kids, was my superior in everything apart from words, which were my weapons. He could punch harder but I could inflict longer-lasting damage with my acid tongue. In between fighting, we were constant companions who regularly wandered off on our own. We'd usually end up at Parramatta Westfields, where the store owners would see us and call Mum to come and pick us up.

When he was about six, he got lost and Mum had to call the police. She had asked a friend to look after me for the afternoon and he must have been bored or lonely at home on his own. He left our little unit across the road from Parramatta Park and set off alone along the Great Western Highway to Greystanes—seven kilometres away—with the idea he would just get me and take me home. He knew the way; he just didn't realise how far it was on foot, a little boy alone on one of Sydney's busiest roads. He was gone for hours and it was dark when the police found him. He'd almost made it. By the time the police returned him, Mum was frantic. While he revelled in tormenting me by turning his eyelids inside out or hanging my Barbie dolls from the light fittings by their necks, he also looked out for me.

I don't remember ever having a conversation with him about our father. He was just not with us and we didn't talk about it. Children don't know how to voice what they're feeling unless someone shows them how. Or asks them. They just accept situations as they are, so we accepted our father wasn't around and we weren't told why. We rarely mentioned his name and the rare occasions we saw him at our grandparents' house, we didn't call him Dad. We called him by his first name. Mum would go quiet if we said we'd seen him at Grandma and Grandpa's and we knew not to talk about it anymore.

Mum was always going to a building in Parramatta with a long hall-way lined with glass bricks in different colours—orange, blue, green, yellow. It was the seventies. I was captivated by the colours in that wall, with the light streaming through them. It was something to look at on those long visits.

Mummy said she was seeing the solicitor. I watched her walk down the hall in her brown knee-high boots, A-line skirt and tight top with blue and orange and brown stripes. She had shiny, long brown hair and was the prettiest mum at school. I was proud of her and I loved her, even though she sometimes lost her temper and whacked us with the end of the feather duster.

'What's a solicitor?' I asked my brother.

'I don't know,' he said, looking down at the ground.

We sat on the floor with our backs against the colourful glass bricks and waited. My brother's bottom lip always stuck out when he was sad.

The boy scampers off to find his next victim and I look back at the jungle and try to sketch its beauty. I can barely draw stick figures, so I don't know why I think I can capture something as complex as the Amazon. I look around the deck. Some passengers are staring at the jungle in the same mesmerised state I am in. Others are playing dominoes, some are chatting.

Chas and Lisa, with their lily white English skin, are determined to get tans and are spending the day sunbathing. Chas is tall and slim with receding ginger hair and a full beard, while Lisa is pale and petite with a perky upturned nose and long mousy brown hair. They're very English and very polite, travelling together as platonic friends. I think Chas would jump Lisa at the first opportunity, but they say they're just mates and that Lisa has a boyfriend back home.

As we cruise deeper into the jungle, the river narrows. Naked children, no older than three or four, row canoes over to the boat while the Brazilian passengers on board throw them food and clothes. The children have big white smiles and their slight bodies move swiftly as they collect their booty and disappear back into the jungle.

The lunches and dinners on the riverboat are not even vaguely vegetarian. A big meaty stew with black beans, carrots and potatoes is the mainstay. We stick to spaghetti, rice and packets of chips from the kiosk. On the second night, we stay up late on the top deck chatting with the other travellers in the humid jungle night air. Franky, Silvia and Nina share stories of their lives back home and how they came to be in South America.

'I have been travelling for five years,' Nina says, lighting a cigarette. She is quietly spoken and usually sits silently, listening to everyone else. 'It's easy. I steal zee bicycle, I sell zee bicycle. I steal zee car, I sell zee car.' Well, at least she doesn't tell us the name of her lover.

Silvia stands up and begins to juggle and I join her. I'm still learning, but I can do the basic three-ball routine. She tells me about a hallucinogenic cactus from Peru and Bolivia called San Pedro, which contains mescaline. The Andean people have used it for thousands of years to heighten their spiritual connection to nature.

'It is not like the flat peyote cactus in Mexico,' Silvia says. 'It's a tall green cactus.' She holds her hand up as high as her head.

'Where can I find it?'

'You don't find San Pedrito, hermana.' She calls me sister. 'It finds you. When you are ready for its secrets, it will find you.'

She begins to dance around the deck singing 'San Pedrito, San Pedrito', twirling in circles, her arms out wide, her long dark hair flying free behind her. I watch, too self-conscious to join in. I don't want to be like her; I want to *be* her. She's so beautiful and carefree and I bet men fall in love with her all the time. I imagine she dances her way through life, sprinkling gypsy magic over everyone she meets.

By the third day we're desperate for vegetables, so Silvia marches downstairs and demands the cook allow Emily, Chas and I to cook our own meal for lunch, and after a hearty chuckle, he agrees. We descend into the bowels of the boat, where the noise of the engine is so loud you can't talk over it. Large animal carcasses hang on hooks, swaying in the open air, unrefrigerated, covered in flies. I'm shocked this is what they are feeding the passengers. We make a modest meal: boiled potatoes, carrots, onions and rice with a bit of salt. Amid glances, sniggers and outright laughter from the kitchen staff, we make a meal even they think looks edible. They nod their approval but stop short of having a taste.

That afternoon, we pull into a small dock that leads to a village hidden somewhere in the trees, to offload bags of beans and rice. I spot a vendor selling homemade, creamy looking cheese from a small fold-up table. My body is crying out for nutrition, so I buy a block of cheese and scoff it without a second thought.

That night I wake with a stabbing pain tearing my stomach to shreds. I fall out of my hammock onto the floor and crawl to the toilet. Diarrhoea begins to pour out of me and I vomit so violently I'm worried my intestines are about to spew out of my mouth.

I stagger over to Emily and shake her awake.

'Emily! I'm really sick,' I moan. 'I think I have food poisoning from that fucking cheese.'

She swings out of her hammock without hesitation, sterilises some water and makes me an electrolyte drink. She takes care of me all night and I feel like I have my mum with me, looking after me. Emily may be sarcastic, she may be cynical, but she's the most compassionate person I know.

The hell continues the next day. There are only two toilets for the entire deck, so when they're occupied, I writhe around on the filthy floor banging on the door, desperately trying to contain the fluids that want to explode out.

Connie gives me a charcoal tablet, which is supposed to stop the diarrhoea, but it only makes it worse. Black liquid pours out of me and I am becoming increasingly dehydrated and delirious. I don't have the strength to get in and out of my hammock above the table anymore, and a kind Brazilian lady offers for me to string my hammock up near her family's, at the other end of the boat and low to the floor. I spend the last couple of days of the trip in a semi-conscious state in my hammock with women and children squashed on top of me. They sit on my legs or on the side of my hammock, using me as a backrest while they laugh and chat, loudly and incessantly, and I don't have the will to protest.

The boat stops for a day in Santarém and half the passengers get off. I tell Emily to go and explore the town without me, relieved to be left in the hammock in peace. She leaves with Connie and Franky and a few hours later, returns with cold lemonade. As soon as I take a few sips, the vomiting and diarrhoea begin again.

A month has passed since we left Australia and we're coming to the end of our time in Brazil. We have two months left before we leave for London and still have to see Bolivia and Peru. I don't have the strength. All I want to do is get off this fucking boat and fly to London where I can have clean food and water, and see a doctor who speaks English. Maybe I'm not cut out for this kind of travel. I've made a big mistake coming to this shithole and dragging Emily along with me.

The sickness is defeating my spirits. I'm delirious, sweating, drifting in and out of sleep, just wanting it to be over. But in that state I hear a faint voice telling me to keep going. I'm living my dream and I have to take the bad with the good. I just have to make it to Manaus. Then I can fly to Buenos Aires and see Gabriel. He will take me to a doctor. God, I miss him. I want his arms around me again, I want his beautiful smooth skin next to mine again. I want to kiss him and watch his fingers twist wire around stone until a beautiful piece of jewellery emerges that will make women smile.

I have to get back to him, but I can barely lift a drink bottle to my lips, let alone carry my backpack. I lean over the side of the hammock, grab my backpack and pull my journal out. I'm too weak to write, so I flip through its pages until I find the photo. It is real; he is real. The blurry second image of me sitting alone transposed on the side of the photo doesn't have to mean anything. Maybe it's not a sign I'll end up alone. Not everything is a sign from the fucking universe. Maybe what we think are signs are nothing more than mistakes in the exposure.

By the time the boat arrives in Manaus, I am a shell. I've stopped shitting and spewing and now I'm starving. In this wretched state, I wonder how much weight I've lost. There has to be an upside.

Connie and Franky help me into a cab while Emily carries her back-pack and drags mine behind her. We flick through the guidebook looking for vegetarian restaurants and find a Hare Krishna centre. The cab driver takes us straight there and when we knock on the door, a peaceful face in orange robes greets us. My heart sinks when the Hare Krishna man tells us it's a spiritual centre without a cafe attached, but when I explain how sick I've been, he invites us in. He prepares two trays of beautiful, clean, tasty vegetarian food for us. It's the best meal I've ever eaten in my life. In fact, I think it actually saves my life. My strength returns quickly and by that evening, I have regained my spirit and sense of adventure. I'm not going to cut my trip short for anything.

We meet up in a bar with other travellers from the boat and drink caipirinhas, play pool and chat to the jungle boys who fondle my hair in amazement. Rather than frizzing, it has woven itself into long ringlets in the humidity. I lap up the attention and flirt shamelessly with many brawny young Brazilian men with shiny brown bodies. But flirting is as far as I go. I'm already taken.

Chas and Lisa turn up, sore and sorry. They're burnt to a crisp from five days of sunbathing on the boat. They've decided to change their itinerary. Instead of taking another boat to Venezuela, they're flying to La Paz, a cooler climate where winter clothing will protect their burnt skin. We'd also thought of taking a boat to Venezuela, but I never want to see another boat as long as I live.

The heat of Brazil, the expense, the language difficulties and my illness have taken their toll. The crisp air of the Andes is beckoning. We book a flight with Chas and Lisa and fly from the hot heart of the Amazon to the soaring city of La Paz, 3,650 metres closer to the South American stars.

Chapter eight

SUNRISE PAINTS THE mountains pale pink, illuminates every face on the plane, both dark and light. The flattering glow makes everyone look beautiful and at peace. Snow-capped peaks surround us and we shift in our seats, trying to get a good look through the small plane windows. A crisp new day is breaking across the Andes and this is a view usually reserved for mountain climbers. That will never be us, so we make the most of this vista—the immense cordillera, its sharp spine stretching as far as the eye can see.

The Andes are breathtaking in their size and beauty, a dramatic contrast to the tropical tangle of the Amazon, which we were immersed in only hours before. Two kinds of wild, each as captivating as the other.

As we near La Paz, I soak up the final moments of the flight and this glorious morning light. After weeks of long, bumpy bus rides and the noise and filth and sticky heat of the boat, it's a luxury to splurge on a plane trip and sit on clean seats in air-conditioned comfort.

As we disembark from the plane, a shock of cold air bites at our faces. Brazil's heat and humidity are behind us; we are now breathing dry, icy thin air into our unprepared lungs. We've given no thought as to how cold it will be here, and how the climate and altitude will affect us. We haven't packed many warm clothes but we know Bolivia will be the place to buy them.

Chas, Lisa, Emily and I bundle into a mini-bus waiting outside the airport. Pale morning light streams through the windows and the soft sound of panpipes plays on a crackling radio. It lulls the passengers, who are mostly indigenous, into a dreamy silence. The music seems born of the landscape, as if its wispy notes have floated directly out of crevices and caves and valleys.

I'm squashed next to a plump *cholita*—the once derogatory but now affectionate term for indigenous women of Aymara and Quechua descent. I smile and try to ignore her overpowering body odour, a mix of woodsmoke and faeces. Descending steeply, we round a bend and see the city of La Paz shining in the sunlit valley below, encircled by the Andes rising around it. The magnitude of the mountains, the haunting panpipes, physical exhaustion and sheer relief at having left the intensity of Brazil hit me all at once.

Tears stream down my face, but I'm not unhappy. I feel closer to Gabriel than I have since I'd first met him in Buenos Aires four weeks earlier. This is the landscape of his ancestors. I see his skin, his eyes, his hair texture and his cheekbones in the people on the bus. The Andes cordillera runs along the western side of the continent from Argentina and Chile, through Bolivia, Peru, Ecuador, Colombia and Venezuela. I imagine the mountains connecting me to Gabriel, like a timeless geological cord that stretches from where I am, to where he is. We have stood together in these mountains before. Or maybe that time is yet to come.

As we descend from the *altiplano*, or high plain, the stark differences between Brazil and Bolivia became apparent. Brazil is all sweat and sex and swagger and bare skin. Here, in this landlocked country, the air is dry and cold and stocky bodies are rugged up in alpaca wool. The cholitas stand out as they go about their daily business dressed in their finery: full skirts called *polleras* over puffy petticoats that give them a rotund look, colourful shawls wrapped around their shoulders, chubby babies with chapped, rosy cheeks in slings on their backs, dangly earrings, two long black plaits and the fashion item they've made their own—bowler hats.

Indigenous Bolivian women adopted the English bowler hat in the 1920s, when a supplier of bowler hats in Manchester sent a shipment to Bolivia for British railway workers. They were too small for the men, so the English expats distributed them amongst the locals and they became an integral part of cholita fashion. Perched high on a cholita's head at interesting angles and held on with bobby pins, they are a delightfully impractical yet supremely stylish form of decorative headwear for these proud women. Once shipped in from England, they're now made locally, embellished with a ribbon or a bow; the finer the hat, the wealthier the woman.

Founded in 1548, La Paz is one of South America's oldest settlements, but the Spanish colonial architecture is mixed with modern skyscrapers to create a city with a strange blend of old and new. Despite a cacophony of horns from cars, buses and trucks blaring through the streets, it doesn't feel like a city as much as a big, homely town, wrapped in beautiful mountains.

In a steep cobblestone lane, we find a hostel for forty bolivianos a night, about US$5, run by a quiet man called Marco. He is around thirty, with Andean features not unlike Gabriel's. But he's smaller and very conservative. He doesn't wear chunky beads around his neck like Gabriel and his short hair is combed neatly. His weathered brown trousers are too big for him and have been patched up in numerous places, but they are neatly pressed, and a faded blue business shirt is tucked in. He seems like a respectable man and I feel safe staying at his hostel. We pay Marco and he shows us to our room, where we dump our bags and straight away set off with Chas and Lisa to explore the city.

It doesn't take long for headaches and nausea to strike. We wonder if we've picked up a virus in Manaus, but then we realise what's going on—altitude sickness. We've flown from sea level to an altitude of 3,650 metres with no time to acclimatise to the decreased levels of oxygen. We're nauseous, drowsy and lethargic, with sore muscles and pins and needles in our hands and feet. My body had taken enough of a beating on the boat; I'm not sure how much more I can stand.

We drag ourselves back to the hostel. Marco draws us a map to an English-speaking doctor and we head to Plaza Murillo. The doctor is a distinguished looking gentleman in his fifties who speaks English fluently and says if our altitude sickness doesn't abate by the following day, we'll have to descend to a lower altitude and give our bodies time to acclimatise before returning to La Paz. In the meantime, he suggests we buy some coca leaves from the cholitas at the market and make coca leaf tea.

The locals walk around chewing mouthfuls of coca leaves stuffed into their cheeks to steel themselves against hunger and cold. The tea doesn't do much for us and I wonder what the plant's more infamous product is like. Scoring cocaine in La Paz is easy. It's cheap and pure, and there are bars around La Paz that sell it over the counter.

But we're not interested. I love a few drinks and the occasional puff, but hard drugs? No way. I am not going to end up like him. I'm not going to let drugs destroy my family.

I was about thirteen when I learnt the truth about my father. Mum didn't tell me, my paternal grandparents didn't tell me, and my dad certainly didn't tell me on those rare occasions I saw him. It was my outspoken maternal grandmother, Granky, who let it slip one day when I was trying to work out why my father had been a ghost all my life.

'It was the drugs, love. That's why you couldn't see your dad.'

'What drugs?' I'd asked, laughing. The wrong words were being spoken, words that made no sense. Words that thumped against my skull.

'The heroin.'

'What?'

'Didn't you know, love? Your dad was a heroin addict. Not when your mum and him first got married, but soon after that. He got in with a bad crowd. That's when things got nasty.'

'What do you mean, nasty?'

She turned her back, started making a cuppa. I waited.

'Well, he got himself into a lot of trouble, love. Your mum had to get you kids away.'

This explained a lot, yet raised more questions than it answered.

'Your mum did it pretty tough, till she met your stepdad.'

My stepdad entered our lives with dishes of pasta bake on rainy Sydney winter nights and tickets to the circus. We liked him straight away. He never tried to pretend he was our father; he was a friend and a provider and he was nice to Mum. Best of all, he was funny. They married when I was eight and a year later we left Sydney and moved to Katoomba. I duly crossed my surname off all my schoolbooks and replaced it with his surname.

I tried to match the image of a drug addict with the father I'd had sporadic contact with and pieces of the puzzle began to fit. Vague flashes of my paternal grandma encouraging me to talk to him, spend time with him. She must have been desperate to help her son, give him something to live for, a reason to stay off the drugs. I was supposed to feel something for this man I barely knew. What I felt was the suspicion a child feels towards a stranger. The weight of his and grandma's sad-faced hope. Their grasping, futile hope that I would love him when all I wanted to do was get away from him, because I thought something about him was bad. If Mum didn't like him, how could I? Worse than a stranger, he was my father. Some part of me that was supposed to be open to him was hidden behind a wall, locked, closed. At the same time, a tiny part of me that had been pushed way, way down yearned for his attention.

Mum later confirmed what Granky had said. There were stories of drugs hidden in my nappies, alleged threats of violence if she fought for custody. But pain distorted her face when I pushed for details, so I dropped it and made damn sure I didn't talk about it again. But at that moment, when I found out how my father had endangered and neglected our family, I made a decision never to touch 'hard' drugs. I separated the drugs that to my mind were bad, like heroin and cocaine, from those that weren't, like alcohol and pot. I judged my father harshly; perhaps too harshly. I knew nothing about the causes of addiction, had no idea what had happened in his life to lead him down that path, had no sympathy for him. I vowed I would never be like him. So, no thanks amigos, no hard drugs for me. Even if South Americans snort coke like Australians drink tea, I don't want to get caught up in those circles. I've seen the destruction it causes.

Still battling altitude sickness, Emily and I manage to check out a bit of the city and I'm taken with its cheerful blend of old and new, laid out beneath the mountainous backdrop. Cars and trucks clog the roads, beeping their horns continuously, and the climate switches from freezing one minute to sunny the next. The narrow cobblestone laneways are crammed with minivans, shoe shiners and popcorn sellers. The cholitas sit on the footpath outside modern shoe stores, selling herbs, coca leaves and dried llama fetuses.

In local superstition, the earth goddess, Pachamama, requires llama fetuses to be buried beneath the foundations of any new house as a good luck offering. The bigger the house, the bigger the fetus required. It's a beguiling city with peculiar customs, and one I can picture myself living in, if it were not so cold and full of dead llama babies.

When Emily is resting at the hotel that afternoon, I sneak out and call Gabriel, but it's not the heartwarming conversation I'd hoped for. He sounds different. It's a weird, stilted conversation. I can't understand much of what he says. He's talking fast, racing from one thing to the next, saying something about going to Iguazu Falls. I'm not sure if I understand, but it sounds like he doesn't know when he'll be back in Buenos Aires, or if he'll be able to meet up with me. It's as if he doesn't care whether we ever see each other again.

My heart sinks. He does not sound like the Gabriel I remember. I want to say so much, but I don't know enough Spanish yet. I pay 124 Bolivianos, which is about US$40 for the call. It's extravagant, and when I finally hear the words 'I love you', it's worth it. But he doesn't say it in Spanish, he says it in stilted English and it sounds strange. Like he has become someone else.

The phone call leaves me unsettled. Maybe I can stay in La Paz, find work teaching English, and Gabriel can meet me here. Or I could cut the trip short, fly straight to Buenos Aires and see him. Possibilities stream through my throbbing head. I can't think straight.

Emily and I suffer through the altitude sickness another day, staring at the peeling, windowless walls of our hostel, in between napping in our lumpy single beds and shuffling to the market for supplies. Marco helps himself to our backpacks. He pulls out our dirty washing, including our undies, and returns it to us clean, ironed and starched. He then sticks out his hand for payment upon delivery of our spotless, stiff clothes. In the state we are in, we appreciate his tenacity and hand him ten bolivianos with no haggling.

By day three, we're worse. It's time to retreat to a lower altitude. The guidebook tells us Rurrenabaque in the north of the country is the best place to take trips into the Bolivian section of the Amazon, so we buy tickets for a bus leaving at 3pm that afternoon. We'll spend a few days at low altitude and take a trip into the jungle, give our blood cells time to recuperate.

Chas and Lisa decide to join us, and the four of us head to the market to buy supplies for the bus trip. The market is crowded and people press in on us from all sides. Emily and I have our passports and our money inside our boots, as usual. We buy bottled water, dry biscuits, bread rolls and avocados and emerge from the crush of people into the street on the other side of the market. Lisa stops suddenly, rifling around in the pockets of her jacket.

'Oh no! I can't find my wallet.'

'Where did you have it?' Chas asks.

'In my pocket,' she says, pushing her hand further in until it pops out the other side. Her pockets and the lining of her jacket have been slashed and she's lost her wallet with money and a credit card inside. We're all shocked out at how quickly it happened.

'At least I left most of my money at the hostel and I didn't bring my passport,' she says. She doesn't have much time to find a phone, exchange traveller's cheques and cancel her credit card before our bus leaves, so we go our separate ways for the morning. Emily and I go back to the hostel to pack our bags, having arranged to meet Chas and Lisa for a late lunch at a vegetarian restaurant not far from the bus terminal. We need a good vego feed before venturing off into the jungle.

The restaurant is large and clean and smells of nourishing, fresh plant food. Heavenly. A buffet laden with vegetarian spaghetti, lasagne, curries and veggie burgers beckons and Emily and I load up our plates and take a seat near the front door. Travellers from Germany and Sweden join us, then Chas and Lisa arrive, give us the thumbs up to let us know everything is sorted, and head for the buffet. Lisa is the first one back to the table.

'I just met an Australian woman over at the buffet who was in a jeep accident. She says she fractured her neck. Her vertebra fractured diagonally all the way through but didn't separate. She's in a brace. Lucky she's still walking.'

'Oh the poor thing. Did she say where in Australia she was from?' I ask, munching on a veggie pattie.

'Sydney. She was on Easter Island and was a passenger in a jeep. The driver skidded and they rolled three times on the side of the road.'

I stop chewing mid-mouthful. Jenny. Jenny is a friend and work

colleague from Sydney. We'd planned to be in South America at the same
time, but she was going to Easter Island and taking a different route to La
Paz, so we'd given up trying to meet up. It wasn't going to work. I stand
up and look towards the buffet.

'Jenny!' I run over to the other side of the restaurant. She's sitting on
her own, thin and fragile.

'What happened?' I say, embracing her gently.

'You're not going to believe this. I was in a jeep accident on Easter
Island. There are zero cars there, but the driver lost control when she hit
the brakes on a completely deserted dirt road. The jeep was all shell; no
padding, no seatbelts. We were so lucky. It took twenty minutes until
anyone knew we were there. Two guys came by with a donkey and eventually, another vehicle came past and they stopped and took me to the
hospital. It was just a tin shed with one intern who spoke only Spanish and
a nurse. They X-rayed me on a machine that was so ancient I was terrified
my insides would be fried. And they gave me some sort of painkilling shot.
The results of the X-ray were so blurry it was useless.'

'Jesus Christ! What did you do? Did you stay at the hospital?'

'No way, I wanted to get out of there. The doctor just scribbled on a
piece of paper in Spanish: 'Get help wherever you go next'.

I stifle a laugh. It's so typical of South America.

We race through all the adventures I've had, from meeting Gabriel to
Iguazu Falls, Carnival and the boat trip down the Amazon.

'Jen, I'd love to stay with you but our bus leaves in about twenty
minutes.'

'It's okay, it's just good to see a familiar face,' she says.

We sit in silence for a moment, stunned at the coincidence. We'd both
read books about synchronicity and how coincidences like this one were
inherently meaningful. If the universe was sending us a message, neither
of us knew what it was. But it was great to see each other, even if it was
bittersweet. There was so much to say and so little time to say it.

I tell her about the altitude sickness and how the bus trip we're booked
on to take us to a lower altitude is notoriously steep and dangerous.

'We'll be back in La Paz in about a week. Will you still be here?'

'No, I've only got three days left and then I'm flying back to Santiago to see my doctor at the hospital. Hopefully, he'll clear me to go to Machu Picchu before I head home. I was supposed to start my trip there.'

I consider cancelling the bus trip, but I know we won't get our money back and Emily and I really can't stay at this altitude any longer.

'Well, good luck, I hope you find a better driver than I did on Easter Island,' she says, giving me a hug.

'You too—I guess I'll see you back in Sydney.'

'Do you know when you'll be back?' she asks.

'No, no idea at this stage.'

The thought of going home leaves me cold. I haven't done enough, experienced enough. I haven't changed enough. Australia feels dull compared to South America, and all its culture and colour and vibrancy. It will take a lifetime to explore all of it fully. I could stay for months, years even. I want to stay for as long as it takes to learn the language fluently, to feel the deep roots of the place wrap tightly around me. I don't want to go home where I'm rootless, lost, invisible. The deeper into the continent I travel, the more my skin changes, the happier I become.

The bus is late, of course. The scheduled departure time is 3pm, but we're on Bolivian time, so that means it could leave at 4pm, 5pm, 7pm, or not at all. Since we've arrived in Bolivia, we've heard the phrase *más o menos* tacked on to the end of many sentences, especially when they relate to schedules. It means *more or less* and a ticket printed with a seat number and a departure time is no guarantee the bus will leave at that time, or that we'll even have a seat. The ticket may as well say: '3pm—sort of'.

When the bus arrives, it's already full of locals. A family with a baby and a young boy on their laps are sitting in our allocated seats—seats we've paid considerably more for, no doubt. The mother and father pretend not to see us. As guilt-ridden as we feel about it, we decide we want to get what we've paid for. In the state we're in, we can't imagine standing or sitting in the aisle, full of people holding chickens or sitting on large sacks of rice, for the next twenty hours while the bus bumps along unpaved roads. So we flash our tickets at the parents and they begrudgingly move into the aisle with their children.

Eventually, two hours late, the rickety old bus with its shifty-eyed driver who clearly thinks he's on a racetrack takes us hurtling out of La Paz and down the Yungas Road. The 410-kilometre trip takes a minimum of eighteen hours—if you make it there alive. It's known as the world's most dangerous road. The Death Road.

The guidebook doesn't detail just how deadly the road is, though its name should have given us a clue. Had the book spelt it out for us: 'Do not travel on this road by bus to Rurrenabaque under any circumstances; take a plane or risk certain death', we may well have followed that advice. But we do everything the cheapest way possible, so it doesn't occur to us to take a plane.

It begins smoothly enough. We climb out of La Paz to the arid altiplano, around 4,650 metres high, past police and military checkpoints where our passports are checked. The road then descends sharply from about 4,500 metres to 1,200 metres near Coroico, and in many parts is only the width of a single vehicle.

It's always a little off-putting when you see crucifixes lining a road. We're a few hours into the trip when it becomes terrifying. A dirt road crudely sliced into the side of a mountain has to take the weight of buses, trucks and cars and withstand rock falls and heavy rain. The edges look about as strong as a nibbled biscuit. In some sections, there are gaping holes, which the bus has to swerve around to avoid falling through. When trucks and buses try to pass each other, it's our bus that has to stop and reverse on a knife-edge to let the oncoming traffic pass on our right. No guardrails and a sheer six-hundred-metre drop to the bottom.

I have the window seat, as usual, so I'm on the side closest to the edge of the road. I can see straight to the bottom of the canyon, where wrecks of buses and cars lie in a scrap metal graveyard. Emily is leaning over me, stricken with fear.

'This is outrageous, how can they allow traffic on this road?' she cries.

'Well, we're here now, there's not much we can do other than get out and walk.'

'I think I'd rather walk actually. Even if it takes five days. This is a fucking suicide mission.'

She's shifting uneasily in her seat, looking around to see whether the other passengers are worried. They are blasé, as if they're not really fussed whether we stay on the road or roll off the cliff. I pat her on the leg and attempt a joke.

'Just don't jump up and shout, "would somebody stop the fuck-ing bus"!'

She doesn't laugh.

I'm trying to lighten the mood, because I'm scared too. Petrified, in fact. But then something happens, a shift takes place, arising out of acceptance. Fear falls away, a wave of euphoria washes over me and I become light and carefree. I'm not in a bus travelling precariously along an unsealed clifftop road. I'm weightless and hovering above the gorge, floating, flying above the mountain peaks. The bus could plummet over the edge at any second, but I'm fearless and free. I embrace this moment in my life, on a precipice between life and death.

'Woo-hoo,' I holler out the window. 'This is what we came for, Emily! This is what it's all about.'

'We're on the edge of a fucking cliff!' she shouts, gripping my arm. 'How is this even legal? This country is so dodgy. This is the stupidest idea we've had on the trip so far.'

'No, it's amazing, just go with it Emily, enjoy it.'

'Enjoy it? The road could give way underneath us at any minute! I can't believe I let you talk me into this trip. We should've just gone to India or Thailand, lazed around on some beaches getting pissed and going to full moon parties.' Her eyes slam shut.

I open my eyes wider and watch the arid altiplano merge into tropical rainforest as we edge further into the Yungas mountains. The scenery is staggering and I want to grow wings and soar through the deep ravines and up to the mountaintops and back down again. If I die in a bus crash in the jungle-covered mountains of Bolivia, so be it.

We drive under waterfalls and I stretch my hand out the window to let the fresh, cold water spray up my arms. In the fading light of dusk, the outline of the mountains disappears against a darkening sky and after two hours, we've passed the most harrowing part of the road. We relax a little and try to sleep, but it's too bumpy. Twenty hours after leaving La Paz, we're back down at sea level, speeding across a long, hot and dusty road to the little jungle town of Rurrenabaque on the Beni River, which flows through the Amazon basin.

We book into a hostel, have a cold shower and change clothes. We're on a high after surviving The Death Road, and chat excitedly with Chas and Lisa and a few other travellers. We meet an English girl called Sue, who speaks fluent Spanish and says she's living in La Paz, teaching English. I'm starting to pick up more Spanish, but I'm relieved to let her take over as translator. She asks us which bus company we've come from La Paz with and when we tell her, she's horrified.

'That bus company lost two buses over the cliff at Christmas,' she says.

'Gee, wonder why they didn't mention that to us when we bought our tickets,' Emily says.

We don't want to spend more time than necessary in Rurrenabaque, so we pile into the hostel's office and book a jungle trip to leave the next day. They can take six people: me, Emily, Chas, Lisa, Sue and a skinny German guy with thick glasses called Claud, who doesn't say much and smiles a lot. The trip costs $US50 and will take us in a canoe down the Beni River and deep into the jungle, camping out for three nights.

We leave our big packs at the hostel and pack our daypacks with the barest essentials, hop into a sturdy long wooden canoe with our guides, Chino and Negro. Chino is half-Bolivian, half-Japanese, a small but solid man in army camouflage shorts and a white singlet, with eyes that turn slightly inwards. Negro isn't actually black, but tells us he was conceived on a dark and stormy night and came out darker than his brothers and sisters. Negro is tall and wears a white baseball cap backwards and a freshly washed button-up shirt with red, white and black panels. It looks a little fancy for a jungle trip.

'Como te llamas?' Chino asks me as I settle into the canoe.

'Me llamo Leigh,' I answer.

'Like Bruce Lee,' he jokes.

Bolivians love kung fu and are obsessed with Bruce Lee, so whenever I tell them my name, they inevitably bring up the kung fu master. I've come to expect it.

We spend most of the first day cruising down the river, looking for a place in the jungle to dock the canoe, stopping every now and then to look at a multitude of monkeys—spider monkeys, white-faced capuchin monkeys, squirrel monkeys—and a rainbow of birds, from electric blue macaws to orange-billed toucans. We're a long way from civilisation and the jungle along the riverbed is dense and seemingly impenetrable. Without warning, Chino jumps out of the canoe, swims to shore and disappears into the trees.

He whistles and Negro pulls the boat in behind him. It's a tiny clearing and the instant we get off the boat, we're blanketed by bloodthirsty mosquitos the size of small dogs. We've all worn long-sleeved shirts, but the mozzies still bite us through the fabric. Chino pulls a lighter out of his pocket and lights a plant with fuzzy white domes on its fronds, which starts sending thick plumes of smoke out and repels the mozzies.

Then he pulls out a machete from underneath the seat in the canoe and starts hacking away at the trees, making a clearing for us to set up camp and whipping up tables and a bench from wood he finds in the jungle. He cuts just enough to make the space we need, then goes off in search of more building materials, while we sit around chatting with Negro, feeling like useless tourists.

Negro speaks English and does the talking, while most of the heavy labour falls to the industrious Chino. He comes back with an armload of straight branches and sticks them into the ground at even intervals, then hangs a large white mosquito net over the top. The net is divided into eight compartments, one for each of us. He places a large tarp on the jungle floor and dusts his hands off on his pants. Our camp is done. We each roll out our sleeping bags in our own compartments inside the mosquito net—it's about as primitive a camping trip as you can get and I couldn't be happier.

Chino sets up a gas stove and makes us all a cup of Nescafe with about seven teaspoons of sugar, then sets to work making a vegetable curry with rice for dinner as darkness falls and we huddle together to talk and drink whisky.

It's too hot in my sleeping bag, so I lie on top, listening to the music of the jungle. The pungent smell of damp earth and foliage thickens the air, everything electrified by recent storms. Howler monkeys roar across the wilderness and a cacophony of noise emanating from wild creatures I can't identify keeps me awake. I wonder what protection we'd have against a jaguar.

My thoughts drift to Gabriel, as they usually do just before sleep.

Lying on the jungle floor of the Bolivian Amazon, I am a million miles from him. I remember his words in the letter and try to stay hopeful, but I'm still confused about our phone conversation. There was something wrong with him, and I can't work out what it was. Has he met someone else? Has he lost interest? I have to believe I'll see him again, but I don't know how or when. Or if he'll be the same sweet Gabriel I met in the park. And if we do see each other again and fall so madly in love we can never be apart, what then? Can I make a good life in South America?

I finally fall asleep and some time in the early hours of the morning, a noise wakes me. It's something big, fossicking around the camp. I'm too scared to open my eyes and everyone else seems to be asleep. I lie frozen, not breathing, until it eventually wanders off into the depths of the jungle.

We spend the next two days cruising the river, spotting wildlife. There's nothing but trees, water and sky and we could be the only humans on a prehistoric Earth. One morning, I'm staring up into the trees watching monkeys scamper through branches, eyeing us off inquisitively, when I see something brown and furry oozing down a tree. I point to it and Negro shouts to Chino to cut the motor. It's a sloth, nature's most chilled-out animal. A rare sight according to Negro.

Pink river dolphins glide shyly out of the water, with just their heads poking out, and Negro tells us to jump in and swim with them, so we do, fully clothed. They assure us there are no piranhas in this part of the river, but if there were, we wouldn't have been able to see them. The water is inky black and whatever lurks below is invisible.

On the last night, we sit in the smoky campsite drinking disgusting Nescafe and chatting. Sue says she'd been offered a job at the hostel in Rurrenabaque, which she's not going to take. I'm envious; I picture myself being offered a job to live in a little village in the depths of the Amazon. Every time I meet a foreigner living and working in South America and becoming part of the local culture, I feel a pull to do the same.

After dinner, we take the canoe out for a cruise. When Negro shines his torch at the riverbank, five pairs of red glowing eyes flash back at us. Black caiman. They hadn't warned us these beasts with sharp teeth were in the river when they'd encouraged us to go swimming. We've cheated death yet again.

A full moon illuminates the surface of the water. The air is warm and sweet and the jungle is never silent, never still. Sitting back in the boat, I trace the silhouettes of palm trees against the moonlit sky with my finger and allow all the wild sounds to move through me. I ask Negro to cut the engine and we drift along in silence. The tip of the canoe slices through the black glass of the river and eight of us are lulled into a sense of wonder.

That night, lying with my head on the jungle floor, with no pillow, at the mercy of whatever animal wants to eat me, I sleep peacefully.

CHAPTER NINE

BACK ON THE Death Road. It's the only road back to La Paz but this time, we're ascending and it's marginally safer. Our bus skirts along the inside of the mountain, while passing vehicles descend on the outside, perilously close to the crumbling edges of the road.

Halfway up the Death Road, we get off the bus and spend a few days at the pretty hilltop village of Coroico. We say goodbye to Chas and Lisa, and Emily promises to contact them when we arrive in London. I give them a farewell hug, but make no promises. I doubt I'll see them again. That's the difference between Emily and me: she never stops making new friends, while I take a lot longer to trust people. To let them in. When it comes to men, however, I let them in too quickly, trust them with my heart and my body before I should.

We arrive back in La Paz on Thursday, March 23, 1995, the 160th anniversary of the day Bolivia lost its piece of ocean. Bolivian flags are flying to commemorate the Day of the Sea. When Bolivia declared independence from the colonial Spanish in 1825, it had the option to become part of Peru, part of Argentina or go it alone. It chose to become a separate nation and since then, has lost over half its original territory. It lost its slice of sea to Chile in the Guano War of 1879 to 1884—the area now called Antofogasta. It also lost its rubber-plant-rich territory of Acre in the north to Brazil. A chunk of its southern border was lost to Argentina and 50,000 square kilometres of the Gran Chaco desert was ceded in a 1932 war with Paraguay.

The result is an impoverished nation, one of South America's poorest. Despite its struggles, Bolivia is friendly and relatively safe, treacherous roads notwithstanding.

We return to Marco's hostel, dump our bags and go shopping for our trip to the high southern plains. We buy handwoven alpaca wool jumpers, ponchos, beanies and socks and take silly photos of ourselves draped head to toe in brown alpaca wool.

The thick wool steels us against the icy chill in the air, as we wander La Paz in search of somewhere to have lunch. We stumble across a café run by Israelis and order two veggie burgers. We're reflecting on our jungle trip when a traveller with an English accent, dreadlocks and wild eyes begins shouting outside the restaurant.

'The barcodes! The barcodes!'

'What's he on about?' Emily asks, bemused. We're both staring at him, which prompts him to run into the cafe and straight to our table.

'Do you know about the barcodes?' he shouts, shifting from one foot to the other. The whites of his eyes are showing and he's tugging frantically on his woven Bolivian vest.

'What barcodes?' Emily asks.

'The US military are planning to tattoo everyone with barcodes. Right here on the wrist. You have to get out of here.'

'Really? Wow, thanks dude, we'd better hurry,' Emily laughs.

'And the lettuce,' he whispers, leaning in. 'Don't eat the lettuce.'

'What's wrong with the lettuce?' I ask.

'It's got a worm in it. It gets into your bloodstream and eats your brain.'

He runs out of the restaurant and disappears down the road, still shouting.

'Too much coke?' Emily asks.

'Yeah, probably.' I look down at my burger. 'I don't think I'll eat my lettuce. Just in case.'

'Me either.'

I love travelling with Emily. Her sense of humour, her willingness to follow me into stupid situations in the name of fun and adventure, her capacity to forgive and forget. She gets on my nerves sometimes, but she's loosening up the further we get into the trip. She's not as cynical as she was, and I'm not as flaky as I was. I'm still visualising white light around us without Emily knowing, but I'm keeping it to myself. It's just not her thing and I'm okay with that. Each to their own. Maybe we're maturing.

'I miss Vegemite,' I say.

'Me too. Vegemite on toast with loads of butter.'

'Oh my god, I'd kill for Vegemite on toast and a decent cup of tea. What else do you miss from home?'

'Going out to hear live music and have a few beers. You know, just our old life.'

That night, we head out to a club in downtown La Paz. A rock band is playing Nirvana, Smashing Pumpkins, Stone Temple Pilots and Pearl Jam covers and we drink a lot of beer and jump around like we're in the mosh pit at a music festival. It's a little slice of home and we don't hold back. The Bolivians are demure and stand back, watching two drunk Aussie girls go crazy on the dancefloor.

'I miss Newtown,' Emily says, leaning on me to hold herself up. 'I miss seeing bands at The Sando and focaccias with eggplant and sweet chilli sauce at Café 381.'

'I don't,' I slur. 'I don't miss anything about Australia.'

'You do so! You miss Vegemite!'

'Oh yeah. But that's all I miss.'

'We'll get some as soon as we get to London.'

I don't answer.

I just can't see myself in London. I'm not finished with South America yet, and it's not finished with me. After our trip to Uyuni, we'll be going to Peru. Gabriel's homeland. I'm going to call him as soon as we arrive in Cusco and tell him I miss him and want to go back to Buenos Aires and be with him. I need to find out what was wrong with him last time I called but whatever it is, I know we will work through it. Unless—he really has met someone else. That would explain why he sounded so distant, so detached. But why wouldn't he just tell me on the phone? In my inebriated state, I can't think clearly but there's a hot, heavy pain in the pit of my stomach.

We stumble into Marco's hostel at 2am and find our bedroom door locked. Giggling and falling into the walls, we knock on his office door and in broken Spanish, ask for our room key. He's asleep on the floor at the other end of the room, with our key on a heavy wooden keyring in his hand. Disgruntled at being woken, he groans and without even lifting his head, pelts the key across the room and it hits Emily square on the forehead, sending us into fits of laughter. He shouts at us to go to bed and rolls over. Poor Marco, dealing with drunk and drugged-out travellers on a daily basis must get tiresome.

The next evening, we set off on a 5.30pm bus for Uyuni, fifteen hours from La Paz towards the southwest altiplano of Bolivia. At an average altitude of 3750 metres, the South American altiplano is the largest high-altitude plateau on the planet after Tibet and the place where the Andes are at their widest. The bus climbs and climbs, and we reach the altiplano just in time to see a blood orange sunset fade to peach, pink, mauve and purple over a serrated mountain horizon.

It's a bitterly cold bus trip, even with our alpaca jumpers, ponchos and beanies on. The driver is watching Bruce Lee videos at full volume on a television perched high on the windscreen so he can watch the movie while keeping one eye on the road. Freezing, huddled under my poncho and trying to block out the sounds of kung fu, I fall asleep and dream I am hemorrhaging blood from all of my orifices. My throat has swollen up so much I can't breathe. I wake with a start. I can't work out what the dream is telling me—maybe that I'm going to die on one of these dangerous bus trips. No, too literal. Maybe it's a hangover from the altitude sickness, my brain trying to make sense of what my body went through. Or maybe it means my blood is finally leaving my body to make way for the new blood I want inside me, the blood that will fill the hole.

I'm busting to do a wee and ask the driver to stop.

'*Por favor señor, necesito ir al bano,*' I say. He nods and pulls over. I'm pleased with how my Spanish is coming along. We're in the eighth week of the trip, and the past four in Bolivia have been easier than our time in Brazil, where we struggled to understand Portuguese. I can't wait to learn more Spanish so I can have a proper conversation with Gabriel. Find out what's going on with him.

It's some time around midnight in the vast emptiness of the altiplano and I walk around the back of the bus for some privacy. I squat on the bare, dry earth and as I look up, I gasp: the sky is ablaze. I try not to wee on my feet as I gaze up in awe, mouth agape. Even in the Blue Mountains, away from the city lights, I've never seen so many stars. Somehow, there are more stars than space in between them. How many are stagnant stars and how many are wandering stars, like me? I'm shivering in the icy air but I barely notice because I'm enveloped in light, floating in space. I could stay here all night and would probably die of hypothermia, but it would be a lovely way to go. People back home would cry and say I died looking at the stars in the Bolivian desert while doing a wee. The driver beeps and jolts me back to reality. I rejoin the bus, the dulcet sounds of kung fu still blaring.

We arrive in Uyuni early the next morning, book into the Hotel Avenida, grab some breakfast and meet an English girl, Kate and her friend Xavier, from Quebec. We have to find three more travellers to make up our own tour group to visit the Salar de Uyuni, the world's largest salt flat. We wander the town's dusty streets, asking various travellers to join our group. We hook up with a bleached-blond German guy called Boris, a pink-faced German girl called Monica and an Israeli, Eres. So there are seven of us and a tiny Bolivian driver who doesn't change his baggy brown slacks and green jumper for four days.

The Salar de Uyuni spans 11,000 square kilometres, the remains of a prehistoric lake that dried up and left a desert-like landscape of white salt. At an altitude of 3656 metres, it's an otherworldly landscape of pure white crystalline perfection.

It's a four-day trip staying overnight in mud-brick huts with concrete floors and rock-hard straw mats to sleep on, visiting cactus-covered rock formations and lakes inhabited by flamingos. The first tiny settlement we reach has a higher population of llamas than people and they scratch around the rocks, looking for food while the human inhabitants are nowhere to be seen.

I can tell Emily likes Boris. He's exactly her type: tall and thin, messy blond hair with dark roots giving him a punk vibe, beautiful brown eyes with thick lashes. She sits next to him on the bus and chats him up. I'm happy for her. But somewhere along the bumpy dirt road into the vast desert, Boris decides to sit next to me. We've both studied journalism at university and we get along well, finding common interests, while Emily broods in another seat. I'm enjoying the attention. She's prettier than I am. Skinnier, better legs, smaller boobs, so she can go without a bra if she wants to. I don't see myself as beautiful, so when a man pays me attention, I'm surprised and delighted and it's like crack cocaine for my ego.

Boris is spunky and smart, but I have Gabriel. This trip is mind-blowing and I'm fully immersed in it, but I'm also counting down the days until I see him again. The bus falls silent as we drive for hours on end through the surreal moonscape of white horizons and big skies and eventually, I drift off to sleep with my head on Boris' shoulder.

We arrive at the Laguna Colorada about 4pm. Its water is the colour of blood. I've never seen anything like it.

'I think it's the iron in the water that makes it red,' I say to Emily as we wander around its perimeter.

'No, the red colour is caused by algae and sediment,' Emily snaps.

'No, it's iron.'

'Leigh, I read it in the bloody guidebook! I do know some stuff you know.'

What's *her* problem? She's obviously pissed off because Boris likes me.

'What's up your arse?' I ask.

'I didn't sleep very well last night,' she shoots back.

'Why?'

'Because people were *fucking* in the room all night.'

'Really? Who?'

'You and Boris!'

'What are you talking about? We were NOT!'

'You were so! I could hear it, the moaning and stuff. I know you two got it on. And you *knew* I liked him. You've been putting me down, undermining me. Trying to steal the limelight.'

'What? We didn't do anything other than pass out. Seriously, what the fuck are you on? I was probably moaning in my sleep because I was freezing my arse off all night. You are out of line, Emily. And how have I been undermining you, anyway?'

She bursts into tears, runs off across the rocks. A wave of guilt and shame washes over me. What is wrong with me? I am obsessed with a Peruvian artisan I know nothing about, ready to devote my life to him based purely on lust and a gut feeling that he is a good person, when he could be anything but. He could hurt me, do terrible things to me, the worst being to make me adore him and then betray me, lie to me, leave me. Fall in love with someone else. I would do anything to be with him, take any risk. And yet, here I am seeking attention from another man I have no interest in.

Why am I never at peace, never happy in my own skin? I'm only happy when I'm pissed or stoned, or listening to loud music that blocks out my thoughts of self-loathing. No man will ever love me, because I am unworthy of love. If my own father did not love me, if he could just disappear from my life, why should any other man love me?

I catch up to Emily and grab her by the arm.

'Look, I'm sorry I was flirting with Boris. I just liked having a sexy guy paying me attention.'

She doesn't say a word. I'm rooted to the spot by her big, blue glare. Everyone is walking back to the bus and the red water is turning deep crimson. I shudder in the crisp air and pull my poncho around me. Emily wipes tears away and I soften my voice.

'Look, I really miss Gabriel. I don't know if I'll ever see him again.'

'What? You are *still* hung up on some guy you met on your third day here? I thought you'd forgotten about him.'

'No. I've been thinking about him constantly. He has never left my mind, Emily. I got a letter from him in Salvador and he says he feels the same way I do. But now I'm worried he might have met someone else.'

'What? Why didn't you tell me?'

'Because, you had the shits back in Puerto Iguazu and I thought I'd better shut up about him.'

'Yeah, well. I think I had good reason. You ditched me for Gabriel in the first week of our trip!'

'I know. I'm sorry, Em. I was an arsehole. You didn't deserve that.'

She's not letting me off the hook.

'We came all this way to travel together—you and me—and you just discarded me.'

'Em, I'm fucked up. I'm not very rational when it comes to men. I know I did the wrong thing but if it's any consolation, I didn't leave you on your own for just any guy. I really felt something with Gabriel. I still feel it.'

'So you're not interested in Boris then?'

'No, not at all. He's all yours.' I put my arms out for a hug, and she leans in. All the fear, the excitement, the stress, the anxiety of the past eight weeks come gushing out in a flood of shared tears.

'I'm sorry, I shouldn't have accused you,' she says. 'But you do put me down a bit, make me look like an idiot. You think you're smarter than me, you know more Spanish than me now, so you're always taking over. And you always think you're right.'

'Do I? I'm sorry, I didn't realise. I'll try not to put you down, that's pretty shit of me. But you've got to admit, I am right most of the time.'

She doesn't laugh.

'You know—your sarcasm kind of gives me the shits too,' I say.

'Yeah? Well, it's not the first time I've heard that. I can't help it. I was born that way. I find the best way to deal with sarcasm is with more sarcasm.'

'Okay, I'll try. But I'm not a sarcastic cow like you. That's your talent. I'm more of a know-it-all pain in the arse.'

'I won't argue with that,' she says. 'Race you to the bus.'

Emily sits next to Boris as we drive to the Laguna Verde, or Green Lagoon. Here, the water does a cool party trick by changing from a dirty shade of brown to a dazzling aqua in the space of fifteen minutes. It's one of the many masterpieces of nature in this strange and beautiful country.

Emily, Boris and I catch a bus back to La Paz together and I give them space. Boris has taken a shine to Emily and seeing them together makes me miss Gabriel even more. I want to be with him, and only him. I will do anything to make it happen, make any sacrifice, cross any boundary. I pull the mandala out of my brown suede bag and hug it to my heart for the entire trip.

Boris is flying to Cusco from La Paz, but we're going by bus to Copacabana, near the Peruvian border, to see Lake Titicaca first. We arrange to meet Boris in Cusco in a week. In case we don't cross paths again, Boris and Emily swap contact details. He asks her to visit him in Germany after she arrives in London in a month, and she's the happiest I've ever seen her.

London. I am numb at the thought of it and the day I must tell Emily I'm not going with her is drawing closer.

CHAPTER TEN

WHEN THE SUN shines, Lake Titicaca is cobalt blue, like the Mediterranean Sea. Standing on the Isla del Sol, in the southern section of the lake, surrounded by Inca ruins, surrounded by rocky earth, surrounded by still water, I have entered a new realm.

It is said the Inca god Viracocha created the universe, the moon, stars and time. He rose from the serene blue waters of Lake Titicaca during the time of darkness to bring forth the light. In one legend, he had a son called Inti and two daughters, Mama Killa and Pachamama. Inti and Mama Killa gave birth to Manco Cápac and Mama Ocllo on the Isla del Sol, the Island of the Sun, and they went on to found the great Inca empire at Cusco.

Exploring the Island of the Sun, I ask our guide about the inhabitants of the island in Spanish and I manage to understand most of his answers. I'm thrilled with how my Spanish is progressing. By the time I return to Buenos Aires in four weeks, I'll be able to have basic conversations with Gabriel. Get to know who he really is.

We spend the night in Copacabana on the Bolivian side of the island. Early the next morning, I leave Emily showering in the hostel and climb the Cerro Calvario, a hill overlooking the lake with small monuments representing the fourteen Stations of the Cross. I have to stop every fifty steps to catch my breath. At this altitude—3810 metres—any exercise is difficult. When I reach the top, my heart is pounding in my chest and I sit on the ground and lean against one of the monuments. The fresh morning air carries a hint of woodsmoke and in the distance, the Island of the

Sun seems to glow in the still and expansive lake. Behind Copacabana, the Andes rise up, patchworked with cultivated land growing broad beans, quinoa, maize and potatoes. This place feels familiar and timeless.

I begin to meditate, focusing my eyes on the vast blue canvas before me. The lake and the sky became one and I'm lulled into stillness. I want a message from the lake, from the Inca gods, from my spirit guides, something to direct me towards a spiritual revelation. What is my spiritual quest? What am I being led towards? Do I have a destiny in this place, or am I just stumbling blindly along? Once I trek to Machu Picchu, I'm sure I will receive a revelation that will explain what my life has been about and what I need to do. Where I need to go. Peru holds answers for me.

A bird flies towards me, so close it nearly smacks me in the face. I snap out of my meditative state with no revelations, no realisations. They will come. At Machu Picchu, they will come.

We set off for the Peruvian border town of Puno the next day. I've heard bad stories about Puno, and Peru in general. Robberies, druggings, beatings, rapes, murders. But I'm not scared; I know I'm protected. In Puno, we consider whether we should splurge on a flight to Cusco or take an overnight bus. We're getting low on money; my book of American Express Travellers Cheques is dwindling, so we decide to take the bus. It's twelve hours to Cusco and we've been warned it's a dangerous journey, our route crawling with bandits. Also, it is the eve of a federal election, a volatile time. The bus company warns us the bus could be held up on the way to Cusco, advising us to hide any valuables.

Some travellers we meet say they've been robbed in Puno, so we don't want to hang around. We take our chances on the bus, which stops regularly throughout the night. Our backpacks are strapped on the roof and every time the bus stops, people climb up to take bags on or off. We're convinced our bags will be gone when we arrive in Cusco, but I visualise them surrounded in protective white light. I hope it works for bags, as well as people. At various intervals, we see men with torches running back and forth in front of the bus and grab each other's arms, but the bus continues on with no mishaps. After a sleepless night, we arrive in Cusco at 5.30am unscathed—money, passports and backpacks intact. It's miraculous.

In Cusco, I feel perpetually wrapped in a warm blanket of security.

This beautiful colonial Spanish city is built on Inca foundations so strong they survived numerous earthquakes, while the Spanish buildings collapsed. It feels familiar, as if it already exists in my psyche. Perhaps these memories of long ago come from the books I read as a child. Or maybe I really have been here, lived many lives here, with Gabriel by my side.

Cusco's cobblestone streets radiate out from the Plaza de Armas, the name of all the main squares of every town in Peru. The Plaza de Armas is the hub of each village, a central meeting place and a pleasant communal area. On the northeast side of the Plaza stands the Catedral Basilica of the Assumption of the Virgin. Built on the foundations of an Inca temple called Kiswarkancha, it's a Gothic-Renaissance style cathedral that houses the famous black Christ—El Señor de los Temblores, or Lord of the Earthquakes.

Centuries of candle smoke and dust have turned it black and it has never been cleaned. We're in Cusco for the Lord of Miracles procession during Holy Week, the Monday after Palm Sunday. It's the one time each year the black Christ is removed from the cathedral and paraded around town. Cusco's streets become a living artwork, with colourful flower carpets in intricate designs decorating the square and surrounding streets in the lead-up to the procession. We watch as the townsfolk work together to create the flower carpets and even the police pitch in and help. People gather in the square and on the balconies of the buildings that surround it. Halfway through the procession, it begins to rain. Large sheets of clear plastic are quickly draped over the Christ and the procession continues through the streets. The people toss their prayers onto this black Christ wrapped in plastic and strain to catch a glimpse of him as he passes by on the shoulders of strong men.

The main squares of Peru are where all the musicians and artisans gather to ply their trades, lovers stroll and tourists mingle. Street vendors sell Inca Kola, a popular Peruvian soft drink the colour of radioactive urine and grubby children beg tourists for money. Along the three sides of the square facing the cathedral are travel agencies selling tours to Inca ruins, cafes, restaurants and stores selling traditional artefacts and crafts.

We choose a tour company, Lys Tours, and book our trek to Machu Picchu. It's possible to catch a bus and train all the way to Aguas Calientes, the nearest town to the ruins, but no way in hell are we going to miss the chance to do the Inca Trail. We will hike for four days through the mountains and arrive at Machu Picchu the correct way.

The travel agent is an indigenous man with dark eyes and pinpoint pupils. He stares at me intensely. I take a step back and look at Emily. She doesn't seem to notice anything unusual about him.

'You will discover many spiritual advantages of walking the Inca Trail,' he says, his eyes never leaving mine.

'What sort of spiritual advantages?' Emily asks, smirking at me.

'You will be spiritually cleansed and you will connect deeply with the cosmos.'

'There you go, just what you're looking for,' Emily says, nudging me.

He takes a step closer.

'Why you come here? Why you come to Peru? To Cusco?' he asks me. His intensity is unnerving.

I see Gabriel's features in his.

'It's a long story,' I say, backing away from him.

What I should say is I've come to find myself. To discover something about who I am, because I am so lost. The New Age books say just love yourself. I've read plenty of them, but I still don't know how to do it. How do you love yourself when deep inside, in an untouchable place, you don't believe you are lovable?

'C'mon, let's go to the Hares,' Emily says, tucking the tickets into her daypack. 'I'm hanging out for a veggie curry and rice. And halva. I love their halva.'

I nod, dazed by my encounter with the travel agent. I look back; he's watching me as we leave. I don't know what that was all about, but he did something to me—cast a spell or perhaps, removed one.

Emily charges ahead towards the Hare Krishna restaurant, the surest bet for finding vegetarian food in Cusco, and I trail behind her. I'm so glad to have her in my life. She keeps me grounded. I'd be a total space cadet if I didn't have Em to bring me back to reality.

We sit near the front window at the Hare Krishna restaurant and a roving panpipe group wearing woven ponchos comes in. They play *El Condor Pasa* and the familiar tune carries me into the sky and above this town, this country, this lifetime. It stirs me to the bone and when a little boy who looks no older than three dances for us, I can't contain my tears. He's dressed in traditional costume, hopping up and down, almost losing his balance. When he comes over with his little hand held out, we don't hesitate to give him some money. He bows, thanks us and leaves.

That night, we meet up with Boris and catch up on the past week since we left Bolivia. We play pool at an English-style pub, then go dancing at Mama Africa, a club on the first floor of a building in one corner of the Plaza de Armas. Packed with tourists and young Peruvians, everyone is dancing to an Andean folk group with a rock edge. Every arty, hippie boy here reminds me of Gabriel. One kisses the back of my neck while I'm dancing, another grabs my hand and kisses it. The attention is both flattering and embarrassing.

Boris is leaving on an early bus so he calls it a night. Emily walks him out of the club and half an hour later, floats back in.

'Oh my god, Boris and I just kissed,' she says. 'He's so beautiful, I am in total lust. Or love. I'm not sure which one.'

'See, I told you he liked you.'

'We're going to catch up again when we get back from the Inca Trail and then I'm going to visit him in Germany after we get to London.'

'Wow, so you think you two could actually be together?'

'Yeah, I hope so.'

'What about all these sexy Latinos?' I look around the room. 'You wouldn't go for any of them?'

'As if! They're all yours. Too short for me. I love how tall Boris is. Over six foot.'

'Well, they don't have to be that tall for me—they just have to be tall enough. And Gabriel is.'

'You really want to see him again, hey?'

'I am *dying* to see him again.' This is my chance. Carefully, I choose my words.

'Em, would you mind going to London on your own? We have until the end of May to use our flights to London. After we leave Peru, I want to go back to Buenos Aires and spend a couple of weeks with Gabriel.'

'But you'll still come to London after that won't you?' She says it flippantly, like it's a given.

'Of course! I'll be stuck in South America with no money and no way out if I don't use that plane ticket. But I can't leave South America without seeing him again. I have to see if what we felt in Buenos Aires is still as strong.'

Emily is feeling loved up and magnanimous.

'Well, I suppose it would be okay. My mum's cousin Helen will be meeting me at Heathrow anyway and she says we can both stay at her house. So I'll just wait for you there.'

'Really? You'd be cool with it?' I'm so relieved I want to throw up. Or, maybe it's the toxic mixture of beer and pisco sour we've been drinking all night.

'Yeah. It's fine. Just be careful with this guy, Gabriel. You don't really know him. What will you do if he's not there to meet you at the airport? You'll be stuck in Buenos Aires not knowing anyone.'

It's a possibility. It has been three months since I saw him.

'I'll just go back to the hostel in San Telmo until I can get a flight to London. But don't worry, he'll be there.'

CHAPTER ELEVEN

SILVIA, THE FREE-SPIRITED Spanish girl on the boat in the Amazon, said you don't find San Pedro, the hallucinogenic cactus. It finds you. We're strolling the back streets of Cusco, buying chocolate and toilet paper to take with us on the Inca Trail, when San Pedro does indeed find me. We pass a little market where women with long black plaits and brown bowler hats sit on the ground, selling woven bags, ponchos and textiles in shades of brown striped with bright pink, red and blue, as well as yucca and corn, and an assortment of herbs. One woman sits with a single cactus in front of her. It looks like an overgrown cucumber, about thirty centimetres long and fifteen centimetres wide, with light-olive green skin and little white spots along the shaft where its spikes have been removed. I stop and bend down.

'Hola señora, es San Pedro?' I ask.

'Sí,' she answers blankly.

'Cuanto cuesta, por favor?' I look around. I don't know if it's legal for me to buy it, totally out in the open like this.

'Cinquenta centimos,' she answers quietly. Fifty Peruvian cents. How odd, to sit around all day waiting for someone to buy one cactus for such a small amount of money.

'What are you going to do with that?' Emily asks.

'Eat it at Machu Picchu,' I smile. 'It's the hallucinogenic cactus that girl Silvia told us about on the boat in the Amazon.'

'What? You're going to lug that thing all the way up the Inca Trail?'

'Yep.'

'But we can only take our day packs on the trip. You won't be able to fit anything else in your bag.'

'So? What else do I need apart from my water bottle, chocolate and toilet paper?'

'A change of clothes?'

'Nah. I'd rather carry the cactus and wear the same clothes for four days.'

I have visions of arriving in the early morning mist at Machu Picchu, ceremoniously eating the cactus and hallucinating as the sun spreads its corn-coloured light across the Andes. The universe has guided me to the lady in the market, just in time for the trek to Machu Picchu. Silvia said people find San Pedro when it's the right time in their spiritual evolution. This is it. This is my time. I'm going to have an epiphany at Machu Picchu.

Our minibus picks us up at 5am on Easter Sunday and then circles Cusco picking up passengers from various hotels for about an hour, before we set off for the four-hour drive to the start of the trail, known as Kilometre Eighty-Two, which indicates how far along the train line it is from Cusco. Our guide, Hernan, is a slim man who speaks only a few words of English. He has a noble face and a quiet voice. While the travellers chat loudly, Hernan sits silently gazing out the window. How many times has he walked the Camino Inca, in his ancestors' footsteps? There are also three tiny porters who speak only Quechua, and carry all of our camping equipment and food on their backs.

There's no bridge across the raging torrent of the Vilcanota River, the upstream section of the Urubamba River. A little man in a beanie who could not weigh more than fifty kilos is balanced on a rickety timber platform suspended by ropes. He hauls us across the river on the platform, one by one, and we begin the trek.

The first day is undulating and easy, with as many downhill sections as up, and the twenty-two trekkers chat happily and get to know one another, while taking in the spectacular mountain views surrounding us. There's only one other Australian in the group, plus some British, Kiwis, Swiss, Israelis and Americans. Hernan walks silently at the front. Our porters run ahead to set up our camp and prepare our meals so everything will be ready when we arrive. We are privileged travellers who have to carry only our small daypacks and enjoy the walk.

Day two is a killer. The path takes a steady uphill climb to Warmiwa-ñusqa, or *Dead Woman's Pass* at 4,200 metres. For four arduous hours we hike up the steep mountain pass, the air growing thinner and thinner, my legs growing heavier and heavier, my daypack weighed down by the cactus. This is the most difficult physical feat I have ever attempted. We've given no thought to training for the hike, so our fitness is average, but we have youth on our side. My muscles burn, my back aches, I am breathless and dizzy from the altitude and my heart is thumping against my rib cage. My mind is as tortured as my body. *I can't do this. I'm not going to make it.* My head swirls with self-doubt. I bargain with God: *Please, help me get to the top. If you help me make it to the top, I'll be good till the day I die.*

I shift my gaze from my boots, plonking heavily one in front of the other, each step slower than the last, to the scenery. The Andes tower above us, covered in deep green vegetation with patchy snow on the highest peaks. I sense an affinity with these mountains. They are embracing me, keeping me safe. The sky is a cloudless cerulean and a cold, clear mountain stream gushes alongside the track. The beauty of the scenery takes me out of my body, out of my pain.

The final arduous steps feel like I'm dragging a dead horse behind me, but finally, we make it to the top of the pass. The sweeping view across the Andes is worth every step and we're elated. I ask one of the other trekkers to take a photo of Emily and me at the top of the pass, arms around each other, hair blowing in the breeze, big smiles of victory and relief.

Our guides set up camp and cook a vegetable stew with rice. Emily and I find a quiet spot to smoke a joint—a little gift from one of the guys at Mama Africa. We're sharing the tent with two English girls, Jess and Mia. Jess is athletic, with short dark hair and intelligent eyes. Mia is rounder, with a doll-like face and long, sandy blonde hair. We persuade them to share the joint with us and we sit together on a rock, waiting for the moon to rise from behind the black silhouette of the mountains. The moonlight on the clouds is as bright as daylight and then, a thin white crescent appears over the mountaintops and the full moon slides into view.

Back in the tent, the pot has a strong effect and the four of us giggle and tell stories about home. Emily excuses herself to go to the toilet, which means finding a secluded place behind a tree or a rock, doing your thing and burying it or covering it up with leaves. She's gone for what seems like a long time and I'm starting to worry she's fallen off a cliff. Eventually, she runs back in, talking loudly about how hard it is to find a private place to squat.

'Can anyone smell shit?' I ask, trying to focus my eyes in the dark tent.

'Yeah, I think I can,' Jess says.

Mia turns her pert nose up, sniffing like a bunny.

'Yeah, I can definitely smell something.'

'You're just stoned,' Emily says. 'You're imagining it.'

But just in case, she turns her torch on and checks the tent. Brown footprints lead from the tent door to where Emily is sitting.

'Oh my god! I must have walked in someone's shit!' she cries.

We scream with disgust and rush to find rolls of toilet paper to wipe it clean. We tip our water bottles all over the poo and fish around in our daypacks for spray-on deodorant, but the pot amplifies our sense of smell and we go to sleep with our noses and mouths filled with the stench of human shit.

On the third day, the trail winds around mountains, climbs up and down ancient stone stairways and passes ruins of Inca settlements, forts and crop storage houses. Hernan explains the significance of the ruins, partly in English and partly in Spanish. He shares his knowledge of the Inca Empire with us, the largest empire in pre-Columbian America, and that night, we crash early out of sheer exhaustion.

The next morning, we wake up wet. A storm has hit during the night and flooded our poorly erected tents. Our clothes are soaked, we've slept in late and I'm worried we're not going to arrive at Machu Picchu early enough to beat the tourists. We still have a few hours to walk before we reach the famous citadel. I want to get there early and take my precious San Pedro in private.

Emily is in a filthy mood. She likes her clothes clean, dry and folded neatly in her bag. All I can think about is seeing Machu Picchu for the first time. We reach the top of the staircase to Inti Punku, the Sun Gate, once the main entrance to Machu Picchu for travellers arriving from Cusco in the southeast. It is dedicated to the cult of the Inti, the Sun God and each year on the summer solstice, the Incas would conduct sacred ceremonies here as the golden rays of the rising sun shone through the gate. Hernan explains this as all eyes shift to the Lost City of the Incas laid out before us in all its splendour. The group is silent. Awestruck.

But Emily is complaining. With her back to Machu Picchu, she is pulling her wet clothes out of her bag and wringing them out, draping them over rocks to dry in the sun.

'Emily! Look, there it is. Machu Picchu!' I cry.

'Yeah, I'll look in a minute.'

'But… it's Machu Picchu. We've walked for four days to see this view. The tourists who come on buses don't get to see it like this, from the Sun Gate, with the morning sun lighting it up. Look how beautiful it is.'

She begins re-packing her bag as the rest of us spring excitedly down the stairs towards the ruins. I follow behind, scanning the ruins for somewhere to eat my cactus. Then, my eyes fall upon a row of coaches parked at the entrance to the ruins and my heart sinks. We're too late. Tourists are already marching around the ruins in their shiny hiking boots, fat cameras around their fat necks, spoiling my fantasy with their loud banalities. How can I take the San Pedro now?

We follow Hernan around the ruins. He explains what each of the buildings are and I listen half-heartedly. The ruins date back to the fifteenth century. The Incas were masters of this style of architecture, he says. They built dry-stone walls without the use of mortar by carving huge blocks of stone to fit tightly around each other. Something about the Inca emperor Pachacuti, something about a mystery. I'm not really listening. I'm gutted, a sulky child with a scowl.

I really am just another tourist. I wander away from the group, and find a secluded rock at the edge of the mountain to sit on. I try to meditate but my chest is aching, my head throbbing. I've come so far, so far to find answers in this sacred place. I look at the mountains around me, trying to take my focus outside myself, to project my childish misery onto their strong frames. This ruined city is protected by a battalion of mountains rising steeply into the clouds in shades of deep forest green, emerald, jade. It is a place of staggering beauty and serenity, but I am racked with disappointment and deep sadness. I've been compelled to come here, to this very place, since I was a child. I don't understand why. Why was I drawn here? What was I supposed to learn? I unzip my daypack and take out the cactus. I turn it around in my hands, examining it for answers. It holds nothing for me. In a fit of rage, I pelt it over the edge and watch it disappear into the valley below, vaguely hoping it doesn't hit someone.

I have nothing but disdain for the tourists who arrive by bus, who haven't earned the right to be here, who haven't walked the Camino Inca. I want them all to fuck off. They're all getting in the way of my spiritual experience, the connection I so desperately needed to find here. Tears stream down my cheeks and chin and drop onto paths where Incas once walked. I am so alone and weary, so tired, tired of trying so hard, tired of never feeling good enough. Of feeling utterly worthless.

But Gabriel comes from this place, this beauty. These mountains are in him and he is in them. I want him to be as solid as these mountains, for his love to be eternal and unwavering. To never let me down, to cradle me in his arms the way this lost and broken city is embraced by the mountains that rise up around it. If Gabriel wants me, this pain will end. And I will be happy.

Chapter twelve

AFTER TREKKING FOR four days through the mountains to reach Machu Picchu, it only takes a few hours to get back to Cusco by train and bus, which is a little disorienting. It felt like we'd gone much further. Upon our return, I dump my bag at our hotel and immediately head to the Plaza de Armas to find a phone box.

'Hola? Hola?' He answers straight away and my belly flips at the sound of his voice.

'Hola Gabriel.'

'Mi amor! Que bien, donde estas?' He calls me his love, asks me where I am. This time he sounds like the Gabriel I know and love. He sounds genuinely happy to hear from me and I don't detect any women's voices in the background saying come back to bed.

'Estoy en Cusco,' I say confidently. After ten weeks of travelling, my Spanish has improved and I'm able to tell him I miss him, that I want to return to Buenos Aires in two weeks and see him.

'Sí, sí, sí,' he cries. 'Por favor!' He tells me he's been thinking about me every day and that I can stay as long as I like at Elsa's apartment.

'Gabriel, last time we spoke you said you might leave Buenos Aires…'

'No mi amor, I will stay here and wait for you. I am selling well at the markets, I have money. When you come, I will take you out for dinner, take you out dancing. You can come to the market with me and help me sell my artesanias, no?'

These are the exact words I need to hear. Now I know I can trust him to be who I imagine he is. Who I need him to be. My fear that he was with someone else vanishes as quickly as my cactus did when I threw it over the cliff.

He encourages me to call his brother Jorge when we arrive in Lima. He says it's a dangerous city and Jorge will show me and Emily around. When people tell me to be careful, I pay attention but don't let fear stop me doing anything I want to do—if it ever did. I have my methods.

When I walk through cities with my backpack on, I'm always vigilant. When I stop at a crossing, I sway from side to side so I will feel if thieves are trying to slash my bag. I always look behind me to make sure I'm not being followed. I continue to stash my money and passport—now wrinkled and reeking of sweaty socks—in the sole of my boot. I don't dress like someone who has money and I try to travel without drawing attention to myself. I like to think of myself as streetwise and sensible. But I also have a private safety net, my white light bubbles, as well as an armada of angels who are always looking out for me.

Along the journey, we meet travellers who've been robbed, or even drugged. One German girl tells us she met some friendly Peruvians in Lima who offered to buy her a drink at a club. They spiked her drink with a drug called *burundanga* and she woke up two days later in a park, her money and passport gone.

Even when I hear stories like this, Lima doesn't scare me.

We have two important sites to see before we arrive there: the Colca Canyon and the Nazca Lines. We splurge on a flight from Cusco to Arequipa in the southeast, a beautiful city of baroque architecture and buildings made of the local white sillar rock from the city's three surrounding volcanoes. Arequipa is the gateway to the Colca Canyon, which at 3,270 metres deep, is twice as deep as the Grand Canyon and is the habitat of Andean condors. I have no preconceived ideas about it and after my disappointment at Machu Picchu, I have deliberately let go of my spiritual fantasies. If something amazing didn't happen at Machu Picchu, it's not going to happen. I know that now. Maybe it happened and I missed it while I was wallowing in self-pity. Maybe I need to drop my expectations and just be in the moment.

The Colca Canyon is 160 kilometres northwest of Arequipa and the bus passes through arid, rocky land, snow-capped mountains always dominating the horizon in this part of the country. We pass terraced farmland and shepherds with flocks of alpacas and llamas wearing colourful pompom earrings. The bus slows as we pass and the llamas stare at us with a bit of attitude as we snap photos. We're staying overnight in the dishevelled village of Chivay in the Colca valley. The toilets at our little hostel are mere holes in the ground with cement footholds on either side, covered in shit. The restaurant serves guinea pig, quinoa and *lomo saltado*, a Peruvian stir-fry of steak, chips and rice. We stick to the quinoa, chips and rice. Since Brazil, I've steered clear of cheese, salads, tap water and anything else likely to kill me and I've managed to avoid any more gastro bouts.

After a deep sleep brought on by the crisp mountain air and long road trip, we rise early to reach the canyon at 7am. It's a sparkling morning with superb visibility. Our group of eight sits on the ground at the edge of the canyon, waiting to spot the first condor soaring through the great gash in the mountains in search of prey.

And in the distance, we see them, growing larger and larger as they glide gracefully into the canyon on air currents that support their massive three-metre wingspans. I need to be alone to fully immerse myself in this experience, to let it burn a permanent place in my memory. I wander away from the group and find a rock to sit on, my mind blissfully empty, my eyes wide open, admiring every feather on these magnificent creatures. Then without warning, a condor swoops in a metre above my head, so close I can almost reach up and touch its black and white wings. I've been anointed. I slip into a meditation, my eyes fixed on the mountains on the far side of the canyon. I am still, my mind is silent, I am in the moment. Then something strange happens, something I've never experienced before: I see the aura of the mountains. Running along the uneven horizon is a strip of electric blue, so bright it's almost white. The mountains, trees and rocks merge into each other and I am sucked into them. The mountains are no longer far off in the distance, but near me. Or, more accurately, they are me and I am them. There is no distance, no space, no time. I am at perfect peace, perhaps for the first time in my life.

El Condor Pasa plays on high rotation in my head as we leave the place where I was not expecting anything and was shown everything. I was shown that separation is an illusion. We are in each other, in the mountains and the trees, the sky and stones, rivers and oceans. We are part of an intricate web of gossamer threads that connect us to this Earth and to the entire universe, but we lose sight of our place in it. We lose sight of who we really are, we become lost and lonely, depressed and anxious. But the answers are all around us in the music of mountains and in the breath of birds, which is also our breath and our children's breath.

From Arequipa, we take a ten-hour bus trip to see the Nazca Lines, hundreds of petroglyphs etched into the desert floor more than 2000 years ago. There are strange lines and stylised animals—a hummingbird, a spider, monkey, fish, sharks, orcas and lizards. Theories abound as to who created them, with the most logical being the local indigenous population. I prefer to go with the least plausible theory—aliens.

We also visit the Cemetery of Chauchilla, an ancient burial ground plundered by thieves who stole treasures from the graves and left corpses strewn across the desert floor. Over thousands of years, the dry desert climate has preserved the bodies and many still have skin, hair and nails. Skeletons and disembodied skulls lie exposed, a stark reminder of life's impermanence.

We stay overnight in Nazca and the next morning, book bus tickets to Lima. The bus is scheduled to leave at 9am, but we know by now not to take any notice of that. We sit on the ground outside the bus terminal for two hours, waiting, watching life go by. Minivans called *colectivos* and decrepit cars pull up continuously, packed to the brim with passengers, but the drivers are always open to shoving more in, shouting out destinations like Ica, Ica, Ica, before tearing off and leaving clouds of dust in their wake. A vendor wheels his fruit cart filled with oranges right up to us and parks it at our feet. He takes out a microphone plugged into an amplifier and announces to us over and over again that he has oranges. *Naranjas! Naranjas! Naranjas!* He stares at us for a minute, then pushes his little cart away when we shake our heads. A mentally ill man sitting a few metres away picks imaginary substances off his jeans and eats them. Men leer at us, try to chat us up and call us *linda*, which means beautiful or lovely, a phrase we hear multiple times a day in Peru, regardless of how tired we are or how bad we smell. We eat chocolate bars, melted in their wrappers, to pass the time. Finally, the bus arrives and we're on our way to Lima.

We arrive into the chaos of the city as the heat is dying down in the late afternoon and catch a taxi straight to the Hotel España, a grand old Spanish-style building close to the Plaza de Armas and the Convent of San Francisco. As soon as we arrive, I call Jorge on the hotel phone and arrange to meet him later that night. He says Gabriel has told him all about me and he's excited to meet me.

Elated, I hang the phone up and skip up the stairs to the hotel's leafy rooftop, where Emily is chatting with a group of travellers. Everyone's lounging around drinking beer and getting stoned, so we settle in for the night and I completely forget about Jorge. I call the next day and apologise, promising to meet up with him when we return from a trip up north to the ruins of Chan Chan and Trujillo. His voice is friendly and upbeat, like Gabriel's. He's not put out at my standing him up. These things happen, he says. I promise to call him as soon as we return.

On April 29, there is a solar eclipse, visible at various points in Peru, including Trujillo. We choose that day to visit the Huaca del Sol—the Pyramid of the Sun, an adobe brick temple built by the Moche civilisation. The temple is one of several ruins found near the volcanic peak of Cerro Blanco. The other major ruin at the site is the nearby Huaca de la Luna—or Pyramid of the Moon, a better-preserved but smaller temple. Walking around the top of the Pyramid of the Moon, I am only half-heartedly looking at the ruins and the excavated areas showing Moche artefacts. I'm dreaming of Gabriel and what our reunion will be like. I've had enough of sacred sites and ruins and I'm sick of travelling rough. I just want to be resting in his arms again. Not long now.

Emily is deep in conversation with some guys she's met at the base of the Pyramid of the Sun; Sean, an Australian, and Pepe, a French Canadian. How does she manage to meet people so easily, just strike up conversations and have them laughing within minutes?

I stand quietly, looking at the top of the pyramid.

'It looks pretty hard to climb,' I say, squinting into the sun, my hand shading my eyes.

'No, it is not so hard if you are fit,' Pepe says, smiling.

'Well, that counts us out,' Emily says.

Pepe laughs and attempts to persuade her.

'Sorry Pepe, after doing the Inca Trail I refuse to do anything that involves walking upwards,' she says.

'C'mon girls, don't be slack arses,' Sean says. 'There's a solar eclipse happening right now. What better time to climb the Pyramid of the Sun?'

'I'm up for it,' I say.

'Okay, meet you down here,' Emily says. 'I'll be sitting on my arse somewhere in the shade.'

'Race you up!' I challenge the guys, and start running. Knowing there's a solar eclipse happening infuses me with energy and I take off at breakneck speed. It doesn't take long for them to pass me. It's a steep climb with no real path and I'm not as fit as I imagine. Once at the top, I look around at the vast, flat, dry landscape and plant myself on the highest point I can find to meditate. The Pyramid of the Moon is in front of me in the distance, with a pyramid-shaped mountain directly behind it.

Stuart Wilde's name keeps popping into my head. He's a metaphysical author who lives in London. My Sydney employer and good friend Leon Nacson is his Australian promoter and he's given me Stuart's number, suggesting I look him up when I arrive in London to see if he has any work. I'm not even sure I'm still going to London, so I don't know why I keep thinking about him. If it works out well with Gabriel in Buenos Aires, I will forfeit my ticket to London and stay in South America indefinitely.

The first thing I do when we get back is call Jorge. I still feel bad about ditching him.

'Hola,' a lady's voice answers.

'Hola, soy Leigh,' I say.

'Sí,' she says.

'Puedo hablar con Jorge, por favour?'

'No, está en el hospital,' she says, her voice trembling.

Did I understand her correctly? The hospital? It has only been a few days since we spoke.

I shout louder into the mouthpiece, the way people do when they're trying to make someone who speaks another language understand them.

'*PUEDO HABLAR CON JORGE?*'

'Señorita, el está en el HOSPITAL.' She shouts 'hospital' back to me and breaks into sobs.

'Lo siento.' *I'm sorry.*

She goes on a long ramble, most of which I can't understand. But I do understand: *accidente*.

I don't know what to say other than I'm sorry. What else *can* you say, even when you know the language?

I call Gabriel. He tells me in a voice calmer than I expected that Jorge was driving around the clifftops of Lima with his mates on his birthday and had a head-on collision near the upmarket suburb of Miraflores. His best friend died and Jorge is in a coma. If he comes out of the coma, the doctors say he will have permanent brain damage. When I spoke to him only days earlier, he sounded so full of life.

I feel terrible for Gabriel and his family and I feel even worse about not meeting up with Jorge now. Gabriel tells me he's desperate to see me, to hold me, to seek comfort in my arms. How this will change things between us, I don't know. But I tell him I'm coming to be with him and to meet me at Buenos Aires airport at 1.35pm the next day. He says he'll be there waiting as soon as the airport opens and will not leave until he has my hand in his.

CHAPTER THIRTEEN

HIS HAIR HAS grown. It's the first thing I notice about him when I emerge from Customs into the chaos of nervous lovers and hopeful families and frenzied cab drivers jostling for passengers as they holler across the airport.

Jet-black hair, falling in thick waves past his shoulders. A necklace of chunky brown and white stones around his neck. Jeans and a red jumper. Even more beautiful than I remember.

'Mi amor!' he cries and hurries towards me, shoving his way through the crowd and scooping me up in his arms.

A kiss, three months in the making. A kiss I've imagined in the dark of night on jungle floors and in dingy hostels and writhing in pain as black liquid pours out of me in the Amazon and as my muscles burn on the Inca Trail. A kiss that, after all this time, does not disappoint.

'Es increíble,' he says on the bus into the city, never taking his eyes off mine nor his hand out of mine.

We have never been apart. The natural order of the universe has been restored. A soothing wholeness permeates my being and in this moment, I know I will do anything to keep it. Elsa has gone to Lima to be with the family while Jorge is in hospital, so we have the apartment to ourselves. That night in Elsa's bedroom, our bodies and souls merge, and our bond, which we know began in some other lifetime, is sealed.

Gabriel is devastated about Jorge but he doesn't have the money to fly to Lima and he thinks he only has two weeks with me before I go to London, so he will wait until I leave before he hitches rides in trucks all the way back to Lima. He knows nothing of my hope to stay with him in Buenos Aires, travel South America with him as artisans, marry, have children, and live a life of art and music and freedom somewhere in the mountains or by the beach.

Emily is somewhere over the Atlantic Ocean, on her way to London. Our farewell the previous day was a mixture of sadness and relief. We'd laughed about the funny parts of our journey, recalled the generosity and warmth of the people we'd met and agreed we were fortunate to have travelled rough for three months through some of the most dangerous parts of South America without any major mishaps. We hugged goodbye, but didn't cry. It had been an incredible adventure and we made excellent travel partners. But we were ready for time apart after the intensity of spending every day and night with each other for three months. She had no doubt I'd be joining her in London in two weeks, so there was no need for tears.

I'd left her in Lima, swallowing the urge to confess it might be a lot longer than two weeks until we saw each other again. The time had come to see whether I had blown a holiday fling way out of proportion or if it was indeed the soul connection I believed it was, in which case, I had to make some decisions about my future—our future.

He sits drinking coffee with his shirt off. Sunlight pours through the kitchen window and casts his hairless brown chest in a golden glow. It is the first morning of our new life together, and I have no doubt he is the man I want to spend my life with. He's making me a pair of earrings with carnelian beads in the deep orange-red of a summer sunset, a warm colour to replace the cold grey hematite earrings I've been wearing since we first met. I examine my nails while he works. I've bitten them as far down as I can without making them bleed, so I start on the area around the nails, tearing off little sheets of skin with my teeth and swallowing them. It's a lifelong habit that gives me a little buzz, but makes my fingers look horrible. He finishes the earrings and I stop eating my fingers, placing my new carnelian earrings straight into my earlobes. I check myself out in a wall mirror. I love the earrings. And I love him.

We exist outside time, making love, eating at irregular hours, watching TV, walking through Buenos Aires parks hand-in-hand, cruising around the city with our fingers permanently interlocked. We sit on the back seat of the bus, where we can wrap around each other and kiss without drawing too much attention to ourselves. We wake up when we want, drink beer for breakfast, eat breakfast at night, talk and listen to the Rolling Stones and Los Rodriguez. Over and over we play an album called *Poncho al Viento* by a young Argentinian folk singer, Soledad Pastorutti, a phenomenon of folk with a voice beyond her years, who is bringing the genre to the youth and making it cool. I listen to her emotive songs so much I begin singing them in Spanish without even trying. Every corner of Elsa's apartment is in disarray and we are concerned with nothing other than learning more about each other.

We sell Gabriel's jewellery in markets around Buenos Aires—he calls them *ferias*. We have a table at *la feria de Recoleta*, and I am at ease sitting beside him, helping him sell his jewellery to tourists who don't speak Spanish. In my mind, I am no longer a tourist, or even a traveller. I live here with my Peruvian boyfriend and that's the story I tell.

When fellow artisans ask Gabriel how he managed to fall in love with an Australian girl, he tells them it's his karma. He tells them I am his and I don't flinch at his sense of ownership of me. I want to be his. He speaks no English and I like it. Spanish is a better language for love. There are two ways to say I love you: *te quiero* and *te amo*. When he says *mi vida*, it means I am his life, when he says *mi reina*, it means I'm his queen. He has no money but he has words that feed every need I have in this life.

Walking home from the markets one day, we pass a florist.

'I love you so much, I could buy you every single one of those flowers,' he says.

'Really?' I ask, calculating the cost.

'Yeah, but don't tell him that!' he laughs, winking at the vendor.

Instead of flowers he gives me necklaces and bracelets and earrings he infuses with love and beautiful stones like rhodochrosite, turquoise, rose quartz and jasper, treasures I can keep forever. I am not a diamonds and pearls girl and never will be.

During these dreamy Buenos Aires days when I get to know my lover, I have never been happier. As we stroll the city streets arm in arm, the world is as it should be and I can't imagine anything bursting this bubble. I am staying, but first I need to call Mum.

'Mum, it's me.'

'Oh love! You sound so far away.'

'I'm okay, don't worry about anything.'

'Oh thank god, I haven't heard from you in so long. I was getting worried. I called Emily's mum and she said Emily is in London, but you stayed in Buenos Aires.'

'I met a guy…'

Silence.

'Mum, are you there?'

'Oh. Who is he?' She's trying to sound calm but I sense her terror.

'Mum, he's really nice. His name is Gabriel, he's an artisan. I'm staying with him in his sister's apartment. Don't worry, everything is fine.'

'Are you sure? I'm going to worry even more now.'

'Mum, it's all fine, I'm safe, trust me. I'll call you when I get to London. Love you.'

'Love you too, please stay safe.'

'Don't worry, I will.'

I do not stop to think how my risky adventures might affect my family. Mum is the one who worries most, but she knows I would have hitched a ride on a shark to get to South America if I had to and there was no stopping me. She knows I am tenacious, that I never give up on anything until I'm completely defeated. Like the time when I was five, running in a race at the school athletics carnival. I was coming last and refused to give up. I had tears streaming down my red face and I remember pushing myself so hard my chest was burning and I almost vomited. But I was determined to finish that race.

I hang the phone up and Gabriel wrestles me on the bed, then lies on top of me. He starts to take my clothes off, speaking in a menacing voice.

'You no safe miss,' he says in broken English, which has the opposite effect of scaring me. 'I am dangerous Peruvian man. I kidnap you.' He pretends to choke me and I go along with it.

'No! Policia, policia!' I shout.

'Ssssh,' he says, pinning me on the bed and kissing my neck. The hint of danger excites me, but only because I know I'm safe with him.

'Te adoro,' he whispers. *I adore you.* He holds our arms up in the air, side by side, comparing our contrasting skin.

'Cafe con leche,' he says. Coffee with milk. I know from this point on, living in my skin without it touching his will be unbearable. I have never felt more loved, more beautiful, more accepted. We lie together and he asks me a question I'm not expecting.

'Cuánto pesa mi reina?'

'Qué?'

'Cuánto pesa mi reina?' *How much does my queen weigh?*

I weigh sixty-eight kilos and I want to weigh fifty-eight, but I'm not telling him that. I feel bigger than I am. I'm not even overweight, but I want be skinny. I'm curvy, and I hate my curves. I thought Latinos were meant to like curvy women.

'I don't know what I weigh, why?' I try and brush him off.

'No importa.' He says it doesn't matter, but that I should find out what I weigh because I'm a little bit *gordita*.

Chubby. The bubble of bliss bursts. I am not prepared for such a direct criticism about my body. It's so early in our relationship and I wonder what else he's going to find wrong with me. My insecurities are triggered, I feel he doesn't accept me as I am, and my guard goes up.

He invites two friends over for dinner the next night to meet me. Manuel and Danny are sweet Peruvian artisans, quiet and gentlemanly. We sit on the floor of Elsa's apartment eating spaghetti and drinking cheap red wine. They say they've never seen Gabriel so happy.

'Para la Pacha,' he says, pouring a few drops onto the floor.

'Para la Pacha,' I say and do the same. It's my ritual now.

Then he does something I was not expecting. Something that shocks me, because he does it casually, like it's no big deal. He pulls a little plastic bag out of his jeans pocket. It's half-full of white powder.

'Tómalo,' he says, handing it to Manuel. He tells him it's good stuff; totally pure.

Manuel's little fingernail is girlishly long—long enough for him to dip it into the bag and scoop out a decent chunk of what I know is cocaine. He snorts long and hard and immediately begins clenching his jaw. His personality changes from subdued, to outgoing. He passes it to Danny, who pours a little on the side of his dinner plate, chops it into a line with a bank card from his wallet, and inhales it. The shy artisan, who hasn't talked much during dinner, becomes chatty.

'Has tomado la cocaína loca?' Gabriel asks me, stroking my hair. 'No te preocupes, es bueno, no te pasa nada.' *Have you tried cocaine crazy girl? Don't worry, it's good, nothing bad will happen to you.*

I should refuse. Using coke will be crossing a line I never wanted to cross.

I watch him snort a line and his light grows brighter. He's calling me his queen, assuring me I will love it. Assuring me I can trust him. They're all watching me, waiting to see if I'm cool or not. If I'm one of them.

Fuck it.

Gabriel tips a little pile of coke onto a book, chops it into a thin line with Danny's bank card, and hands it to me. I block my left nostril and inhale the line hard into my right nostril. It burns at first, a metallic taste trickling down the back of my throat. But then…

It's a revelation. My anxiety, gone. Self-consciousness, gone. Low self-esteem, gone. Within a minute, my teeth are tingling, my jaw is tightening and when that stops, I am the most confident person on the planet. I am awesome. I am invincible. I am witty, charming, intelligent. I'm also *quite* good-looking. Why do I always give myself such a hard time about my looks?

The four of us chat at full-speed about jewellery and semi-precious stones, how stone suppliers are making fake turquoise these days and the tourists don't know the difference, how one day we'll go to Mexico and buy jade and amber. We talk about the cities and villages of South and Central America where artisans can make the most money, places where you can live cheaply by the beach and sell in US dollars to Americans who willingly pay $100 a necklace. We talk about the cost of silver, and how one day we'll graduate from cheap alloy metals to real silver, maybe even gold. I include myself in these conversations, as if I too am an artisan.

That night in bed, Gabriel gets teary and asks me to stay. He can't imagine his life without me now. I tell him I want to stay with him forever.

The next morning, I wake up before Gabriel, tip-toe into the bathroom, sit on the toilet and burst into tears. What am I doing? I had no idea Gabriel was into coke. Then it dawns on me—he was high that day I called him from La Paz. My head spins with the realisation. That's why he sounded so strange. So cold and distant. Like someone else. I'm brutally hungover and the cold light of day gives me a reality check. Gabriel doesn't make a lot of money at the markets and, really, how are we going to live off that? I'm out of money and my best chance for work is in London. I'm now living off a credit card I was keeping for emergencies only.

I hate the idea of losing my financial independence, especially in a foreign country where my employment possibilities are limited. I can't expect Gabriel to support me. My plane is due to leave in two days. If I miss it, my ticket to London will expire, along with any chance I have of leaving South America. If I go, I can work, replenish my savings and come back. It doesn't have to mean our relationship is over.

Gabriel's up and making a mushroom omelette and milky coffee when I emerge from the bathroom, wiping my eyes.

'Buenos días mi reina!' he says in his usual sunny way. *Good morning my queen!* He's standing shirtless in a pair of white cotton pants that hang low over his hips, black hair falling loose across his brown shoulders. I briefly consider changing my mind.

'Cómo estás mi amor? he asks, enquiring how I am.

'I'm sorry Gabriel, I have to go to London. In two days.'

'Como? No, mi amorcito!'

He drops the pan and embraces me, pleading with me not to go, asking if it was the cocaine that has scared me off.

I tell him about my father, how I had vowed never to take heroin or cocaine or any drug I deemed capable of wrecking lives. He assures me he only has it now and then and it's not a problem, that in South America, it's just a fun thing people do, like having a social drink. It puts my mind at ease, but still, I need to go and earn some money in London.

Before I leave, we make love one last time in Elsa's crumpled, squeaky bed. Someone in the apartment below bangs on the roof with what sounds like a broom handle. The radio is playing Simon and Garfunkel's *The Sound of Silence* and there is no moment in my life happier or sadder.

We take a long time to say goodbye at the airport. I'm crying, he's trembling, a security guard is rolling his eyes. I finally tear myself away from him, pass through Immigration in a daze and collapse onto the first seat I can find. My flight is already boarding, but I don't hear the calls. Names are being paged on the loudspeaker in a blur of sound I pay no attention to. I'm paralysed, caught between my heart's desire to run back to him immediately, and my head, which I know for once in my life, I need to pay attention to. It won't kill me to use some common sense.

'Miss… excuse me. Is this you?' A breathless man in an Aerolineas Argentinas uniform holds a list of names and points to mine. 'You are supposed to be on the plane going to London. We have been calling your name. The plane is fully boarded and we are leaving. You must run if you want to get on the plane.'

'London?'

'Sí, London. Are you okay miss?'

'No, I'm not okay.'

'Do you want to go to London, or no?'

He's holding a two-way radio in his hand, ready to make the call.

What the hell. I can always come back.

'Yes, I'll go.'

He speaks into the radio, saying hold the doors and pointing me in the direction of the plane.

I grab my daypack and will myself to sprint, like a determined little girl with a tear-streaked face who refuses to admit defeat. This is not over.

I step onto the plane and a perfectly groomed male flight attendant looks at me sternly.

'May I see your boarding pass please?'

'I'm sorry I'm late.' I hand him my pass, puffing hard and looking down the aisle at a plane full of disgruntled passengers I've kept waiting.

'We were about to close the door, miss. You made it with only a few seconds to spare.'

'I'm sorry, I didn't realise the time.'

His expression softens as he hands me my boarding pass.

'Did you have a good time in South America, señorita?'

Mountains, deserts, oceans and rivers flash through my mind.

'Sí señor. Muchas gracias.'

CHAPTER FOURTEEN

WAITING IN THE long immigration line at Heathrow Airport, I begin chatting to a fellow Aussie girl who has just arrived from Sydney to begin her working holiday. Fresh off the plane and elated like I had been when I landed in Buenos Aires, she has planned a year of bar work and partying in London, with side trips to Ibiza and Santorini. I'm nodding and smiling, not really listening. All I can think about is Gabriel and how far I am from him now. But then she mentions how we have to show proof of 2000 pounds cash to enter the country and reality brings me crashing down. I've forgotten I need money to enter the UK on my Commonwealth working visa.

I'd been meticulous in my preparation for South America, but completely negligent when it came to England. I don't even have one pound to catch the train from Heathrow into London. What will they do, send me back to Australia? I don't have a flight back to Australia. This flight is the end of the line for me.

My legs and arms grow heavy and the amplified airport voices announcing flight arrivals and departures fade. Adrenaline surges through my body and I begin to sweat and bite the little strips of white that have grown back on my nails. My credit card is maxed out and I have no cash. I'm stuffed. I pray, repeat affirmations in my head, visualise myself cruising through with no problems. I'm so nervous when I reach the desk, I can barely speak.

'Good morning,' The immigration officer wears a poker face. 'What do you plan to do while you're in the UK?'

'Look for some temping work, save some money and do some more travelling.'

Damn. Why did I mention money? My legs are about to give way.

He stops and looks closely at one of the stamps in my passport. Oh shit. What?

'Did you know the consular general who stamped your passport in Peru was Carlos Castaneda?'

'Ah, no. Like the author?'

'Yes,' he says, looking a moment longer. I watch his face intently, readying myself for the next question. But there isn't one. He flips to a blank page and brings a big silver stamp down with a heavy click.

'Welcome to the UK.'

I'm in. I'm not sure I want to be in, but I'm in. I make my way to the baggage carousel and find my beaten up blue backpack spinning around like an old friend. We've come so far together.

Once through Customs, I head for the train station and then do the only thing I can do: beg. I could easily be mistaken for a homeless person, but my skin is tanned and I'm wearing a woven purple and pink patchwork vest from a market stall in Peru. I certainly look the part of a destitute backpacker fresh off the plane from South America. People are wary when I first approach them, but a few are happy to hand over a pound or two and it doesn't take long to get enough money for a train ticket and a phone call to Emily.

She's staying in Beckenham with Helen, her mum's cousin. Helen and her husband David have kindly offered to put us up until we find a share house. It's late spring and the sky is a putrid grey, which suits my mood. I face at least a year of working in a soul-destroying office job to save enough money to get back to Gabriel. Rather than being excited about the opportunities London has to offer, I'm depressed. I couldn't care less about Big Ben or the Tower of London.

'Hello you crazy hippie,' Emily says down the line. 'So, you finally made it.'

'Told you I would,' I answer. She'll never know how close I was to not making it. 'I'm at Victoria Station. Had to borrow money to catch the tube from Heathrow. I should get to Beckenham Junction by about 12.30pm. Could you and Helen come and meet me?'

'Yeah, no worries. Helen and David are really looking forward to meeting you. They're so lovely.'

'Great, I'm looking forward to meeting them, too.'

It's comforting to have somewhere to go, a hot shower and a clean bed. They live in a row of identical two-storey brick houses, with their two sons, one in primary school and one in high school. David is a statistician; Helen is a slightly eccentric art student who previously worked as a nurse. He's shortish with balding grey hair and a deep, resonant voice. She looks like a prettier Princess Di, with short blonde hair and gentle blue eyes.

It's great to see Emily again. I didn't realise how much I'd missed her warm smile and easy humour. She's met up with other friends of ours from Sydney who are already established in London and she's in her element. Her mother is English so she's right at home. These are her people. I feel an absolute foreigner, much more than I ever did in South America. But Helen and Emily set me up in my own bedroom and make sure I feel at home. I've missed Emily's nurturing ways and I am deeply grateful for Helen and David's English hospitality.

A few weeks after I arrive, Helen organises a party to welcome us and introduce us to some of her art student friends. Pining for South America and Gabriel, I drink way too much red wine and throw up in the kitchen sink before passing out. It's not very ladylike of me, but Helen and David don't judge.

'Morning, how are you today?' Helen asks breezily, as I drag myself downstairs and into the kitchen, holding my head.

'Sorry about my behaviour last night.' I slump on a chair at the kitchen table.

'Oh no love, that's fine. We found it really entertaining. Don't be sorry. You might be interested in this, though. I found it in your vomit.'

She places a glass jar on the table in front of me. It contains a white worm with a tinge of orange, about ten centimetres long and half a centimetre wide, pointed at both ends.

'Oh my god! What's *that*?'

'A parasite,' she says. 'I looked it up in one of my medical books. I think it's this one.'

She reads out a passage about roundworms, how they infect you after you ingest their eggs, which are contained in water and food contaminated with human shit. I'm almost dry retching, but she reads on.

'The eggs hatch in the intestines. The larvae then move through your bloodstream to your lungs. After maturing, the roundworms leave your lungs and travel to your throat. You'll either cough up the worms—or in your case, spew them up—or swallow them. Then they travel back to your intestines, where they mate and lay more eggs.'

With that, she puts the book down, takes a bite of toast and goes back to making breakfast.

I have never been more disgusted by anything in my life. I can't take my eyes off the worm. It isn't moving.

'Are you sure it didn't crawl up through the drain and into the sink?'

'No, we've never seen anything like this before. It was well mixed up in your vomit. You might want to go to the doctor, love. Take a course of anti-worming medication.'

'Ah, here she is!' David springs into the kitchen and greets me in his jovial way.

'I'm so sorry about last night, David,' I say. 'I must have drunk about three bottles of your best red.'

'Don't be silly, we haven't had that much fun in ages.' He laughs a deep belly laugh.

'I vomited up a worm. How disgusting is that?'

'Well, that's what you get for going on exciting adventures to South America,' David chuckles.

'It's not over for you yet, is it love?' Helen asks, handing me a plate of tinned spaghetti that looks disturbingly similar to the worm, along with fried eggs and toast. I can't stomach it. All I can manage is a cup of tea. Thank god for tea.

'Well, I'm hoping to go back and see…'

'Her boyfriend! The beautiful Peruvian artisan,' Helen says, before I have a chance.

Emily charges into the kitchen, right on cue.

'Not him again,' she says, groaning. 'You just got here. You're already talking about going back?'

'Well, not yet. But as soon as I can save some money—maybe in a year? Earlier if I can manage it.'

'I don't blame you,' David says, biting into a piece of buttered toast. 'South America is a damn sight more interesting than England, if you ask me. Better weather, better music, better food, better beaches. I'll have that if you're not eating it.' He pulls my plate of spaghetti and eggs towards him and tucks in.

'And a lot hotter. I'd love to get a tan like yours,' Helen chimes in. 'Look at the colour of you both.'

'You can stay here as long as you like,' David says. 'If you want to get your savings off to a good start.'

'Yes, and then you can get back to your Latino lover sooner,' Helen says breezily. 'And have a baby!'

'Helen!' Emily shouts. 'Don't give her ideas.'

'Why not? There's nothing wrong with having babies at a young age. I love babies. I'd have ten if I could.'

She's standing at the stove, looking longingly at David. He walks over and envelops her in a bear hug.

'Yeah, just don't tell *her* to have a baby," Emily says. 'She's too bloody impressionable, especially when it comes to Latinos. The first thing you need to do is organise some work, anyway.'

'Yeah, you're right. I've got Stuart Wilde's number. He lives in Notting Hill. Leon said to call him when I arrive.'

That afternoon when my hangover has subsided, I call Stuart and leave a message. I call every day for five days with no response. Over the next couple of weeks, I call various magazines to pitch travel stories and do a few unsuccessful tryouts for temping jobs in offices in London. At night, alone in my room, I listen to Andean music on my Walkman. I stick the photo of Gabriel and me together in Buenos Aires on the wall next to my head, so I can look at it as I fall asleep.

Never knowing if my letters will reach him, I write to him. London is cold and dreary and I have no money, no suitable clothes for work and I want Gabriel so much my bones ache. I have to find work; it's the only way back to him. I'm about to give up on Stuart Wilde when I realise I haven't been dialling the right prefix. I try one last time and get him. He sounds taken aback that I'm calling, like he barely remembers meeting me in Sydney. But Leon is a mutual friend and for that reason, he agrees to meet me for a beer the next day.

That night, Helen and David take us out for dinner to a local tapas bar called El Molino's, where I meet a woman from the Canary Islands. When I tell her my story, she doesn't hesitate to give me her opinion.

'You must go back sooner mi amor,' she says. 'One year is too long for anybody to wait. You cannot expect him to wait for you. You will lose him.'

'Yes, go back and have a baby with him,' Helen adds, smiling a cheeky smile as Emily slaps her on the arm.

I make a firm resolution not to wait a year. I'm going back in six months. I don't know how, but I'm going to pay off my credit card and save the money I need to meet him wherever in the world he might be by November.

Having made my decision, I am better able to cope with life in London for six months. I feel upbeat when I meet Stuart at a pub in Notting Hill and we have a lively chat about South America. One beer turns into two, then three, then four. He keeps ordering as he asks me question after question about my adventures. He's fascinated, especially when I tell him about the hallucinogenic plants you can find there. San Pedro. Ayahuasca. Peyote. He offers me a job one day a week as his personal assistant. One day becomes two, then before long, it's a full-time job, cash in hand.

Emily and I are invited into an established share house with a bunch of Aussies at Blackhorse Road, Walthamstow, set up by our lovely mutual friend from Brisbane, Elaine. I like my room; it's large and bright with a window that faces a busy road. I have no coat hangers so my clothes stay in piles on the floor. The only decorating I do is to stick the photo of Gabriel and me onto the wall next to my bed and buy a candle, some incense and purple material to hang as curtains.

Within a month of arriving in London, I've fallen on my feet. I have a great job with Stuart and a fun house with a cool bunch of Aussies who are a lot more enthusiastic about being in London than I am. They organise trips to Camden markets, Islington, Brick Lane, Greenwich, Wales and the Glastonbury Festival.

To help ease my South American sickness, the girls take me out to a Latin dance night at El Barco Latino, a party boat on the Thames. It's packed with Latinos dancing salsa in pools of sweat. The music, with its happy horns and infectious rhythms, takes me straight back and I realise my soul will not rest until I return.

I settle into the job with Stuart quickly. I convert his spare bedroom into an office and he gives me his chequebook and sends me off to buy a desk. I'm amazed he trusts me.

'Don't buy anything new and ugly,' he says. He would have hated to have a soulless piece of furniture in his house.

I find a vintage furniture store and buy a plain, old-fashioned timber desk that he seems to approve of. It looks like something Jane Austen may have written on. Every task he sets for me, I carry out in the hope of pleasing him, terrified I will make the wrong move and he'll tell me not to come back. I need him more than he needs me, but he always makes me feel valued.

At fifty, Stuart is at the height of his fame: an author, metaphysician, speaker, music producer, writer, poet. Sometimes, I open his mail to find a letter and a full-length photo of an adoring female fan propositioning him. His girlfriend is often away for work, so he spends many nights at home alone. Sometimes, he asks me to stay after work and eat dinner with him. He looks at me over the top of his glasses and says, 'A man eating dinner on his own is terribly sad, don't you think?' He's world famous and successful, but to me, he seems lonely.

One night he takes me out to one of London's top restaurants for dinner and I can sense snooty eyes on us, wondering what a stylish silver-haired man is doing with someone like me.

He doesn't seem to care in the slightest what I wear to accompany him—or if he does, he doesn't say so. He doesn't give a fuck what people think of us and he's quite protective of me, demanding the waiter brings me a vegetarian meal immediately, after I've been served a meat dish. He makes me feel as important as everyone else in the restaurant.

Our work days are filled with writing business letters, checking his stocks, paying bills and dealing with the builders who are constructing his adobe mud brick mansion in Australia. In between all the admin stuff, he gives me jobs I find truly fascinating. One day he hands me his cheque-book and says, 'Hon, I have to do a seminar on lucid dreaming next week. Go and buy as many books as you can on the subject and write me up some summaries.' He pays me to go shopping for books, read them for him, and report back to save him some time. And he pays me handsomely, in cash. Always in cash.

Stuart teaches me about money; not necessarily how to manage it or save it, but how to make it and spend it. How to keep it flowing. He knows I am burdened with a crippling poverty mentality and he makes it his job to fix it. I left Australia thinking money was evil and people who pursued it were greedy capitalist pigs lacking in creativity and spirituality. It doesn't take long for Stuart to ingrain in me the opposite mindset: abundance mentality. He shows by example what it's like to not have to worry about money, to spend it freely, as if the more I spend, the more I will make. I come from a family of Aussie battlers and this attitude is a revelation.

In July, Stuart invites me to live in his apartment for six weeks while he goes to Taos, New Mexico. His company, Tolemac, is based there and he runs workshops called Warrior's Wisdom. It's shamanic consciousness stuff, delving deeply into metaphysics and self-empowerment. Stuart is renting his Notting Hill apartment from a friend of his girlfriend's who lives in New York. His rent is discounted because he's looking after her cat. It's a beautiful, airy apartment in Campden Hill Gardens, not far from Notting Hill Gate tube station, Holland Park, Kensington Gardens and Portobello Road.

It has polished floorboards and high ceilings, and abstract murals of naked women adorning the light blue walls, as if floating through the sky. The large bedroom has a four-poster bed in the middle and a bay window at one end with bright blue timber shutters. I can't believe my luck at having a luxurious London apartment for free. It's strange to think that in the space of two months, I've gone from meeting Stuart for a beer to staying in his apartment, deliciously alone. The depression that has hung over me since arriving in London lifts. I've never lived alone and I love it.

The work Stuart leaves for me can be done at night and on weekends, so I find a full-time day job as a receptionist with the architectural firm, Arup and Associates, based near Tottenham Court. I buy conservative clothes from op shops, brush my hair for the first time in months and buy some makeup. I'm now employed by a London firm, dealing with architects and engineers, organising couriers to deliver plans, typing letters and answering the phone. Stuart has left me the job of checking his stocks and has taught me where to find them in *The Times*. So while I sit at the front desk and answer the phone, I look through the stocks and bonds pages and type up reports for Stuart to send to him in the US. One day a senior architect walks past the desk.

'Stocks and bonds, eh?' he asks, his brow furrowed.

'Yep, just keeping an eye on things.'

He stands for a minute, watching me write down the stock prices, looks at me again, then walks back to his desk, puzzled. I don't fit his image of a stockmarket investor and it's fun pretending I'm some sort of financial whizz-kid.

I make 250 pounds a week at Arup. This, added to the money Stuart is paying me, coupled with the fact I have no rent to pay for six weeks, allows me to save money a lot faster than I imagined I would. Within six months I'll have thousands saved, in pounds sterling, not Australian dollars. I won't have to wait a year to see Gabriel. I can pay off my credit card and go back in November, only six months after arriving.

When I tell Emily I'm leaving, she isn't surprised. She has a good group of friends and a job and is loving London life. She's been to Germany to see Boris, but the relationship hasn't worked out. Back in his home country, he was different; cockier. He was also interested in someone else by the time she arrived. She'd left with a broken heart but recovered quickly as she settled into a graphic design job by day and a bar job by night. She doesn't long for South America the way I do, though she hopes to go back and see a bit of Central America one day. Maybe even meet up with Gabriel and me.

Gabriel is back home in Lima, helping to look after Jorge. He's out of the coma, but as the doctors predicted, he has been left brain damaged from his accident. I make long phone calls to Peru about once a week on Stuart's phone, with no idea how much it costs. I use Stuart's fax to send

Gabriel letters and he replies from his father's office fax. Sometimes, I hear the fax go in the middle of the night, jump out of bed and rush to the office, reading every line as the fax machine spits the paper out. When it finishes, I tear it off and take it back to bed to read and re-read until I fall asleep.

One night in August, Gabriel calls me on Stuart's phone.

'Hola loca!' he almost shouts down the phone line.

'Hola mi amor, que tal?'

'Bien, bien. I am so happy you're coming back. I think about you all day and all night, my love. I want to be with you forever. You don't know how much I love you; I love you with all my soul.'

Tears stream down my face. I've missed him so much over the past three months.

'My friends want to kill me because I never stop talking about you and showing them your photos,' he says.

He always makes me laugh, lifts my spirits. Hearing his voice simultaneously calms and excites me, and I promise to be back in Lima in three months. He says if I'm not, he's coming looking for me in London.

Stuart has given me the apartment to mind because he has two jobs he needs done while he's away: I have to water the plants and feed the cat. I forget to water the plants and they die. I lose the cat on the first day. When Stuart comes back, he isn't even mad. I've racked up a phone bill of 1000 pounds calling South America. He asks me how I'm going to pay for it. I tell him I'll work it off and he simply says, 'Don't worry about it, hon.'

We go back to work, me in the spare room, him in the lounge room on his laptop, cigarette hanging out of his mouth while he writes furiously, calling out for a coffee every hour or so.

Some days he comes into the office and sits on the couch by the window, and we have long discussions about metaphysics. Or about great thinkers throughout history. Or about aliens. One day he comes in, plonks himself on the couch and stares at the floor.

'What's up?' I ask, stopping my typing.

'I don't know, hon. I've worked all my life and I thought I'd have more money by now.' His bright blue eyes have lost their sparkle.

'I thought you had a fair bit, Stu.'

'I did. My ex-wife got a lot of it. And I've spent way too much building my house in Australia. This business of books and seminars isn't as lucrative as people think. And I've had a couple of big losses on the stock market this year.'

I don't know what to say. It's as though this New Age guru who tours the world imparting his wisdom to thousands of spiritual seekers is looking for answers—from me! What would I know?

'Um... maybe it's time to develop a new teaching.'

'I think it is. I don't feel I've finished my work yet.'

'No?'

'No. I still haven't really explained the reason for everything. The real purpose of the whole journey. I know I have more to offer. I think I've just lost a bit of confidence.'

'Why?'

'I don't know, hon.' He looks down into his coffee for a minute, thinking. 'I think I'm just sick of teaching. People aren't ready to hear what I want to teach.'

'Write a new book, Stu, something really amazing. Tap into the energy of someone like Isaac Newton. A man who changed the world.'

'I would like to be that man.'

'You can be, Stu.'

With that, he seems to cheer up.

'Stop working, hon, let's order some Indian and watch a movie.'

Some days he strolls into the office with twenty pounds and sends me out to buy a box of fine chocolates for us to share. Or he invites all my Aussie mates and me out for pizza and wine. He always pays the bill and doesn't flinch when one of the girls passes out drunk with her head in a pizza. Stu likes his food and wine, but he doesn't like the round belly he's found himself with since he turned fifty. He often complains about his weight, telling my Australian girlfriends he wants to be skinny like them. But with his penchant for wining and dining and his distaste for exercise, it's a losing battle.

Every day is different with Stuart. Some days, he wanders his apartment all day, deep in thought, smoking. He stands his cigarette butts up on the marble mantelpiece, or on pieces of furniture, and leaves them there. One time I find a gift I've given him—a solid Buddha I've had carved out of Mexican amber—lying on its side on the mantelpiece, carelessly knocked over and covered in cigarette ash. At first, I'm hurt. But then I brush it off and set it back up the right way, realising material possessions just aren't Stuart's thing. Wealth, yes. Stuff, no.

Some days I arrive and there's a house full of Stuart's Irish mates, or New Age celebrities like Shakti Gawain, hanging out in the lounge room. I nervously serve them coffee and go back to my office. Other days, I arrive at 9am and he's still asleep. I have my own key, so I begin working and he eventually calls out from the bedroom and asks for a coffee, then emerges in nothing but his undies, his hair a mess and a cigarette hanging out of his mouth. He stands in the doorway of the office, big bare belly hanging out, a mischievous grin on his face and wiggles his fingers at me, like a wizard casting a spell. It's his way of having a bit of fun. Stuart is almost always up for having a bit of fun.

Sometimes he tells me not to disturb him because he's going to meditate. One rainy London day in autumn, he's meditating, lying on his back on the lounge room floor, and I hear him snoring. Later I tell him he's been asleep and he denies it.

'No, hon, I was just in a very deep meditation,' he says. I don't let on about the snoring.

He is the least guru-like guru I've ever met. Back in Sydney, Leon Nacson had introduced me to authors and teachers like Wayne Dyer, Louise Hay and Deepak Chopra. To me, Stuart is by far the most interesting. He often says the most outlandish things and I can't tell if he's for real. I tell him I've been learning Astanga yoga and he warns me to stay away from yoga because it's dangerous and gives people a sense of spiritual superiority. It's such a hilariously 'Stuart' thing to say. He becomes interested in aliens and tells me he saw a UFO land on the roof of his apartment building. Then he tells me he thinks he's been abducted and asks me to inspect his nostrils for ball bearings, which he believes the aliens have inserted up his nose. I can't tell if he really believes it, or if he's just winding me up. With Stu, both possibilities are plausible.

His teachings are not everyone's cup of tea and he can be prickly if he's in a bad mood, but I don't care because he takes me under his wing with such kindness and with a complete and utter absence of judgement that I feel happy around him. Special, almost.

We work closely, just the two of us in his apartment, and I come to love Stuart Wilde and all his idiosyncrasies. His public persona is often brash, belligerent, even downright offensive. But in person, Stuart Wilde is one of the kindest, funniest, most generous and caring people I have ever met. He teaches me to stand up for myself, to aim high, to live in the moment and enjoy life to the fullest. And not to fear money.

'It's just a form of energy that gives you more choices,' he tells me. 'It gives you freedom.'

No word resonates as deeply in my being as the word freedom. I am a bird, a butterfly, a beast—a wild thing that will not be tamed.

Stuart sees me truly, because he's a wild creature too. We share a distaste for rules and regulations, for the mundane. He calls mainstream society 'tick-tock' and the people who live outside the status quo, 'fringe-dwellers'. He tells me to avoid tick-tock, to steer clear of group-think. He tells me not to worry about buying a house unless I can pay up front, because a life of debt, chained to a bank, is not an empowered life. He doesn't say I should be climbing a career ladder or settling down. He says I should embrace life, embrace freedom whenever possible. Do what I love. Be a fringe-dweller. For that short time in my life, when I am trying to figure out who I am, he is like a father to me.

The leaves are turning orange and there is a chill in the air as the time comes for me to go. I am happy to miss the English winter. I don't see the Tower of London or Madame Tussaud's. I don't even visit Ireland and Scotland. They are my heritage, my culture, exactly what I want to escape from. I'm transforming myself, becoming South American. London has been kind to me, but I don't belong here. I just blow in and out like a dandelion on the breeze and my presence is barely felt.

'You're doing the right thing you know, hon,' Stuart says, as we hug goodbye on my last day in London. I'll be back in Peru the next day.

'Thanks, Stu. I know.'

CHAPTER FIFTEEN

I AM UNDER house arrest. A willing prisoner. Gabriel lives in Callao, a dangerous part of Lima, and his family won't allow me to leave the house alone. It's about as far as you could get from Westminster and there would be few reasons for a tourist to visit. So of course, I'm in my element. But danger is only exciting when it keeps its distance; not when it creeps up and smacks you in the face, shows you how your life could end at any minute.

Gabriel's house is nothing like I imagined. White brick, two storeys, windows tinted black and a large exterior wall lined with spikes. It's one of the nicer homes in a run-down old street with few trees and very little green. Everything is brown. Brown concrete houses, brown dirt, brown air. Lima is one of South America's most polluted cities and the sky hangs low in a perpetual blanket of smog.

Gabriel's father, Ernesto, welcomes me with a bear hug and a kiss on the right cheek.

'Bienvenida hija,' he says. *Welcome daughter.* A short, obese man with a warm smile, he's more welcoming than Gabriel's mother, Manuela, who is courteous but eyes me with suspicion. Her caramel hair is streaked with grey and pulled back into a tight bun. Her face is a mixture of exhaustion and concern. She's very religious and doesn't approve of us sleeping together in Gabriel's room, as a non-married couple. Gabriel tells me she was hoping he'd meet a nice Argentinian girl.

We sit at the family table in the kitchen, drinking tea and attempting to get to know each other. My Spanish has deteriorated after six months in London and I'm almost back to square one. The kitchen door opens and three black-haired dolls walk in and kiss me on the cheek: Javier, eight, Isabella, six and Lucia, almost four.

'Candy!' Lucia says, touching my face. Gabriel explains the children's favourite show is an American cartoon called *Candy*, about a young girl with curly blonde hair. It's the first time the children have met anyone with my hair colour, and they're transfixed.

They are Jorge's children. I'm dreading meeting him. I still get pangs of guilt when I think about standing him up last time I was in Lima and now, what state will he be in? Gabriel takes me into the lounge room, where a plump man in his late twenties sits, staring blankly ahead.

'Jorge, es Leigh, mi novia,' Gabriel says, introducing me as his girl-friend. He speaks slower than usual, his voice filled with tenderness for his brother.

'Hola Jorge,' I say, bending down to kiss him on the cheek. He slowly turns his head and nods, then goes back to staring at the wall.

Ernesto employs two security guards, Martin and Martute, who sit beside Jorge in the sunny lounge room at the front of the house, reading newspapers and keeping him company. Martin is a muscular black man with a gap-toothed smile and Martute is short and tough and has been in jail for fifteen years. Gabriel says it's necessary to have security guards to protect the house and the family, as thieves know his father makes decent money with the truck. He tells me about a night some men came knocking on the front door, asking for Martute. Through a window, Gabriel saw they had guns and knives and he shouted at them, said fuck off, Martute wasn't there. He says he was shitting himself.

'Does Jorge remember me?' I whisper as we leave the room.

'No, he doesn't remember much of anything. His skull was cracked open from his forehead to the nape of his neck. The doctors say he will probably stay like this, but I won't accept that. I will take him to a shaman if he doesn't improve. His spirit is lost somewhere and I know a shaman who can find it.'

He tells me the children's mother disappeared when Jorge had the accident, leaving the children behind. The family employs Carmen, a pretty live-in nurse with big brown eyes, to look after Jorge. She says she's in love with him and wants to marry him. Perhaps out of frustration at her own situation, she sits at the kitchen table openly discussing with Manuela how long it will be before I fall pregnant.

Manuela adores her grandchildren and her weary eyes light up whenever they enter the room. Javier is full of life, like a mini Gabriel, and always wears a mischievous grin. Isabella's black eyes are rimmed with thick lashes, her bouncy hair tied back on one side with a pink bow. Lucia has something wild about her, like a little Isabella, but with a tough edge.

Gabriel has explained I'm vegetarian to his mama, but it's a concept she either can't or won't understand. She offers me meat for lunch and dinner and asks me whether I can eat it. When I say no, she looks perplexed. We eat cereal or bread and cheese for breakfast. The main meal of the day is lunch, usually a soup followed by a meat stew with rice or pasta, white bread rolls and bottles of Coke. Dinner is a light supper with warm milk boiled on the stove to kill bacteria, white bread rolls and butter. Ernesto hollows out the bread rolls by eating only the soft white insides and goes through about ten a night.

Gabriel's bedroom is on the roof of the house, a small room built into the corner of an open patio, beside the laundry. Standing on the roof, I scan the neighbourhood. Every house looks as though it's still being built, with steel reinforcing bar poking out of every dwelling. Peruvians don't have to pay property taxes until a house is finished, a loophole just about everyone takes advantage of. It's rare to see a nicely finished home minus the eyesore of rebar, not just here, but throughout the country.

We sleep on a double mattress on the floor. The room has its own bathroom, a small TV in one corner and a Janis Joplin poster on the wall. It's here I come to retreat, to be myself away from the scrutiny of the family. Manuela is often outside the door, doing mountains of washing. It doesn't occur to me that I am adding to her burden, nor do I think to offer her help. I drift through the days in a dreamlike state of infatuation, spending every second of the day and night with Gabriel, mostly in his bedroom.

The family soon grows tired of this, and Ernesto begins to shout Gabriel's name early each morning, waking us up.

'Why does he call you every morning?' I ask him as we lie entwined.

'Porque soy el alma de la casa,' he snaps. *Because I am the soul of the house.*

With Jorge so unwell, his responsibilities have fallen to Gabriel. He's required to work with his father, visiting factories around Lima to ask for the money they're owed for their salt deliveries. Sometimes he's gone all day and I stay in his room alone, listening to the radio, writing in my journal and writing letters home. Now I have a fixed address, I can receive mail. Mum sends me a koala T-shirt she has had my family and friends sign, and some Vegemite—which the kids think is disgusting—and I receive a letter from Grandma and Grandpa. Grandpa has had a stroke and can't walk very well, Grandma writes: 'Now you've got a couple of wobbly old grandparents.'

I cry when I read these words. I've never lost anyone close to me and I don't want it to happen while I'm here, so far away. I listen to the sounds outside. The dogs next door that never stop barking, that seem to bark louder and more passionately when important soccer games are on. The planes that thunder overhead directly above the house on their way to and from Callao Airport. An assortment of bells, horns and distant voices shouting things I can't understand. I try and guess what the people ringing the bells and honking the horns are selling—ice-cream, bread, milk? It's all a mystery to me.

My Spanish is crap. I can understand Gabriel, but I have trouble understanding his parents, which makes my stay awkward for everyone. I begin to dread sitting at the kitchen table while the whole family fires questions at me. Sometimes, I even find myself missing London, if only for the joy of effortless conversation.

The kids take it upon themselves to teach me Spanish. We sit at the dining room table and Javier puts the fruit bowl in front of me.

'*Na-ran-ja*', he says slowly, pointing to an orange. Naranja. Orange.

'*Naranja*', I repeat.

'Sí, sí, sí!' he claps.

'*Man-zan-a*,' he says, pointing to an apple. Manzana. Apple.

'*Manzana*,' I repeat.

Javier, Isabella and Lucia add to my limited vocabulary each day, taking me on tours of the house to teach me what things are called. Gabriel watches on with delight and Javier sidles up to him and says he wants to be just like his uncle when he grows up.

Gabriel's mother surprises me by giving us a knowing smile and I feel welcomed by her for the first time, as if all the time I've been spending with the kids has won me some points. She asks me if I believe in God. I sense it's important to get the answer right.

'Yes, I believe in God.'

I'm not sure I do, at least not the Catholic version. But now's not the time for a theological debate.

'Bueno, vamos a la iglesia mañana,' she says. *Let's go to church tomorrow.* I'm not sure if she wants me to purify my sins or just show me off at her congregation, but the next day we all dress in our best clothes and catch a taxi across Lima to a mansion in Miraflores, where the priest stands on a pulpit and releases a flock of two-hundred doves into the air. There's a swimming pool and a cafeteria, a cinema screen at the front and TV monitors all over the church. Young children and nuns, dressed in white and wearing headphones, operate video cameras, which record the service. The altar is a stage, the priest a rockstar.

Father Roberto is a balding, bespectacled Spanish man who is like no Catholic priest I ever saw when I was growing up. Halfway through the mass, he sends the children off for popcorn and Inca Kola and a large statue of Jesus is carried through the congregation. People kiss the statue affectionately and stroke his body. The mass is more like a show than a spiritual service. I prefer my gods in trees, mountains, oceans and deserts, but after I take Communion in this luxurious church, Manuela seems more comfortable with having me in her home.

The next day is a rare day in Lima: clear and sunny, with a brilliant blue sky. Gabriel takes me on a day trip to Chancay, about an hour north of Lima, the seaside city where he grew up. We have lunch at the famous Castle of Chancay, a faux medieval castle built in the 1920s, overlooking the oil-polluted ocean. He points out all the rocks he sat on as a child, fishing with his mates.

'Look chica, we share an ocean.' He's standing behind me, his arms around me, as we look down at the Pacific Ocean, dirtier here than I've ever seen it.

'Sí,' I laugh. 'My house is just over there.' I point to a hazy horizon.

We stand in silence, contemplating the vast ocean that separates our two countries.

'Has being with me been what you expected since I came back?' I ask.

'It's been better than I expected,' he says. 'I've been waiting for you. But not just for six months. I've been waiting for you forever.'

Gabriel has an aunt here, Tia Luz. She has money and he needs to ask for a loan to buy Christmas presents. He says it's normal for everyone in the extended family to ask each other for money in Peru because they don't see them as 'extended', they are just family.

She lives in a whitewashed cement house with a red-tiled roof in the centre of town. We ring the doorbell and hear movement inside, but it takes ten minutes for the door to open. Gabriel's Uncle Pedro stands there, head lowered. Not even a hello. He stands aside and ushers us in. As we walk into the lounge room, I notice a thick red substance all over the floor. I check under my shoes, worried I've stepped in something. Then I realise it's everywhere; on the floor where I haven't yet walked, on the dining table, on cups and plates. The whole house is in a state of upheaval. A sinking feeling pulls me onto a chair and I'm afraid something awful has happened.

Tia Luz finally comes down the stairs and her eyes are red and swollen. I look back at the floor and realise the red stuff is blood. Their daughter, Gabriel's cousin, has slit her wrists. If there was ever a time not to ask someone for money, this would be it. But Gabriel does it and I shrivel in my seat. He hugs his aunt and she hands him a wad of cash, her face dazed and broken. They found her just in time, she says, stopped the bleeding and the ambulance is on the way. We thank them and leave quickly.

On the bus back to Lima, Gabriel tells me his cousin was a manic-depressive, anorexic, pill-popping woman in her thirties with a young son who had a mental illness. After she'd had the baby, she found her husband dead in bed for no apparent reason. She never recovered from the shock.

Back in Callao, Gabriel and I pass the weeks staying up late and sleeping in late, and I can see it's beginning to annoy Manuela. Lima's climate is sticky and humid, its air thick with smog. Gabriel suggests we get out of Callao for a couple of days and visit a sacred site three hours from Lima called Marcahausi, which means *village house* in Quechua. It is a high plateau where festivals and sacred ceremonies have been held by the indigenous Andeans for thousands of years. I can't wait to get out of my jail cell in Callao and have Gabriel to myself.

We leave Lima in a hurry without planning or preparing, taking only a couple of water bottles, sleeping bags and a few joints. Neither of us thinks to take food. We catch a bus out of the city and Gabriel points to the favelas on the outskirts, says I'd be attacked if I dared venture there. The favelas are an ugly but somehow complementary addition to the dull brown hills of dirt on the city's fringes. The ramshackle houses are mostly the same flat brown of the surrounding mountains, with the occasional splash of aqua green, blue or yellow and dark square holes that serve as glassless windows. There are huge piles of rubbish everywhere, putrid smells and an ambience of decay, disarray and poverty.

We arrive in Chosica and change to a smaller bus. Its seats are tied together with string and the whole vehicle looks like it's on the verge of falling apart. It's crammed with cholitos and cholitas, chooks and goats, and we sit on the front dashboard of the bus, leaning up against the windscreen, because it's the only space left. It's a bruising ride, winding forty kilometres up a steep, sheer-sided mountain to the pre-Inca town of San Pedro de Casta. A dangerous road, but nothing compared to the Death Road. I seem to be the only foreigner in town, but cholitas in yellow top hats and short men with weathered faces go about their business, barely glancing at me.

A volleyball game is in full swing in the centre of the village and two teams of cholitas in sports uniforms are belting the ball back and forth over the net in a torrent of long black plaits. It appears the whole pueblo, from grandparents to children, are watching and laughing and we sit for a while, enjoying the spectacle. One of the girls loses balance and ploughs into a spectator, who screams in mock terror at the large-boned cholita potentially squashing him.

As we set off on the four-kilometre trek up into the mountains, the sun is high in a cobalt blue sky and the mountains fold back over themselves all the way to the horizon. We smoke a joint and take our time walking along the dirt track, sparsely vegetated with cacti. Beautiful rocks of deep red, purple and blue line the path, which rises steadily higher. My head begins to throb the higher we walk; my legs grow heavy.

'La ganja… es muy fuerte,' I puff. *It's strong pot.*

'Sí, sí,' Gabriel laughs. 'La ganja Peruana es la mejor.' *Peruvian ganja is the best.* I don't know if I'm hallucinating, but I can't breathe. There's not enough oxygen up here to suck into my lungs. Every now and then a local dashes past us, a woman with a baby on her back or a man carrying a huge bag of firewood and we ask how far it is to Marcahausi.

'Half an hour.'

'An hour.'

'Very far.'

'Very close.'

'Three hours.'

Their answers are inconsistent and we realise their concept of time is more fluid than ours. Gabriel and I don't wear watches and neither do they, so we have no idea what time it is or how long we've been walking.

I trudge behind Gabriel, trying to keep up. I stop to catch my breath and notice the sun is sinking towards the horizon. A thick mist is erasing the deep blue sky, obscuring our surroundings. I'm suffocating on the mist and Gabriel has disappeared.

'Gabriel! Gabriel!' I call, weakly.

'Estás bien?'

'NO! I can't breathe!'

He emerges from the mist and rubs my back, pulling me down onto a rock. Rest, but not for long, he says. We have to reach Marcahuasi in time to have a look around and return to town before nightfall. I drink some more water, catch my breath a little. But nausea is building and my shaky limbs are growing weaker. My head is throbbing, my lips are sticking together. A cloud swallows us and I'm dizzy. I can't walk anymore. I collapse onto the rocky ground.

Far off in the distance, I hear a woman's voice. I'm trying to find her, somewhere in the mist. A donkey is staring at me. Where did it come from? There's the lady, a tiny crone crouching over me, her long black plaits falling in my face.

'Soroche,' she says. Altitude sickness.

I just want to sleep and she tells me not to close my eyes, to wake up and eat some pears. She pulls a handful of tiny native pears from her apron and hands them to me. I sit up and fight off the urge to vomit, biting into the juicy flesh. She looks ancient but her limbs move with the agility of a young girl. She sits silently watching me. Deciding whether I'm going to live or die. I don't know how long she sits like that; I'm aware of Gabriel's voice somewhere in the mountains and her intense black stare. I struggle to my feet and she cackles and wishes me luck. She pulls on the donkey's reins and the last thing I see is firewood on the donkey's back as they disappear into the white mist.

It's dark when I wake to a sky thick with stars. I don't remember getting up and walking, but Gabriel says after the cholita gave me the pears, I mustered the energy to walk to a nearby cave, where we lay our sleeping bags for the night.

'Mira,' he says, smiling. *Look*. He points to a ridge above the cave, to a place about twenty metres away. Towering rocks stand tall against the night sky, the moon rising behind them.

'Marcahuasi,' he says. We were so close. He tells me I had been determined to get there and had pushed myself to walk, but when he saw the cave, he'd decided we should rest for the night.

'I also brought you here so you could see this,' he says, sweeping his hand across the sparkling sky. 'In Lima, the pollution is terrible. I wanted you to see the stars.'

I suck in a big gulp of cool, cleansing oxygen. This is what I love; clear mountain skies. Not the greyness of Lima, not the greyness of London. I love him for seeing that in me; for wanting me to see the stars.

The sun is smudging the mountain sky dusty pink when I wake. I snuggle down in my sleeping bag, breathing the cool morning air. I smell the familiar Andean mountain scent of woodsmoke in the distance. I'm alive. The sky is once again clear and below us on a track, a small man trots along with firewood on his back, waving and calling out hola. I wave back at him and feel the urge to run after him, to ask him to thank the lady who helped me. But I stay where I am in the warmth of my sleeping bag and watch him disappear over the crest of the mountain.

Gabriel wakes and asks me how I am.

'Bien, gracias,' I answer. 'Muy bien.' The headache, nausea and muscle weakness have all gone. I've acclimatised to the altitude overnight.

I don't know how quickly altitude sickness can kill a person, or whether I really was close to death the day before, but I had fallen into a coma in that Andean cave while my blood cells scrambled to keep me alive in the altitude of almost 4000 metres.

We roll up our sleeping bags and walk the final few steps up to Marcahuasi. A grassy plateau stretches out, rimmed by huge granite rock formations shaped like human heads and distorted facial features. It's an otherworldly place, haunted by the spirits of pre-Inca civilisations. Are rocks haunted the way trees are, I wonder?

Something about this place reminds me of the haunted tree I found in Parramatta Park when I was five. My brother and I walked through the park on our way to school each day and one of the trees we passed in a dark corner of the park was the home of a witch. She lived somewhere inside its thick trunk. Its twisted limbs and branches looked like gnarly old legs and arms. This tree looked different from the other trees; its bark was almost black.

One morning, we decided to bait the witch. My brother put a *Star Wars* sticker on the trunk to see if she would come out and take it. When we walked back through the park after school, we ran straight to the tree. The sticker was gone! Snatched by the witch.

But we forgot all about the haunted tree when we were taken away from Mummy to live in a place far from our school, with different looking trees and a big dining room that smelled of porridge. They said Mum was sick. We were taken to St Michael's Children's Home in Baulkham Hills, a home for Catholic children whose parents needed a rest. We called it the cottage. We lived with nuns, sleeping in a long corridor of beds with a curtain around each one, like a hospital ward.

My brother wouldn't talk to Mum the day she left us there. He just sat silently staring at her, his bottom lip stuck out, even when they said they made a roast on Sundays. I was excited. It was a new adventure, new kids to play with. But the nuns were always watching a boring kissing show called *The Restless Years* on TV and wouldn't let us have a drink with our meals. Mum always let us have a drink with dinner. One night, all the kids were running around in the TV room and I fell and hit my head on the sharp corner of the coffee table and it bled. The blood pooled in my hands and I wanted my mummy, but I didn't know when I would see her again. Maybe never. It wasn't fun anymore and I wanted to go home. But I didn't know where home was. Was it here in this porridge-smelling place? Was it with Grandma and Grandpa, where I could play the pianola and the table was always set with a tablecloth, cloudy apple juice and a fresh pot of tea? Was it with Granky? Was it with a father I rarely saw? Or was it with our sick and exhausted mum?

I did not know where I belonged.

I'm not the only one who believes spirits live in trees and rocks. Daniel Ruzo, a Peruvian writer, photographer and archaeologist, lived at Marcahuasi and studied it for nine years during the 1950s. He documented hundreds of human-like rock formations and believed the site contained signs to save humanity from a forthcoming catastrophe. It was also a famous location for UFO sightings.

We spend an hour exploring the eerie rocks before we make the trek back to San Pedro de Casta, a faster trip down the mountain than up. Gabriel has his arm around me as we hitch a ride down the mountain in the back of a truck filled with kids and chooks, and Gabriel pays the driver with a bracelet for his daughter. He wants to go out partying with his best friend Juan and his girlfriend Maria when we get back to Lima.

'Vamos a celebrar!' Gabriel says.

I'm in the mood to celebrate too, after my second near-death experience, and I welcome the chance to check out Lima's nightlife with Gabriel and his friends. Juan has been Gabriel's best friend since school and he wants to meet this Australian girl he's heard so much about. Juan is tall and clean cut with short dark hair, a solid build and a speedy energy about him. Just the kind of person I can get along with, the kind of guy who's never dull, always up for fun. He and Gabriel are similar in temperament, upbeat and always ready for a laugh, only Juan isn't an artisan and dresses more conservatively.

Juan and Maria pick us up and we drive around the clifftops of Lima, drinking beer and smoking pot. In Lima, no one seems to care about driving under the influence, not in Gabriel's circle of friends anyway. I push down a glimmer of concern for our safety. I don't want to be the party pooper of the group, so I go along for the ride. We stop at a lookout where Juan and Gabriel do a few lines of coke and Maria and I decline. I don't know if she says no to make me feel more comfortable, or whether she always abstains. I'm not thrilled about Gabriel taking it, but I don't have any say in the matter.

Maria is small and brunette with a pretty face and a gentle manner and I like her. I need a Peruvian friend; I've been missing Emily and my girlfriends at home. Now high on three different substances, Juan speeds off along Lima's winding coastal clifftops and it's a relief when we reach Barranco, an arty area of the city with a night market. Gabriel greets many of the artisans sitting behind their stalls, has a few brief conversations while I wander the markets with Juan and Maria. Gabriel is well-known here and I'm proud to be with him.

'Hey chica,' he says, returning from one of the stalls with his jaunty gait. 'All the artisans think you look really nice.'

'Oh really? That's sweet—which ones?'

'Oye, don't get ideas. I'm flattered, but I like to think you are beautiful only for me. I am completely in love with you, loca. But I don't want to think the whole world is, too. I've had many foreign girls flirting with me, asking me out, but I'm not a brichero.'

'What's a brichero?'

'Peruvian men who try to meet foreign women, seduce them and get them to buy them tickets to their countries. Or try and marry them as a way out of here.'

'You don't want to marry me as a way out of here?'

'No, loca! I want to marry you one day, but so we can live here, somewhere in South America, a place by the sea that we both love. You are the only girl I have ever gone after. I can never be angry with you. I live for you. All you have to do is say 'rub my leg' and I will give you a full-body massage.'

'Rub my leg!'

'Okay, but not here.'

Juan and Maria laugh, and the three of them chat about old school friends they haven't seen in a long time. They try to include me in their conversation as we wander around the night markets, but I'm happy to watch Lima life passing by and keep quiet. I still get stares from passersby, but I'm used to being the different one now. Besides, I don't feel different to them on the inside. Juan, Maria, Gabriel and I are going to be great friends.

CHAPTER SIXTEEN

BEFORE TRAGEDY STRIKES there is often a period of calm, but it only appears so in hindsight. I'm finally feeling comfortable in Gabriel's house and there are fun times to be had. A life in Peru to be lived, beside my handsome artisan. A love, deep and strong, an all-consuming love. A desperate and addictive love.

Lucia celebrates her fourth birthday and Manuela sews pink satin dresses for her and Isabella to wear to her party at school. I go along and take photos of the girls in their new dresses. The family doesn't own a camera and this is one way I can be useful after weeks of feeling burdensome. The party is held in a dark classroom decorated with balloons and streamers, the desks and chairs pushed to one side. In one corner, a large homemade cake sits on a big timber table. Gabriel hangs a piñata from an upstairs window and the children bash the lollies out with a broom handle, scrambling to pick them up as they fall to the floor. They line up politely for a piece of cake and when they sing happy birthday, they sing it in English first, then in Spanish—a Peruvian custom.

Gabriel and I have bought Lucia a doll that walks by itself and wrapped it in shiny pink paper. The children crowd around as she opens the gift and when Gabriel switches it on and it walks, Lucia is in awe. She sits completely still, watching the doll walk, eyes wide, mouth agape. Then very gently, she picks the doll up and holds her like a real child. I can see she believes it's a real baby by the tender way she cradles it.

I take photos of Lucia and Isabella spinning around in a big circle laughing and holding hands with the other girls, little princesses in their pink dresses

Gabriel's mother does everything for the children and to help ease her load, I tell her I will wash Gabriel's and my clothes. I spend hours hand-washing them in the big tub outside his bedroom door and I am satisfied with my work as I hang our clothes out on the line that stretches across the roof.

Manuela is still bewildered and increasingly put out by my vegetarianism, but has taken to making me cheese empanadas and delicious pie made with choclo, a Peruvian corn with chunky whitish kernels. The choclo is chewy and starchy rather than sweet and golden, like the corn I'm used to, but I'm not complaining.

With Christmas coming up, I decide to take some pressure off Manuela and make a huge vegetarian dish for everyone. I have one specialty: Greek moussaka with eggplant and ricotta cheese. It takes hours to make, frying slices of eggplant in breadcrumbs and layering the dish with vegetables. I cook it on Christmas Eve and take over Manuela's kitchen for the day, making mountains of moussaka for the family and the next door neighbours, Rolo and Julia, who think my romance with Gabriel is the best thing to ever happen in Callao. Manuela watches in silence as I cook. I'm determined to impress her.

For her Christmas gift, I have photos of Isabella, Lucia and Javier developed and buy a large montage frame. I wrap it and keep it in Gabriel's room to give to her after Christmas lunch.

On Christmas Day, the seven members of Gabriel's family along with Rolo and Julia gather around the kitchen table while I serve up moussaka for everyone, anticipating their delight at my cooking. They refuse to eat. They sit and stare at the food, as if it's poisonous. Gabriel and Rolo try to ease the tension by grabbing their forks and tucking in with overzealous compliments. I try mine, wondering if there's something wrong with it. It tastes great. In fact, it's one of the best moussakas I've ever made. But still, they don't eat. Gabriel's mother sits silently, arms crossed, a strange look on her face… I don't know if it's anger or satisfaction.

When we can't bear the awkward silence anymore, she gets up and begins to clear the table, making a loud show of tipping the food in the bin. I am mortified. I don't understand what I've done wrong. Is it because there was no meat? Is she annoyed at me taking over her kitchen at Christmas time? No one says a word and I'm too embarrassed to ask why they won't eat it. I excuse myself and bolt up to Gabriel's room, throwing myself on the bed in tears.

Gabriel stays downstairs drinking with Rolo, leaving me to it. It's Christmas Day after all. The radio is on and a Peruvian pop song I don't understand is playing. Then a song straight from my teen years begins to play. It's *Don't Change* by INXS. The familiar keyboard intro cheers my soul and it makes me cry more. I miss home for the first time. I've been gone almost a year and no matter how hard I try to fit in here, try to learn their language, try to please them, I'm not one of them. I'm not sure I ever will be.

But I'm not defeated. I wash my face and take Manuela's Christmas gift down to her. When she opens it, her face lights up as she admires the framed photos of her beloved grandchildren.

'Gracias, hija,' she says with a warmth I haven't felt from her before. She calls me daughter for the first time.

Then she hands me a gift of her own: two pairs of flared pants she has sewn for me out of the ugliest fabric I've ever seen. She has snuck up to Gabriel's room and taken a pair of the loose cotton pants I wear in boho Indian prints, and copied the pattern. The style is right, but the fabric is so wrong, a loud floral fabric that would make a cheerful tablecloth. I tell her I love them.

'Voy a comer su comida,' I say. *I will eat your food.* I don't want to add to her stress anymore.

'Ah, sí? Y la carne?' *And the meat?*

'Sí, sí,' I answer. Yes, I will eat the meat.

The next day, I eat her lunchtime casserole and become so ill with diarrhoea and vomiting that Gabriel has to take me to the hospital after I collapse in the street in Callao. Fortunately, it's easy to get around Lima. Colectivos speed around the city playing blaring Latin rock and pop, stopping anywhere to pick up passengers, and it seems anyone with a car can write a sign saying 'taxi' and stick it on the windscreen. These taxis range from reasonably safe looking cars to complete bombs with windows missing and doors smashed in. We don't bother waiting for a colectivo, jumping straight into a taxi.

A security guard at the hospital door looks me up and down.

'Que tiene ella?' he asks with a tilt of his chin towards me. *What does she have?*

'Are you the doctor?' Gabriel shoots back as he pushes past.

Sick as I am, I can't help but laugh at the way Peruvians ask the most invasive and rude questions without the slightest hesitation, as if I'm not actually standing right there in front of them. Why is she so chubby if she doesn't eat meat? Why is she wearing those ugly boots? Is she pregnant? Why isn't she pregnant? When is she going to get pregnant?

Navigating the hospital system of Lima is infuriating. After hours of waiting, I'm sent to one window to give my personal details, another window to get a ticket, another window to hand that ticket in, and another window to get a second ticket. I can barely walk and the process seems futile. It's ridiculously convoluted, as if the job of one person has been split into four. When I eventually get to see a doctor, he hands me a dirty jam jar and tells me to do my *caca* into it. I ask Gabriel to take me to a pharmacy where I can buy a sterilised jar to do the deed in. I return to the hospital and hand it in, whereby it disappears into the bowels of the hospital. I wait for results that never arrive and after two weeks of spewing and pooing, my energy returns. I feel great. Rolo and Julia are having a party for Rolo's fortieth birthday and they've booked a live band. We're looking forward to a fun night after the tensions of Christmas.

Before we leave, Gabriel pulls me into his room and holds a cigarette paper under my nose with a small pile of white powder on it. I hesitate for a second, then I snort it. What the hell, I need a bit of fun after all the sickness and the awkwardness with Manuela and the difficulties of being a gringa in this city, always standing out, always watching my back. A little bit won't hurt. I mean, it would be rude to come to Peru and not try the coke, right? It's not like its heroin. We arrive at the party just as its kicking in.

We kiss Rolo and Julia on the cheek and then move around the room, greeting guests with the customary peck on the cheek. In my confusion as to who's who, I kiss the band members and everyone laughs. They all look the same to me. The band strikes up a salsa tune and Rolo asks me for the first dance. I have become a guest of honour and the cocaine infuses me with confidence. I swivel my hips and spin around on Rolo's arm, much to the delight of the guests who tell me I dance salsa pretty well for a gringa. Gabriel is glowing with pride and when the dance is over, we escape to the rooftop to kiss and declare our undying love.

Each day I love him more. He tells me if Jorge doesn't recover, he may have to stay in Lima, work for his father and help bring up the kids. He wants me to stay with him and I ponder the possibility. I can't imagine being without him, so I am willing to go wherever he needs to be. I am convinced of his devotion to me. I can see it in his eyes and the way he wraps his arms around me tightly at night. In the way he caresses my body and holds my face when he kisses me. I know nothing and no one will ever separate us.

We fall into a lifestyle of partying every weekend with Juan and Maria and cocaine becomes a regular fixture when we hang out. We're not addicted; it's just the done thing here. It's so cheap, cheaper than alcohol, and it makes everything seem better. Brighter. It gives life a glossy veneer, smooths out its sharp edges. Fatigue gone, sadness gone, anxiety gone, washed away by this powerful white powder.

On New Year's Eve, we drive through the streets of Lima, burning with effigies of politicians and hate figures, tyres and piles of rubbish. A Peruvian custom I can't help but think isn't wise for the lungs of the city, considering its high pollution levels. We're going to a León Gieco concert, one of Gabriel's favourite musicians, and he's in the mood to party hard. He snorts all night and we dance and kiss, completely uninhibited.

But Gabriel takes it too far. When we return home, he's manic. He spends the night crouching near his bedroom window like a frightened animal. He thinks the police are coming to get him. I keep pulling him back to bed and he's trembling. His heart is beating so hard I can see his pulse throbbing in his neck and his skin is cloaked in sweat. His eyes are bloodshot and full of terror. I ask him if I should call an ambulance, or get his parents. He pleads with me not to; they will never forgive him. I'm scared too—what if he flips out and kills me? I grab my bag, tell him I don't feel safe, that I'm going to sleep downstairs and he pleads with me to stay with him.

As the night wears on and the coke wears off, we sit outside on the rooftop and look at the starless Lima sky. He begins to relax and tells me, finally, the truth.

'The real reason I was in Buenos Aires was because I overdosed and ended up in hospital,' he says. 'Here in Lima, I'm constantly scared. Paranoid someone is coming to get me. I was working for my father, earning money and partying, but I was depressed. I couldn't stand the idea of delivering salt for the rest of my life. I didn't know what I wanted to do. After my overdose, Jorge gave me some money and said, 'get the fuck out of Lima'. I was in Buenos Aires recovering, trying to escape this life. Elsa invited me to stay with her so I could sell artesanias in Buenos Aires. That's when I met you and you gave me a reason to live. I will never leave you, never cheat on you, never hurt you. You are my life.'

I have never felt more conflicted. I am hopelessly in love. I want him, I want his life, his culture, his history, his creativity, his children, but not this. He has to agree to stop using cocaine or I can't be with him. I won't marry him until I know he can stay clean. I love him with the core of my being and I can't leave him, I won't leave him. But this has to stop.

'Promise me you will stop taking cocaine,' I plead with him, stroking his hair.

'Sí, sí, sí, mi amor. You have seen the worst of me now. Please don't leave me. The only way I can be happy is to derive my happiness from someone else. From you.'

The incident rattles me. Our love has been a fairytale until now. Here I am, in a strange city, barely speaking the language, in a house where everyone talks about me and I make them uncomfortable because I don't eat animals. Now this.

We go back to bed. Gabriel passes out and I stay awake, writing in my journal about this beautiful, damaged man. The only way I can deal with it is by getting it out on paper. I write about how I am besotted but shaken. How I didn't know he had such deep-seated problems, but then, he doesn't know about mine. Maybe finding a life partner isn't about finding someone perfect, but finding someone with a dark side you can live with. Maybe it's about loving them *for* their faults, not in spite of them. I close the journal, kiss his smooth cheek, and go to sleep.

The next weekend, Juan and Maria invite us out again but we decline in favour of a quiet night at home drinking maté and watching TV. They go out anyway and as they speed along the clifftops of Lima, where the streetlights and the hazy night sky mingle too close to the edges, a car rounds a bend. Maria is driving. The cars collide.

Gabriel receives the news the next day over the phone. He collapses into my arms, but he doesn't cry. Not yet. Juan is in a coma and Maria has severe internal injuries, but she's going to be okay. It's Juan everyone's worried about. Gabriel and I stand on the street outside the hospital with a growing group of his friends, waiting for any scrap of news, hoping, praying. Our arms around each other, we gaze up at the windows lining the tall white building, wondering which room is his and whether he's breathing in that room, or whether he's fading away. We're not allowed in to see him—in Australia, they'd at least let us in. It's not enough to stand outside and wait, helpless. After five days of waiting, making plans for what we'll do when he wakes up, willing him to wake up, the news reaches us like a headline about someone else: Juan is dead. *Muerto*.

We line up to view his body in an open casket before the funeral, saying goodbye to a man Gabriel loved, a man who had welcomed me into his life and accepted me. His face is like a patchwork doll's, ripped apart and sewn back together. He looks as if he is sleeping peacefully. It's the first dead body I've seen and I didn't know him well enough to be given this privilege, but since I'm here, I feel compelled to spend an acceptable amount of time looking at him. Standing before this man I was just getting to know, staring at his corpse, I am both shaken and fascinated. How quickly a life can end. How little of Juan is left in this Juan-shaped shell.

We join the funeral procession to the crematorium, a line of cars rolling slowly through the streets of Lima, past old ladies who make the sign of the cross when they see the hearse, past businessmen who cross themselves, mothers, fathers, aunts, uncles, children. It's a beautiful custom and one that helps us feel less alone in our grief.

A large group of Juan's school friends gather at the crematorium. Juan's frail mother wails, her legs giving way. An ambulance pulls up and two uniformed men help Maria limp out of the ambulance, bandages around her stomach, cuts and slashes across her face. Juan's mother runs at her, screaming: 'You killed my son!' and is gently pulled away, sobbing. Maria sees Gabriel and me and hobbles over.

'Por favor, you must always stay together,' she cries, holding onto Gabriel for support. 'For Juan and for me, you must always stay together. You don't know what it's like. It hurts so much, Gabriel. I want to die.'

I try to shrink inside myself, hide from fifty or so strangers openly staring at me, wondering who the hell this gringa is at their friend's funeral.

'It's okay, you're with me,' Gabriel says, pulling me close. Yes, I am with him. I will always be with him. I can't imagine what Maria is going through, what I'd do if I lost Gabriel.

After the funeral, Gabriel and another old school friend Julio decide to go for a beer at a bar by the water in the Callao suburb of La Punta. The beach is lined with big smooth rocks the size of cricket balls, and parents with toddlers splash around in the dirty bay. It's far from picturesque, but it's theirs.

Julio and Gabriel order ceviche, a Peruvian dish of fresh raw fish cured in lemon or lime and I eat plain spaghetti yet again. I push my fork around my plate while Julio and Gabriel chat about the old days. Halfway through the meal, Julio disappears to the toilet and when he returns, Gabriel does the same. He comes back only a minute later. Must have been a quick piss. I smile at him and rub his back, asking him if he's okay. Then I notice what looks like fine white granules beneath his nostrils.

'Did you guys just have some coke?' I glare at them, incredulous.

They look sheepishly at each other and Gabriel turns to Julio.

'Esta bien hermano, ella no entiende.' *It's okay brother, she doesn't understand.*

To them, it's normal. To me, it's completely fucked up. Heat rises to my cheeks, prickles down my arms, becomes full-blown rage.

'You've just been to your friend's funeral! The reason he is fucking *dead* is because of this shit, driving around like it's perfectly fine to mix drugs and alcohol then drive along the fucking clifftops! He's still in the furnace burning and you're snorting that shit again.'

I shove the table into them, push my chair back and sprint to the beach. The emotion of the past few days, the past months in Lima, the sickness, the awkwardness of staying in Gabriel's house, the language difficulties, the heat, the food, Lima's incessant murky sky, the sense of danger on every street corner and Gabriel's lies about quitting coke crash onto me, a powerful wave that knocks the wind out of me. I stride along the beach, tripping and stumbling, trying to get away. I have no idea where I'm going, just away.

Gabriel runs after me, calling out to me to stop, saying I don't know where I'm going, that it's not safe for me to walk around Callao on my own.

I turn to him, exasperated, and begin picking up the beach rocks, pelting them at him one by one, as hard as I fucking can.

'Go away! Fuck off and leave me alone!' I scream and throw rocks, while Gabriel ducks and the people of Callao stare at the gringa losing her mind.

Chapter seventeen

I AM LEAVING Lima, with or without Gabriel. The sky is rarely blue here and I have enough money to travel for another six months, maybe even a year if I skip meals and sleep on beaches. Gabriel can't bear to work for his father any longer, standing around outside factories in the grimy industrial parts of the city, waiting to be paid for his father's salt, being sent away empty-handed and told to come back the next day. It's killing his spirit.

'I can't stay here loca,' he says. He's sitting on the floor, leaning up against the wall underneath his Janis Joplin poster. I was surprised when I'd arrived and seen that poster. I often played Janis on the jukebox in the pubs at home, while I drank beer and played pool with Emily. I never expected to find her in Peru.

It doesn't take us long to make up, but things have to change.

'My soul is not meant for selling salt in this crazy city,' he says. 'I need to travel, to make things. My spirit is stagnant here. The first time I went travelling, I returned with long hair and knocked on my front door. My father opened it. Do you know what he said?'

'What?'

'I don't know you. He said, I don't know you.'

'Geez, that's a bit harsh.'

'He made me cut my hair and work for him and I was so fucking miserable. I was trapped and so I started taking cocaine. To cope with this place, with all these responsibilities. And then I went to Buenos Aires and met you. Do you know what, loca? I've never been in love before. I've been with women, but not like this. Not how it is with you. You are my queen and my life. Let me come with you.'

I still love him. Despite the lies, despite the drugs, I still can't imagine ever being without him. So I make him a deal. If I invest my savings in materials to make jewellery, he will teach me what he knows and we will work together while we travel and sell. But under no circumstances can he take any more cocaine.

Deal. He takes me to Polvos Azules, a labyrinthine indoor market near the Catedral de Lima in the city centre and we spend up big. The market is crammed with fake brand label clothes, pirated CDs, toys, shoes—and it's all going cheap. We buy bags of semi-precious stones—turquoise, malachite, agate, tiger's eye, chrysocolla, labradorite, rose quartz and jasper cut into cabochons, discs of varying sizes and beads, as well as metal wire in different strengths and thicknesses, clasps and pliers. We buy hundreds of brown and white porcupine quills, pointy spines that give Peruvian jewellery its distinctive tribal look, and *chaquiras*—deep red and peach coral stones found at Peruvian archeological sites. We buy thousands of *huayruro* seeds from the Amazon, bright red and black seeds that are said to bring good fortune and ward off negative energy, leather cord for plaiting into bracelets, and thousands of hand-painted ceramic beads the size of a cashew, which we can thread onto leather to make beach jewellery. We also buy a backpack for Gabriel and now I'm down to my last $100. My beaten up backpack is filled with clothes; his clean new pack is filled with plastic boxes partitioned into segments that hold the raw materials we will convert into riches.

'What are we going to tell your parents?' I ask Gabriel. I'm lying on his mattress under the watchful eye of Janis, running my fingers through piles of stones in light blues, pale pinks, rich browns, shiny blacks, deep greens and warm oranges. I love these stones, am itching to learn how to work with them, how to transform them the way Gabriel does.

'Leave it to me,' he says, trying to organise the stones into colours as I continue to mess them up. Each stone, each colour, has its own personality, its own power. Imagine such beauty lying hidden in the ground, out of view, until its dug up and cut and polished.

He tells his parents we're going to travel and make money to send back to them, to help care for Jorge and the children. I feel bad taking Gabriel from them—their son, their soul, their prime income earner. But I have to get out of this place before I die.

We tell Manuela and Ernesto we're going to Trujillo in the north for a few days to relax by the beach, then we're going to travel through Ecuador, Colombia, Panama, Costa Rica, Nicaragua, El Salvador, Honduras and Guatemala until we reach the beaches of Mexico. We're going to find our place, a place we can live happily together, make good money selling jewellery, somewhere sunny by the sea. We are leaving, but we will send them money to ease their burden. They know they must let their son go.

We buy tickets for an overnight bus north and before we leave, Manuela conducts a prayer ceremony with the whole family present, to give us her blessing. Words tumble out of her trembling mouth and as she closes her eyes tightly in an extra effort of concentration, tears flow down her tired face. She anoints our foreheads, making a cross with holy water and kissing us on each cheek. I cry as I say goodbye to the people who have taken me in as their own daughter, offered me a bed, food and a family.

Gabriel feels like a traitor for leaving his mother to take care of Jorge and the three children, his father to run the business alone, but this is his chance. He'll make a good life for himself in the north, send money back and return one day having made a success of himself. He knows it will never happen in Lima, where darkness and old ties will continue to drag him down.

We make our plans for the future in a small hotel room in Huanchaco, a surfing town in the city of Trujillo, famous for its long left-hand wave and traditional canoes made of tortura reeds, which are still used by local fishermen. We'll rest here for a few days and sell jewellery with the other artisans by the beach, then we'll catch a bus to Ecuador and begin our journey northwards.

'Mierda!' Gabriel says as we settle into our room. He's pulling everything out of his backpack, checking his pockets. *Shit!*

'Que pasa?'

'No tengo mi pasaporte!' He's left his passport at home, an eight-hour bus trip back to Lima. Off to a brilliant start. He can be so vague and forgetful. It's infuriating.

He leaves on the first bus the next day and I'm left alone in Huanchaco, with no idea how long he'll take to return. You can't trust buses in Peru. I'm beginning to believe I can't trust anything or anyone in this place, including Gabriel. I don't know if he'll go on a bender when he gets home, decide the trip with me isn't feasible.

Oh well, if I want to be an artisan, I may as well go and sell. I pack a brown woven bag with Gabriel's collection of jewellery—elaborate necklaces, dangly earrings and bracelets—and walk down to the promenade by the beach. I spread our *manta* on the ground, a large piece of cloth like a sarong, and begin to display our wares. The local artisans nod but keep their distance, until one comes up and introduces himself, asks me where I'm from in a gentle, hesitant voice.

I tell him I'm from Australia and he says he's a guitarist from Cusco and is trying his hand at being an artisan. Tall and skinny, with straggly hair and two front teeth rimmed in gold, he looks like a gangly teenager with braces. His name is Kike and he looks after me while Gabriel is away, introducing me to the others, helping me feel welcome.

That afternoon, an ancient woman hobbles past the artisans, all sitting on the ground displaying their wares on their mantas. Kike hops up and follows her, asks if she'd like a drink. He sits her down on a seat beside a patch of sunflowers and buys her a glass of cold chicha, a sweet drink made of purple Peruvian corn. She gulps it down and places the empty glass beside her, then sits staring at the ocean. She may not remember all the details of her life on her deathbed, but I hope she remembers the day a long-haired artisan went out of his way for her, to show her someone cares.

I think of my own grandparents, Grandma, Grandpa and Granky. Three stalwarts of unconditional love in my life. Along with my parents, they gave me substantial amounts of money for my twenty-first birthday. They all helped me get here. I need to write to them, tell them all how much I miss them.

Even with Kike to comfort me, I still feel out of place, but I need to make money every day to pay for my food and accommodation. I've got my US$100 note safely tucked into my bra, but it's only for emergencies. I also have a sign I've painted onto a piece of white silk that says *masaje*. I'm offering head and neck massages, but the people here are conservative and unaccustomed to massage being done in public. It's as though I'm offering them sex on the beach in plain view.

Gabriel doesn't return that day, or the next. What the fuck is he doing? I fear this lack of reliability could be a sign of things to come. I quickly push the thought away. I love him too much to entertain any notion of him really letting me down. His coke addiction is bad enough; I hope there are no more secrets.

I get to know the other artisans and become more comfortable, though I never shake the feeling I'm encroaching on their territory. They warm to me gradually and invite me for beers at the end of the day with whoever has sold the most. Maybe I could live this lifestyle without Gabriel, cruising around South America as an artisan. I haven't made a single piece of jewellery yet, but I'll learn.

In the afternoons, young lads play soccer in the street, bread boys carry baskets twice their size and men in uniforms sell bread from bicycles. Señoras set up stalls along the promenade and sell *papa rellena*, a deep-fried ball of mashed potato stuffed with half a boiled egg and served with a generous dollop of chilli sauce or mayonnaise. For a vegetarian travelling in South America, surrounded by meat at every turn, it's sheer heaven. I also find a restaurant selling *Papa a la Huancaína*, boiled and sliced yellow potatoes on a bed of lettuce, smothered in a spicy, creamy sauce made from fresh cheese, yellow Peruvian pepper and evaporated milk. Finding food I can eat lifts my spirits and I even sell a few pieces of jewellery, mostly because the locals are curious and want to find out who I am and what I'm doing here on my own.

I spend the third morning writing letters and postcards home, then send them from a little post office in town. Sitting at her desk, surrounded by photos of her children, Christmas decorations and an old black and white photo of herself as a young woman in tight pants, is Alicia Dominica. While the rest of the post office workers in Peru usually plonk a big black ink stamp on letters and postcards without even looking up, Alicia sells beautiful paper stamps adorned with pictures of local flowers and plants, which she carefully sticks on with special gum. She is fastidious in every aspect of her job, reminding me not to lick the stamps because they're poisonous. While she busies herself carefully tearing stamps off large sheets, she entertains me with stories of all the love affairs she's had in her life. I leave privileged to have met and done business with Alicia the postmistress.

On the fourth morning, I take a trip to Simbal, an hour inland. The artisans have told me it's an idyllic place to swim and spend the day. I arrive to two dried-up public swimming pools and a trickle of water over the rocks. Lush vegetation gives the area a tranquil feel, but I'm horrified to find garbage polluting every spare space. Plastic plates covered in rotten, fly-infested food, beer cans and bottles, used toilet paper, lolly packets. The stench is so putrid I take the next bus straight back to Huanchaco.

Gabriel arrives back on the fifth day. He has his passport and says he's ready to begin a new, drug-free, responsible life. He just needs me to smuggle a large amount of high-grade Peruvian weed over the border for him, hidden in my clothes. They won't check me, he says, but he'll be an easy target for border police.

The stash of weed isn't for sale. It's strictly for personal use. We've come this far together and there's something about his boyishness, his sincere love for me, his determination to begin a new life, that makes me want to help him.

I cut holes into the wide waistband of a pink cotton Indian skirt and feed fat marijuana buds through it, until I look like I've put on a kilo around the waist. Gabriel says if they're going to search anyone, it will be him, and it's safer to cross separately. All I have to do is be a charming Aussie girl and talk about kangaroos and Crocodile Dundee and they'll wave me through.

The border crossing from Tumbes to Huaquillas is one of South America's most dangerous, but I'm not deterred. I know once we pass this final test, we'll be on our way to the tropics, where we'll drink piña coladas and laze around under palm trees while we work. I shower myself in white light, then a double bubble of white light and take a deep breath. I'm going first and Gabriel will follow half an hour behind me.

I have not anticipated sniffer dogs—big German Shepherds that could rip your hand off. I don't know if they're trained to sniff only coke, or pot too, and as I make my way closer to the border checkpoint with my backpack on my back and the drugs hidden safely in my skirt, I pray. I'm aware it's not an appropriate situation in which to call on the power of prayer, but it's worth a shot. Besides, I'm not smuggling heroin or coke, just a bit of weed. The border police won't see it that way if they catch me though. They'll take the opportunity to extort money out of me, probably let me rot in a prison cell, where I'll be raped and murdered and raped again. Every worst case scenario is racing through my mind, my mouth dry, sweat pouring off my face, as I take my first tentative steps towards the checkpoint. I smile my biggest smile as I hand my passport over. The Ecuadorian official simply smiles back, stamps my passport and waves me through, while the sleepy looking sniffer dogs completely ignore me. It's all a bit of an anti-climax.

Gabriel also crosses without any problems and we meet up further down the dusty road for a celebratory kiss, then catch a bus through roads lined with banana plantations to the beaches of Guayaquil, where we stroll the sand with our wares, hoping to make enough money for a meal or a night's accommodation.

People stare and ask if we're hippies.

'Sí,' Gabriel answers proudly. I prefer to think of myself as an artisan.

With Lima far behind us, we're free to be ourselves. We are inseparable, together twenty-four hours a day, full of optimism about the road ahead, laughing a lot, making love, drinking beer and missing meals without noticing.

My Spanish is improving and it's getting easier to talk to him. Each time I hear a Spanish word I don't understand, he explains it so well, I barely need my dictionary. It's just as well, as he still doesn't speak any English and he has no need to. Our entire relationship is conducted in Spanish, and as trying as it is at times, it's opening me up to him and his world in a way I wouldn't have access to if I didn't speak the language.

We have plenty of material to keep making jewellery for months and I still have my $100 stashed away. It's not much, but it's an important safety net. We travel to Quito, Ecuador's capital city in the Andean foothills, constructed on ancient Inca foundations. It reminds me of Cusco and I am at home once more. These old Andean towns and villages always strike a chord of familiarity in me, and I'm happy to stay in Quito and rest for a few days.

Quito has a problem with electricity supply, so each day the city's power is turned off for a period of time in the afternoon. We're staying in a cavernous old hotel with small windows, so when the power goes off, the hotel falls into darkness. On our second day, I decide to take a shower while the power is off and pad to the bathroom, throw my clothes on the floor, shower and race back to the room, where I throw my arms around Gabriel and plant a kiss on his smooth cheek. He's sitting at a small table in our room, twisting wire around stones by candlelight, cocking his head to the side to see how his new piece looks. He works every chance he gets.

I sit on the bed and write in my journal, not in the mood to start learning the craft just yet. A thought arises—a sickening thought. I run down the hall and back to the bathroom. It's gone. My last $100 is gone. I had forgotten it was tucked in my bra for safe keeping and it has fallen out when I undressed to have a shower. In the darkness of the bathroom with the power out, I hadn't seen it on the floor. I fly into a rage.

'Es tu culpa!' I shout at Gabriel. *It's your fault!*

'Why? What did I do? He stops mid-creation, pliers in one hand, an earring dangling from his fingers.

'Because you have no money, because I have to pay for everything, it's your fault I spent all my money on fucking stones and wire and now I have nothing left. You're so bloody vague, you left Lima without your passport. No wonder your father thinks you're a failure. You are a fucking failure!'

He stares at me in shock and I collapse on the bed, distraught.

This has nothing to do with Gabriel, but I'm so full of rage, so full of fear, so full of desperation, I must blame someone. It can't be my fault; I can't take the blame for this. I can never take the blame. I took the blame too much as a child, for things that weren't my fault.

Gabriel is deeply wounded. I have destroyed the pride of a Latin American man. We have a huge fight and he tells me he doesn't want to travel with me anymore, that he's going back to Lima. I wrap myself around him, sobbing hysterically at the thought of him leaving me, and beg for his forgiveness.

It's the first time Gabriel cops my wrath when things don't go my way. It's a deeply ingrained habit I carry. By assigning blame, I don't have to take responsibility. He brushes it off and I calm down, but things are tense. I realise how much I have given over to him, how much of myself I have let go of to become like him, to inhabit his world. I want to live the life of a travelling artisan, but I don't know if I can handle the insecurity that goes along with it, living hand to mouth, being conspicuous in the streets. I needed that backup money and it's gone. I am entirely reliant on Gabriel now and I'm going to have to hurry up and learn to make jewellery, add to our production. Make myself useful.

I'm not good with my hands. Both Grandma and Granky tried to teach me to knit, sew and crochet as a child and I failed at all three. Gabriel tries to show me some basics, how to set a simple stone or make a plain pair of earrings, but when I have to make a loop with the round nose pliers, it never turns out well. Or the stone I'm trying to encase in a piece of wire falls out because I haven't secured it tightly enough. He has an innate talent for this craft, and the essential ingredient: patience. I lack both.

After Quito we visit the charming indigenous village of Otavalo, where the locals wear colourful traditional dress. Men in a blue or grey poncho, white calf-length knickers, a long braid that hangs down their backs and a fedora. The women's dress is the closest to Inca costume worn anywhere in the Andes—white blouses adorned with colourful embroidery, long blue or black skirts, shawls and rows of bold beads and red coral bracelets.

We put our manta down in the street and sell to tourists and the locals don't seem to mind us working on their turf. An unsuspecting German traveller falls in love with a small rodochrosite necklace Gabriel has made, worth no more than $2, and offers us $50 for it. We don't like ripping him off, but we're desperate for the money so we keep our mouths shut. He rushes off to show his friend, who nods enthusiastically.

After replenishing our savings in Otavalo, we head for Colombia. We have no desire to spend time in Bogotá—the drug cartels rule and it's too dangerous for us to sell there. We arrive at the bus station and have a few hours to wait for a bus to the Caribbean coast in the far north, so we sit in a small café to drink coffee and pass the time.

Two foreign girls in their twenties sit at the front counter flicking through their Lonely Planet guides. We're sitting at a small table nearby, holding onto our bags as we always do in places like this. Their large backpacks are on the ground next to them and they've placed their small daypacks on the counter, under the watchful eye of the café owner. They turn to face us and we chat about where we've been and where we're going.

A man walks in and orders a coffee, standing at the counter wiping his glasses. Something isn't right. Its odd, the way he and the café owner keep glancing at the girls. Perhaps they're just eyeing them off. We're deep in conversation about our planned adventures, when a small woman in her sixties walks in holding a blanket and stands at the counter. Then within a few minutes, she leaves the café without ordering.

'Our bags! Our bags!' The girls are screaming.

The bags are gone. Passports, money, everything important. Gone. It's not hard to figure out the three Colombians have worked as a team to pass the bags to the lady, who concealed them under the blanket and walked out.

'What did you do with our bags?' one of the girls shouts at the café owner.

'No se nada,' he says, smiling. *I know nothing.*

It happens all the time, he shrugs. Nothing I can do.

We take the distraught girls to the police station inside the bus terminal and are told the same thing: it happens all the time, nothing we can do. Care factor zero.

We can't leave them alone, with no money and no documents. We change our plans and pay for a taxi to take us all to a nearby hostel, where we spend a couple of days helping them make phone calls to cancel their credit cards and travellers cheques, and order new passports. Then we get the hell out of there on a bus straight to the Caribbean.

It's a sobering reminder: I'm not safe here. The only time I've lost money it was my own stupid fault and I haven't been robbed but still, I'm not safe. I'm a gringa.

A target.

CHAPTER EIGHTEEN

WE SETTLE INTO our shared life as artisans in a remote national park along Colombia's Caribbean coast. Parque Tayrona's jungle grows right up to the edge of powdery white sand beaches, towering coconut palms on one side and glossy water on the other.

A bus drops us off at the entrance to the park and we trek along a dense jungle pathway, passing coconuts that have fallen to the ground and are sprouting baby palm trees. Our heavy packs weigh us down, but we are invigorated by our vibrant surroundings. A green glow illuminates our faces and we congratulate each other on having made it to such a beautiful corner of the world.

Giant electric-blue morpho butterflies flit across the path and disappear into the jungle, the most exquisite butterflies I've ever seen. I catch my breath at their beauty and Gabriel turns to me, takes my face in his hands.

'Tu eres una mariposa,' he says. *You are a butterfly*.

'Por que?' I ask. *Why?*

'Because you are beautiful.'

Beside him, surrounded by fluttering bright blue butterflies in this land of lush delight, I do feel beautiful. Juicy and energised. My skin is hydrated in the humidity and I let go of all the stresses of Lima, our fight in Quito and the robbery in Bogotá. From here, things are going to get better.

We arrive at a small campground, the only accommodation here, hire two string hammocks and tie them up between the coconut palms. We waste no time getting to work, setting up our manta on a little bamboo platform to the side of a café, where backpackers sit around chatting, reading and writing postcards.

I lay out a series of hand-drawn postcards with graphic mandalas I've been working on to sell, along with the jewellery. No one buys them. I've never had any art lessons and have no natural drawing ability, so the postcards look like something a kindergarten student might be proud of. I'm no artist, but I'm avoiding learning to make jewellery, so I've turned my hand to drawing. It seems easier. When Gabriel tries to teach me, I resist, saying I'm too tired or I don't feel like it. I like the image of myself as an artisan, I can picture myself holding a magnificent finished product, but I don't want to do the work required to learn the craft. It's too tedious and my mind flits around like the butterflies in this luscious jungle.

I prefer to watch Gabriel work, admiring his deft hands. I lie down on the platform behind him as night falls. He's chatting to travellers, trying to sell to them as he works, but they're all backpackers on a shoestring. No one has money to buy jewellery here. We're going to have to get working on our cheap beach jewellery line. It's just threading ceramic beads onto leather cord and tying an adjustable knot at the end. Surely I can manage that.

I doze off with reggae beats and animated chatter in the background and when I wake, a pretty German girl is flirting with Gabriel. He looks sexy in a white singlet, which shows off his smooth brown arms, baggy hippie pants, beads around his neck and his hair flowing around his shoulders. I'm barely awake but I'm awake enough to know she's a threat. I sit up and put my arm around him and she backs off slightly.

Gabriel introduces me as his girlfriend. She looks disappointed, makes some small talk, then wanders off. He is friendly with everyone he meets, but he doesn't flirt with other women, doesn't comment on their looks, and I love that about him. I am emotionally secure and solid in our union. I don't doubt we're going to have a long and happy life together and this is just the start.

We spend our days hiking through the jungle, visiting ancient ruins belonging to the Tayrona Indians and looking for private places to swim naked in the warm Caribbean water. We fall asleep holding hands on the beach, wake up and swim some more. On the second day, we're lying about a metre apart in the soft sand when I sense something that makes me open my eyes. Without moving, I shift my eyes toward the water and see a two-metre-long black snake emerging from the blue, sliding up the sand directly towards us. I have no idea what kind of snake it is and if it will chase us if we run, so I decide it's best not to attract its attention. Gabriel is fast asleep as it slides straight up between our bodies. I'm not as frightened as I should be as I watch its pink tongue flick in and out and look closely at its beady eyes, about half a metre away from me. It doesn't disturb us, we don't disturb it and it goes on its merry way, disappearing into the jungle. Had it been a spider, I'd have run away, screaming. They terrify me. But the skin of a snake up close is so exquisite, I am lulled into a state of wonder.

I lie there, wondering what the encounter means, if it's a sign from the universe. Not every unusual encounter is a sign from the universe, I tell myself. Sometimes, it's just life, doing its thing and you happen to witness it. But on a spiritual level, snakes are often seen as a symbol of rebirth and transformation. Is it significant that when the snake slides by, Gabriel is asleep and I'm awake? When he wakes, I tell him about it and he says we're in a jungle, of course there will be snakes, but seeing one so close is a lucky charm.

A week into our stay, as we're swinging in our hammocks and talking about where we're going to go next, an agitated Colombian man rushes past us, stops, then runs over to Gabriel. He says his name is Carlos.

'Here, take this,' he says, sweating and shaking. He whispers something to Gabriel, hands him a white rock and disappears into the jungle.

'What was that all about?' I swing out of my hammock to have a look. It's a rock of pure cocaine, about the size of a golf ball.

'I think he's crazy in the coconut,' Gabriel laughs.

'You're not going to have any are you?'

'No, mi amor. I'll hold onto it in case we see him again and I'll give it back to him.'

'I don't know, chico. Maybe you should give it to me to mind.'

'I don't want you getting busted with it, loca. Colombian police would not treat you well if they found it on you.'

He has a point. But I'm not comfortable about him keeping it either. Nor do I want to throw it away, just in case Carlos comes back for it. I agree to let him keep it for the time being, just until we decide what to do with it. But I'll be watching vigilantly for tiny white grains beneath his nostrils.

We never do see crazy Carlos again at Parque Tayrona and with no sales eventuating from the thrifty backpackers, we decide it's time to leave for Cartagena, an old colonial port city further along the Caribbean coast, where we hope to do a better trade.

We arrive in Cartagena late on a steamy Friday night and check into a peeling old hostel in Calle de la Media Luna, or *Half Moon Street*. It sounds like something from an old Hollywood romance or murder mystery and is buzzing with life even at this hour, with locals and backpackers coming and going.

Our room is bare with a double bed made with synthetic sheets that don't fit the bed and stick to our skin in the oppressive humidity. There's a shower head hanging off the wall in the corner of the room with no cubicle or curtain around it. It's a luxury to have our own shower, but it pours water straight onto the concrete floor of our room.

Cartagena is a sixteenth-century Caribbean city to rival Cusco for its world heritage value. Cobblestone alleyways wind around colourful colonial architecture, with lanterns perched on canary yellow walls and rickety timber verandas decorated with red bougainvillea. The beaches in Cartagena and those of the nearby islands are all turquoise water, white sand and palm trees. We catch buses around the city and they're all decorated with bright colours inside and out. Inside, holy cards featuring an assortment of Catholic saints plaster the dashboard and windscreen, and music is always blaring, usually cumbia—a festive style of Colombian folk music—and Latin American pop music.

We try to sell at Bocagrande, an area of the city popular for its long beaches backed by palm-fringed promenades, but it's an upmarket area and people aren't interested in our wares. Backpackers hold onto their cash and wealthy people go for fine gold jewellery set with emeralds. We give up, pack up our things and enjoy the beach instead. Street vendors sell coffee from carts attached to bicycles. In a box mounted on the front are a selection of thermoses with different styles of coffee, all strong and sweet. A woman with deep black skin and braided hair, wearing a bright red sundress, approaches me and asks if I want my hair braided like hers. It's not something I'd usually spend money on.

'Can I offer her some jewellery?' I ask Gabriel.

'Sí, mi amor,' he says. He's always generous with offering his work to barter when we can't pay cash. I love his giving spirit and even though I haven't made any jewellery yet, I'm starting to realise I can do the selling to tourists who speak only English. It's an advantage we have over other artisans who speak only Spanish.

The woman chooses a pair of chrysocolla earrings the colour of the Caribbean, and sits me on a fold-up chair facing the water, weaving my hair into fine cornrows fastened with colourful plastic beads. When she's finished, I stand up and thank her.

'You're pregnant,' she tells me bluntly, as if she's commenting on the weather.

'What? What did you say?'

'Your belly. You're a little bit gordita, amiga. I think you are pregnant.'

One: I thought I'd lost a bit of weight. Two: I am not fucking pregnant!

The thought horrifies me. I want to have children with Gabriel some-day, but not yet. We're nowhere near settled and I'm far too young. Too many adventures are calling. Gabriel reassures me if I am pregnant, he will look after me. I refuse to believe it's a possibility and I don't want to spend money on a pregnancy test.

I am overcome with anxiety for the rest of the day. That night, lying on the synthetic sheets in our room writing in my journal while Gabriel winds wire around stones and holds them up to the dim light, I bleed. Thank the lord. Thank the angels. I shower in the corner, trying not to flood our entire room and freshen up. A knock on the door. More a pummel than a knock.

'Dejame entrar! *Let me in!*'

Gabriel slowly edges the door open and Carlos shoves it violently and barges in. How does he know we're here? Has he been following us? Did he meet up with Gabriel at some point and do a deal? He's accusing us of ripping him off, saying he wants his cocaine back. Saying if we've sold it, he wants the money. He punches the wall, eyes bulging.

'No hermano!' Gabriel says, unruffled. No brother, you took it back, remember? I know Gabriel did not give it back. Why is he lying? He offers Carlos a puff on his joint. 'Toma loco,' he says. *Take it crazy guy.*

The pot takes effect and Carlos relaxes. Then he strips.

'Loco! Qué haces?' Gabriel shouts. *What are you doing?* He's offended at Carlos' display of nudity in front of me, *his* woman. Carlos jumps into the shower and soaps himself, under his arms, under his balls, chatting about other Australians he's met and asking me whether I know Crocodilo Dundee.

Gabriel tells me to turn away, hands him a towel and leads him out of the room, insisting I lock the door after they leave. I'm shaken and a little amused. This guy is nuts. Period pain is gripping my belly in its familiar vice, and the night is hot and sticky, so I strip down to a black singlet and undies, re-light what's left of Gabriel's joint and lie on the bed, watching the water drip from the shower head straight onto the bedroom floor. That dripping will annoy me later. I throw the match onto the floor, not realising it's still alight, and it lands on Gabriel's only pair of undies, catching fire and spreading quickly to the sheets and mattress.

'Fuck!' I shout to the empty room.

I jump up and grab a blanket to stamp out the fire, then fall into a heavy, stoned sleep.

I dream the kinds of dreams that are like movies, so real you're surprised when you wake up. Carlos is in my dream and he's running around shouting. I think he's saying 'fire'!

Fire! The shouting grows louder. FIRE! Am I still dreaming? It's so hot. Cartagena is so hot. Is the whole Caribbean region this hot? I'm coughing hard, smoke is stinging my eyes and I'm in the air, being lifted, carried. Shouting, flames, the sound of gushing water. My bare feet touching the stone floor, running.

I run up the long corridor past the old men who sit quietly, day and night, smoking cigarettes and watching life pass by. I run out the front doors and into the street. Gabriel is sitting in the gutter with Carlos. He has glowing green droplets in his hands, lit by the street lamps. Emeralds.

He's looking at emeralds in the middle of the night as a fire engulfs our bed and I stand dazed in the street in my underwear.

The scene melts away and I'm six, sitting on a garden bench at Grandma and Grandpa's fibro house, the house of tea and tablecloths and *Reader's Digest* and golf in the backyard. The house of plum trees and flower gardens, of board games and boiled lollies. The house of china painting and Madeira cake and a pianola that lets me imagine I am a pianist. The house my father visits, sometimes. He's sitting next to me smiling, holding a small pile of sparkling green stones in his hand, his skinny arms a tangle of ropey veins.

'Choose the two prettiest ones and I will have them made into earrings for you,' he smiles. 'For your birthday.'

But I don't want emerald earrings for my birthday. I want the Barbie Campervan. He doesn't know anything. Grandma is watching, urging me to choose. I don't want to make her sad again.

'That one and that one,' I say flippantly.

'What do you say to your father?' Grandma says in her soft, wheezy voice.

'Thanks.' I run off to change into my swimmers and jump into the neighbour's pool.

Where did he get those emeralds? Mum said he never paid child support, always cried poor. He made life tougher than it already was for her, a beautiful young woman in 1970s Sydney, prettier than the brown-haired lady from ABBA. I bet she would have loved to hit the disco every Friday night, but was stuck at home with two kids who she loved, but who wore her down, so far down her nerves broke.

He gave me the wrong birthday present. But—he gave me a present. An actual gift.

Standing half-naked in Half Moon Street, a thought stirs: maybe he cared. Maybe he even loved me. He gave me emeralds, asked me to choose the ones I liked. Had them made into earrings, which I wore until I lost them. It wasn't a lot, in the entirety of a childhood. But it was something.

It was something.

'Chica! Que pasa!' Gabriel is shaking me, asking me what's wrong. I'm frozen in the past, in another time and place. His arms around me, telling the crowd to fuck off. Pulling me inside, sitting me down on a chair where the old smoking men sit. One of them covers me with an old man's jacket that smells of stale tobacco and sweat.

I'm trembling. 'Oh my god, I set fire to the bed! I threw a match on the floor and your undies caught fire.

'Loca, they were my only pair of undies!'

'I know! I'm so sorry.'

We're surrounded by concerned faces. An Israeli couple say they'd smelled smoke and knocked on my door. When they didn't get an answer, they tried to open it and found it locked. They ran to get the manager, who opened the door with the spare key and found me unconscious, flames rising on the bed.

Strangely, I am unharmed. Was someone watching out for me? An angel? No, I wasn't saved by angels. I wasn't saved by white light. I was saved by humans; quick-thinking humans.

We're given another room for the night and the next morning, we're called into the manager's office to discuss the damage I've caused. The old men of the corridors nod as I pass, ask me if I'm okay. I'm profoundly embarrassed and Gabriel tells the manager a story that's not entirely untrue.

'She sleepwalks,' he says. 'It's not her fault. She acts out her dreams.'

Poor Mum had many an interrupted night's sleep dealing with my bizarre evening antics, when I would be stuck somewhere between the real world and a dream world. The night I said I had spiders in my mouth and the only way she could get any sleep was to go through the motions of scraping them out with an imaginary spoon. The night I woke up sitting inside my closet with the door closed, didn't know where I was and screamed the house down. The night she heard the front door of our Blacktown rental house slam shut and found me walking down the street in my pink nightie.

The hotel manager nods and smiles, as if it's a plausible explanation, then says the cost of replacing the bed and the sheets will be US$300. I'm a gringa, therefore I must be rich, and he takes the opportunity to upgrade his soft furnishings. We don't have that much money. We're down to our last $50. We've been trying to sell enough in Cartagena to pay for a ferry to Panama, but this will set us back. We'll be stuck here for months paying this off. He has our passports in his safe and will hand us over to the police if we don't pay up. He gives us three days to come up with the money.

That day, instead of selling in the streets, we set up a table across the road at a popular backpacker's hostel, El Doral. The backpackers don't have money to buy anything but the cheapest beach jewellery, but what they do have money for—what they keep money aside for—is drugs.

A backpacker approaching a Colombian stranger to buy drugs is risky. Approaching a Peruvian artisan with his Australian girlfriend? Different story.

They ask if we have any weed. It happens so fast, crossing the line from being artisans to being drug dealers. If you can call us that. We don't think of ourselves in that way. We are artisans who have been presented with an opportunity for a little side hustle because we have a debt to pay. That's all.

Once word spreads that we have good weed, the backpackers' budgets miraculously expand. The cash rolls in faster than we can count it. In two days we've made $600, a fortune compared with the $30 or so we make a day selling jewellery. In three days, we've made enough to pay off the fire damage, recover our passports and buy tickets on a cruise liner to Panama, with money left over.

That night, we dress up and celebrate at a salsa club in Cartagena, spending more on drinks than we usually would. It's a great feeling, having the money to splurge on a night out together. We dance close, more in love than ever, charged with ideas for where we'll sell jewellery when we arrive in Central America. It's going to be a big leap into our new life, leaving South America, starting fresh.

Tourists mix with Colombians, dancing to the festive horns and passionate vocals of a catchy salsa song. A group of travellers huddles in a dark corner of the club, eyes shifting around nervously. Four well-dressed guys in collared shirts and nice jeans and a woman in a neat dress with short brown hair are staring at us.

The woman approaches, tentatively.

'Hi, we're here from London making a documentary for a TV station in the UK,' she says.

I'm impressed. People with real jobs, well-paid jobs, working here in South America. A pang of envy shoots through me.

'Um… we were just wondering if you knew where we could buy some, um, cocaine? We can pay you as much as you want.'

Gabriel and I look at each other. It's one last chance to make a stack of money to propel us comfortably into our new lives. Gabriel whispers that he still has the rock crazy Carlos gave us. I knew it! I wonder what he'd been planning to do with it, if he was going to try and get it across the border to Panama. I push the thought aside. Opportunity has landed in our laps. There's no way these Londoners could be police.

'I'm not sure,' Gabriel tells her. 'I can find out for you. Wait here and I'll be back in an hour.'

I stay with them, chatting about their documentary, fishing for details. They seem legit. They say they're going into the Colombian jungle to film wildlife and I can't imagine anything more exciting to do for a living. I miss the security of a stable job and I wish I could somehow join them, even as an assistant, but I know this is a fleeting moment and we'll all soon go our separate ways.

Gabriel returns and I give him a nod to let him know they're trustworthy. He discreetly hands them an envelope and they're happy to part with $400, which will fund our trip all the way to Mexico.

'That's the last time we sell drugs,' I say to Gabriel as we walk back to the hostel, my arms crossed, his arm dangling around my shoulder. He assures me we won't need to where we're going, that the tourist beach towns of Central America and especially Mexico, are a honeypot for artisans. But now we know how easy it is to sell drugs—easier than doing just about anything else—what will stop us doing it again? It requires no skill and very little effort. It's incredibly lucrative and I fear we have unleashed something—a temptation we won't be able to control.

I should be happy we've fallen on our feet, but a discomfort is growing in my gut; is this who I am now? Is this what I have lowered myself to? Is this the price of my exotic new life?

Drugs are fun, for a while. For the carefree backpackers who will return home to regular jobs and lives, for the filmmakers who will have the time of their lives dabbling in the dark side and go home with memories of a wild night in Colombia.

But both Gabriel and I know how quickly the fun can end. It ended in a split second for Juan and Jorge back in Lima. It doesn't seem to concern Gabriel as much as I think it should. He rarely talks about it and it doesn't make him want to stop drinking, or taking drugs. I begin to wonder what will.

CHAPTER NINETEEN

IN PUERTO VIEJO de Talamanca on Costa Rica's Caribbean Coast, I finally become a real artisan. Gabriel teaches me macramé techniques to turn leather cord into bracelets, chokers and anklets, and I'm pretty good at it. I don't have to wield tools and sitting quietly knotting the cord is meditative. In Panama, we'd stocked up on rolls of hemp twine before heading to Costa Rica. Now I can make beach jewellery with hemp and ceramic beads from Peru and sell them for $1. If I sell ten a day, that's our accommodation paid for. Some of the bead designs we selected in Lima feature the Rasta colours of red, yellow and green, which go down well in Puerto Viejo.

It's a sleepy little village where rustic bamboo cafes play reggae along the beachfront. The standard mode of transport is to walk or ride beaten-up bikes along flat dirt streets lined with wide-leafed foliage and bright pink and purple flowers. Skinny dogs sleep in the shade and the scent of ganja wafts through hot, humid air.

Within days, we meet a friendly bunch of artisans and musos who invite us to rent a room in an old timber share house two streets back from the beach. We're only paying six-hundred colónes a night, which is about US$10 for both of us. I'm thrilled to have a kitchen where I can cook vegetarian food and don't have to order yet another plate of spaghetti or plain rice and beans. The artisans have tables set up in front of the Rasta café and invite us to sell with them there. We become part of the local community, passing the days basking in the sun, swimming in warm clear water, selling enough jewellery to get by and enjoying the sweet life. We have a comfortable and clean place to sleep, somewhere to cook, somewhere to sell by day and outdoor reggae parties under the stars and coconut palms at night, where locals mix with artisans, musicians and travellers. A local saying here is *pura vida*, which means pure life. It's used as a greeting and a farewell and I'm smitten.

In this slow-paced little village, we can stay a while and relax, make some honest money and get healthy. We do lots of walking and swimming, drink fresh tropical juices and coconut water, and cut back on alcohol. One day a few weeks into our stay, I leave the table where we spend most days selling and making jewellery, buy some veggies and make a big pot of vegetarian curry back at the house. I add plenty of butter and spices and make a huge pot of rice for everyone to share. I carry the pots down to the market and hand bamboo bowls around to the artisans and musicians, who accept gratefully and compliment me on my cooking. These are my people; they accept me for who I am; I can be proud rather than be treated like an outsider for not eating meat.

I'm wearing an ornate shiny purple vest with gold and silver brocade sewn around its edges that I'd picked up in a second-hand market in La Paz. One of the artisans, an older local guy, begins to look me up and down.

'Me gusta tu chaleco,' he says. *I like your vest.* He's intrigued not only with my vest, but with my armfuls of bracelets, dangly earrings and chunky necklaces of turquoise and silver.

'Where you from?' he asks.

'Soy gitana,' I answer. *I am a gypsy.*

He nods and says he thought so. I don't have a gypsy bone in my body. But in my heart, that's who I am. I'm not a regular Aussie girl from the western suburbs of Sydney with Irish and English ancestry, I'm a gypsy at heart. I love our transient lifestyle and I have no desire for it to end. It's been a year and a half since I left Australia and the old me is long gone. I have a new identity; I'm not really even Australian anymore, I'm a woman of the world who goes where the wind takes me. No responsibilities, no demands, following a life of love and creativity and art. A fringe-dweller.

Here, in the tropical bliss of Costa Rica, our love deepens and we swear never to be apart. Gabriel cuts long chunks of our hair and plaits them together, making bracelets of woven black and blonde hair, which he fastens with silver clips at the ends and we wear, like wedding rings that bind us to each other. We are two halves of one soul, the dark and the light. We talk of marrying and settling down somewhere peaceful like this, where the days are long and the nights are warm and we have everything we need to be happy.

It has been a long time since I called home and I know Mum will be worrying. I find a small telephone exchange service in one of the back streets and call reverse charges.

'Mum, it's me," I say down a crackling line.

'Oh love, where are you?' She sounds so far away.

'I'm in Costa Rica. It's beautiful. We left Peru and we've travelled through Ecuador, Colombia, Panama and now we're in this little Caribbean town called Puerto Viejo.'

I blurt out a sanitised version of our trip to now and she listens quietly. Too quietly.

'Leigh—Grandma died.'

Her words are a steel-capped boot kicking me in the solar plexus.

'What?'

'One minute to go,' the operator says, a plump black woman who means business. There's a five-minute limit on phone calls and a long line behind me.

'No, wait! I just need five more minutes. Mum, this fucking bitch won't let me talk.'

'Okay you're done.' The operator ends my call. I'm in shock.

'I'm sorry, I shouldn't have called you that,' I say through tears. 'My grandma died.'

Efficiency makes way for sympathy and she allows me to call back.

'Hi love, I'm so sorry, it must be such a shock for you,' Mum says.

'How did she die?'

'An asthma attack. Grandpa found her on the lounge in the morning.'

The dominant sounds of Grandma's house were always the cricket or tennis on TV and Grandma puffing on her inhaler. I clung to her when I said goodbye before leaving Australia and I didn't know why. I wish I'd known it would be the last time I'd see her. I would have told her so much.

I run to Gabriel, throw myself into his arms. I tell him how before I left for South America, I'd written my grandparents a letter telling them their home had been such a stable, loving influence in my life growing up. Knowing Grandma read that letter before she died is my only consolation.

In my distraught state, I clutch my belly. It feels swollen. I can't remember the last time I bled. The idea of being pregnant once again horrifies me and fear mixes with grief in a torrent of tears.

'Chica, you are taking your grandma's death very badly,' Gabriel says.

'Yes, I am. But it's not just that, I'm worried I'm pregnant.'

'Again? You weren't last time. Are you sure?'

'Sí, sí, I'm sure,' I say. Anxiety has overtaken my mind, distorted my thinking, decimated my ability to think rationally.

'Chica, no vas a morir,' he says. *You're not going to die.*

But it does feel like my life is over. My grandmother is gone, I won't be able to make it home for the funeral and now I'm fucking pregnant. I'm nowhere near ready for the responsibility. I wasn't in Colombia. I'm not now. I won't be in Mexico. Not for another ten years, at least. I like my freedom too much. And I need time to see if Gabriel is committed to staying away from cocaine.

'We'll be okay,' he says, rubbing my back. 'Te quiero loca, te quiero mucho.' He tells me how much he loves me and assures me he'd look after the baby and me and I know he will.

But I'm not comforted. I say I need time alone. I stroll around Puerto Viejo's hot, sleepy streets, thinking. Maybe having a baby would force Gabriel to become more responsible. It could be just what we need.

I pass a bamboo hut with a sign that says 'masaje' out the front. It's a luxury I used to enjoy in Australia but haven't indulged in here, as I'm always guarding my money. The massage therapist is a small woman with black hair, wearing a black cotton dress. Her nails are painted black. It's unusual in this part of the world, where women like to wear bright, happy colours. I have an idea. I rush back to our table and ask Gabriel if I can swap a piece of jewellery for a massage. It's a chunky silver necklace with a large oval obsidian stone in the centre, a stone that shines like black glass. She accepts the necklace in exchange for a massage and asks me to remove all my clothing. I lie on a mattress on the floor and the crisp white sheet is cool against my naked skin.

It's peaceful inside her hut and I melt under her strong hands as she kneads my weary muscles and I fall into a state of deep relaxation. After travelling rough, it's a decadent treat. I feel my emotional strength returning. I've been twisted into a tight coil and as I slowly unwind, I feel blood gush onto the white sheet.

'Oh my god, I'm so sorry.' I'm mortified.

'It's okay, I can clean.' She does her best to reassure me she doesn't mind the blood, that it's not the first time it has happened. Relief washes over me. I'm not pregnant.

Gabriel is relieved, too, but says we would have made great parents and he knows we will someday. Boosted by the knowledge my freedom is still intact, my wanderlust returns and I say let's keep going, let's leave this little village and find another one. There are more to be found and this life of travel is not over for us. I'm always looking ahead, always thinking of the future, never really content to stay where I am. Gabriel is the opposite. He lives in the present and rarely plans ahead, to the point where he's always forgetting to organise important documents and details. It wastes time and wasting time infuriates me. I always need to feel in control, moving forward. But I can never be really angry with him; he's too divine. He makes me laugh, he's always in a good mood, he's creative and kind. I'm doing the right thing, creating a life with him. We can face any challenge together.

The artisans tell us about the island of Roatán in Honduras, about Antigua in Guatemala, and about a little town in the Mexican Caribbean called Playa del Carmen. So we pack our bags and say farewell as we hit the road again on a rickety bus blasting out deafening music, with holy cards of the Virgin Mary dangling off the rear-view mirror. We're headed for the capital, San José.

The day we set off is a public holiday and without warning, the bus driver drops us off on a road in the middle of the jungle, saying his shift has come to an end. He tells us to wait, that another bus will come along and take us to San José. The other passengers get off and disperse quickly, leaving us sitting alone by the roadside.

The occasional car or truck passes, but no one stops to offer a lift. No buses pass and we sit in the scorching sun, discussing whether or not we should risk hitching. There's movement in the trees behind us, thick jungle we can't see through, and six men emerge.

'Hola!' I say, relieved we're not the only souls in this deserted place.

'Hola, Americana?' one of the men asks.

'No, Australiana.'

'Ah, Australiana! Crocodilo Dundee!'

'Sí, sí.' The Crocodile Dundee thing is getting old.

While the men laugh among themselves and joke about the 'that's not a knife, this is a knife' scene from the movie, Gabriel whispers, and I don't like his ominous tone: 'Go to the other side of the road and get in the first car that comes past. I'll meet you at the bus terminal in San Jose.'

'But…?'

'Just go,' he says. He puts my backpack on top of his and sits on top of both of them on the hot, dusty ground. I have the same odd feeling I had in Bogotá. A sickening sense of unease.

I stick my thumb out, wiping sweat from my forehead while I wait. Three separate cars slow to pick me up, but then their drivers spot the men and continue on. I return to the group—they seem like nice enough guys.

'Want to see a trick?' one of the men asks, smiling to reveal a mouthful of gold-plated teeth. There's a strong smell emanating from the jungle; the stench of death. Must be a dead animal decomposing.

'Okay, sure,' I answer, looking at Gabriel. He's staring at the ground, head bowed. It's not like him. He's usually so chatty, he strikes up conversations with anyone he meets.

The man with the gold teeth takes out three plastic cups and a little white ball. He places the ball under one cup.

'Guess which cup it's under?' he smiles. Does he think a mouthful of metal instead of teeth is attractive? Or is it supposed to intimidate?

He shuffles the cups around and I try to track the movement of the cup hiding the ball. It's too fast and I lose. We continue the game and I play along, laughing nervously and trying to ease the tension in what is an increasingly unsettling situation. Then the men begin moving around me in a tighter circle and a hot stab of fear cuts through my core. I see terror in Gabriel's eyes. What the hell is going on? I look around for a place to run, but there's only jungle on both sides of the road and that stench is getting stronger.

'Do you like Costa Rica?' A voice emerges from the trees and all heads turn towards its owner, a small man with a gentle face, dressed conservatively, holding a Bible. He has a sense of calm about him, different from the agitated energy of the other men.

'Sí, mucho,' I answer.

'Do you want to know the best place of all?' he asks.

'Er… okay.' Things are becoming increasingly bizarre.

'The best place of all is the kingdom of heaven,' he says, and begins reading his Bible. He reads passage after passage without stopping and the group of six men retreat and sit beside Gabriel. While he reads, the men stay silent, bowing their heads in respect for the Lord's word.

A sound. The deep rumble of an engine. A bus is coming. Thank fuck! A dilapidated bus pulls over and opens its doors. The Bible reader shouts at me to get on the bus while he and Gabriel grab our bags and jump on, leaving the group behind, who hiss at us as we disappear up the dirt road.

'What was that all about?' I ask the Bible guy as we settle into our seats.

'Those men are crack addicts,' he says. 'Thieves. They wait at the bus stop for people like you and rob them to pay for their drugs. They are also killers, amiga. And rapists. You were in big danger, señorita.'

'Wait, what? How do you know?'

'Because I used to be one of them, until I found the Lord Jesus Christ.' He makes a sign of the cross.

'Did you know what was going on?' I stare at Gabriel.

'Sí, I knew we were in trouble. I didn't care about me; I was mostly worried about what they would do to you. I know guys like that. They are merciless.'

'But why did they stop when you showed up?' I ask the Bible reader.

'Because I found God and he saved me from a life of drugs and crime. They will not commit a crime when I am reading the Bible. They see themselves as good Catholic men. While I read the Bible, they will not do anything bad. Since I found God, I come here to this bus stop as often as I can, to help people like you.'

He rides the bus with us to the main terminal in San José to make sure we're safe. I ask him to wait while I buy him a cold Coke to thank him and when I return, he's gone. As quickly as he had appeared.

171

My belief in angels is confirmed that day. Not otherworldly beings who swoop down and rescue us, but people. Real people. Like the man with the Bible, the tourists who saved me in Cartagena, the little cholita feeding me pears in the Andes, Emily looking after me on the boat when I was sick and Grandma, a gentle lady who loved me unconditionally, never said a bad word about anyone in her life and finally ran out of breath.

CHAPTER TWENTY

I HAVE GRADUATED to making chains. Gabriel is teaching me a technique called *punto Peruano*. We sit for hours in dingy, peeling rooms throughout Central America as he patiently shows me how to twist the round nose pliers in circles to make tiny loops, which I then snip off with the cutting pliers. I open and close the loops, interlocking them in a pattern that creates a slim silver snake to hang around a brown neck or a white wrist. I've pulled so much hemp twine through my fingers over the past weeks, they're calloused and bleeding and making chains is a welcome break. But I still can't encase stones in wire to make necklaces and bracelets, the way Gabriel does so effortlessly. There are small grooves carved around the edges of the stones and every time I try to fit the wire into them and secure it, I lose patience and wreck whatever I'm working on, wasting metal and angrily throwing the stone back in the box with its brothers and sisters.

'Watch me,' he says. 'The wire tries to slide free of my hands and the stone tries to pop out of position at every available second. There is a relationship between an artisan and his material. If I don't establish control with a firm grip from the beginning, the material will soon exert power over the artisan. It's like taming a snake.'

'Well sorry, but I don't think I have it in me to tame a snake.'

We hitch a ride through Nicaragua in the back of a truck, lying on bags of cement, and arrive in Honduras, where we spend *Semana Santa*, Holy Week, on the island of Roatán, where we band together with more artisans, musos and backpackers and spend a few weeks selling, snorkelling and partying. Sitting in the sun behind our table, the sea before me, I leave the selling and production to Gabriel and bury myself in a book one of the backpackers has lent me: *Even Cowgirls Get the Blues* by Tom Robbins.

The book has a profound impact on me. It makes me realise how important it is to know how to survive. To live self-sufficiently. I tell Gabriel how the book has inspired me to learn how to grow food, make clothes, make my own plates to eat off, my own cups to drink out of. How to make shoes and music, build a house.

'There's a place in Córdoba in Argentina, where we could live like that,' Gabriel says, holding a rutilated quartz crystal up to the sun to examine the golden threads inside it.

'There's places like that in Australia, too.'

He doesn't answer. He never asks me much about Australia and doesn't seem to have any interest in living there with me one day. I haven't given him any reason to think it's a possibility for us, but still, I wonder why he's not more interested in my life there. Who I was before I met him.

'Maybe we could visit that place in Córdoba one day,' I say. 'I want to learn. I don't know anything.'

'Yes you do, loca. You're very smart, you know lots of things.'

'No I don't. I don't know anything that matters.'

Of all the Central American countries we travel through, Guatemala feels the most familiar, with its colourful textiles and colonial architecture reminiscent of the Andean villages of Ecuador, Bolivia and Peru. I love how the Mayan descendants of the village of Todos Santos wear beautiful traditional dress made of brightly coloured woven fabrics. The men's pants are the standout: bright red and white candy-striped trousers that all men and boys wear, so stylish the tourists buy them to wear back home.

We spend a few days touring the countryside and visit Panahachel, a charming town in the Guatemalan Highlands on the banks of Lake Atitlan, a stunning body of water surrounded by three volcanoes. UFO sightings are common here and we look out for them as we swim in the cold water of the lake of a morning and meet artisans of an afternoon, where we trade materials and share information on good places to sell.

We meet a Brazilian artisan with a mass of brown springs for hair sticking out of his head in all directions. He pulls a small cloth bag out of his satchel and tips a handful of Brazilian tourmaline and agate onto the cloth to see if we'd like to swap anything. At that instant, Gabriel remembers meeting him in Lima ten years before, selling the same stones. He had the same springy hair, but was less wrinkled.

Gabriel tells me how artisans need various fallback plans for when they're not selling well. Those with musical talents hit the peñas and bars to play guitar, drums or panpipes. The bars don't usually pay them, but they're allowed to pass a hat around for a few coins. Those with artistic abilities might draw or paint. Some pierce ears or cut hair. Some buy stones to sell, usually in places far from their country of origin. By buying tourmaline in Brazil and selling it in Mexico, buying amber in Mexico and selling it in Argentina, buying lapis lazuli in Chile and selling it in Costa Rica, jade in Guatemala and selling it in Peru, turquoise in Peru and selling it in Honduras, an artisan can make a decent profit without having clocked up any labour time.

I'm confused. Gabriel has said it's a disgrace to sell *reventa*—things you buy cheap at a city market, which you then sell as your own work in smaller towns.

'There's an understanding between artisans,' he tells me. 'Yes, reventa is a disgrace for an artisan. You are not an artisan if you sell reventa. But most people can't go travelling to the mountains to mine their own stones, have the machinery to cut and polish them, make their own silver wire, paint their own ceramic beads. There is an artisan for each job.'

'Okay, so those ceramic beads we bought in Lima, aren't they reventa?'

'Sí, but we are making them into bracelets and necklaces. I do not have the time or ability to make those beads. You know who makes them?'

'Who?'

'In Peru, there are whole families who make them, including the children when they're not at school. They sit at home and hand-paint thousands of ceramic beads in intricate detail with the hair from a horse's tail. There is a difference between someone who goes to markets and buys everything cheap, then pretends to have made it, and a real artisan. A real artisan is proud of his art. He carries the stones of the earth with him, close to his heart.'

We meet a Chilean artisan who looks like a short, chubby version of Keanu Reeves and never takes off his raincoat, and a Mexican artisan of Mixtec descent with small black eyes and impossibly white, straight teeth. Chubby Keanu Reeves makes pipes in the shapes of very realistic heads, from John Lennon to a stoned-looking witch. He's a bargain king and his every conversation is centred around the cheapest food he has eaten, the cheapest hotels he's stayed in and everything he has ever scored free. The one thing he doesn't skimp on, he says, is buying good quality brown bread freshly baked by a Swiss girl who rides a bicycle around town, selling her bread from a basket on the handlebars. On bread, he is an expert. Bread and ping pong.

They invite us to the house they're staying in, an old timber place near the main street. Over a beer, the Mixtec man tells us a story about the hawk of the Aztecs and the condor of the Incas meeting up in Panama and flying in a circle together to mark the meeting point of each other's territory. For artisans, it seems, there is no territory. Wherever we've gone, we've been welcomed, allowed to put our manta on the ground and sell, sent off with well wishes. There's always trading going on and even gifting of materials when someone is short on some stones or clasps or wire. It's a brotherhood and a sisterhood I am proud to be part of.

We spend the night in the house and I have a dream that I am being burnt alive. I am part of a group of people who decide to commit mass suicide and burn ourselves in a fire. We ascend to a platform on a kind of conveyer belt in groups and upon reaching the top, we jump into the fire, where we sit, waiting to burn to death. One by one, people begin to lose heart and jump out of the fire because even though we are not in pain, it's taking too long to die. I am the last still in the fire and I decide to leave too, but by the time I get out, I am severely burnt. My hands are curled and crackling and I decide I'd better get myself to a hospital. All the people in the fire are people from my past.

In the nearby market village of Chichicastenango—which has the best name of any town in the world—I allow myself a rare splurge. I bargain without beating the vendors down too much; I know how much back-breaking work goes into the intricate woven textiles made on backstrap looms by the women of these villages. I buy a patchwork quilt, long striped skirts, an embroidered shirt, purple overalls, a hat, a red and purple striped vest, table mats and other gifts to send home, all in beautiful handwoven fabrics. I spend US$100 all up and Gabriel is not pleased, but we're close to Mexico now and we'll be selling well soon.

In Antigua, Guatemala's old colonial capital, we buy chunky granules of silver weighed on an old-fashioned scale, and have it melted down and made into rolls of wire. It's a step up from the cheap alloys we've been using. We also buy Guatemalan jade, the sacred stone of the Maya, famed for its powerful healing qualities. It's different to the nephrite of Chinese jade and New Zealand greenstone. This is jadeite, a slightly harder stone than nephrite, and traditionally represented affluence.

In a jade factory in Antigua, we learn how large rocks are removed from the mountains and cut and polished into gems. In its natural state, it appears to be an ordinary rock from the outside, but when it's sliced open, the inside is revealed as a smooth, shiny surface ranging from black, to iridescent green, to moss green, to white. We buy thirty pieces of jade carved into the faces of Mayan gods for ten quetzales each and invest in a stock of chunky jade and silver rings that we know we'll be able to make a profit on in Mexico. We meet a Guatemalan artisan in the main square and trade some of our Peruvian ceramic beads for lime green serpentine stones. We buy fifty embroidered bags for our jade rings, at one quetzal each, from an indigenous lady sitting on the ground selling handmade embroidered textiles.

Artisans relate to each place they travel to in terms of the value of its stones, and Guatemala is all about jade. I see its appeal, but it's not one of my favourite gemstones. It doesn't hold the same magic as the vibrant blue-greens of turquoise and chrysocolla, the stones that always lighten my mood. Around my neck, I wear a large chrysocolla disc encased in a silver rectangular design Gabriel has copied from the Mayan ruins of Copan, in Honduras. Dangling beneath it are deep red Peruvian cha-quiras, which give the piece an earthy, tribal look. I wear it with pride, evidence of Gabriel's talent, which I know will truly blossom when we arrive in Mexico and settle down to our new life.

Our family of stones is growing, but it won't be complete until we buy Mexican amber, the honeyed gemstone travellers love for its varying shades, richer and more beautiful than the bright yellow of Baltic amber. We're prepared to go to the source to get the cheapest prices possible and thereby increase our profit margin. So after crossing the border from Guatemala to Mexico, we go straight to San Cristobal de las Casas in the southern state of Chiapas and from there, take a three-hour bus trip to the mountain town of Simojovel, the home of Mexico's largest amber mine.

We bump along an unsealed and slippery road into the mountains, passing churches strung with streamers, dogs with protruding ribs, women wearing colourfully embroidered blouses called *huipils*, children congregating on roadsides and utes crammed with workers hanging off the back tray.

In Simojovel, everyone seems to sell amber, from the man pushing an ice-cream trolley with a stash of amber underneath, to little old ladies at the market, to teenagers hanging out on the street corner. Amber isn't a stone but a fossilised resin, twenty-five million years old. If you're lucky, you'll find a piece with inclusions like prehistoric leaves and insects. The colours of Mexican amber range from clear lemon to deep cognac to the burnt orange of a summer afternoon sunset.

We spend US$80 and buy eighty pieces of polished amber in sizes varying from a five-cent piece to cabochons the size of a baby's fist, as well as small beads for earrings and large chunks. We're excited about the possibilities amber presents for our business and on the bus back to San Cristobal, we look at each stone and ask it what it wants to become.

From San Cristobal we travel to the Mayan ruins at Palenque, dating back to 226BC, and spend a day playing tourist. I always wanted to be more than just a tourist but now I'm so far removed from that identity, travelling and working as I am with my Peruvian love, I enjoy the day of sightseeing. Like the jade burial masks donned by Mayan kings, I wear the mask of an artisan as if it's my new face, my new identity, my new skin.

We climb the dizzying stairs of the main pyramid, the Temple of the Inscriptions, and descend to its dark and claustrophobic centre to view the beautifully carved sarcophagus of Pakal, the great ruler of Palenque for most of its eighty years. We explore the surrounding structures and cuddle in the grass, watching toucans, with their comically long beaks, fly through the surrounding jungle, thick with mahogany and sapodilla trees.

It's tiring walking up and down the narrow stairs of Palenque's temples, palaces and pyramids and we doze off in the grass, arms around each other as if we're in our own private room, not at a world-famous archaeological site. I wake up before Gabriel and look at him. I am more deeply in love with him every day. We make love often and with a hungry passion that never wanes, and I want to grow old with him. Sometimes, I can't even remember a time before him.

We have one final bus trip to make, ten hours up the east coast of the Yucatán Peninsula to Playa del Carmen, on Mexico's Caribbean coast. It is known as the Riviera Maya and I'm itching to arrive there. I've lost count of the number of long bus trips I've taken in Central and South America and I'm ready to stop, to settle down in a place we can make our home. We've heard about Playa del Carmen, or Carmen's Beach, from artisans and musicians all over Central America. They say it's a little fishing village that is quickly becoming the coolest holiday destination in Mexico, but it hasn't yet been overrun with tourists and ruined by developers. It's a more authentic Mexico, away from the wet T-shirt competitions of Cancun.

We arrive in the scorching heat of early afternoon and the Quinta Avenida, or Fifth Avenue, is quiet. Everyone is at the beach and shopkeepers are holed up in their air-conditioned comfort. We stroll down the paved main street, catching glimpses of the metallic-aqua sea each time we pass a side street, a colour so magnetic I want to run and dive into it, backpack, boots and all.

I love this town's low-rise, laid-back vibe, its brightly painted shopfronts in sunny yellows and oranges and leafy streets, where pink, orange and red bougainvillea crawl over walls and fences and palm fronds hang above thatched roofs and dangle into the streets. Jewellery stores are brimming with shiny Mexican silver, handicrafts stores sell brightly woven striped blankets, string hammocks and cheerful Mexican pottery—chunky plates, bowls, cups and planters in multi-coloured floral designs. Tropical bars tempt passersby to take the edge off the sizzling day with a chilled margarita or a Corona, the scent of freshly made burritos and fajitas wafts into the street and every restaurant serves corn chips and guacamole in ceramic dishes decorated in happy blue and white designs. It's a festive atmosphere, just touristy enough without being garish and tacky and losing its rustic ambience. It's perfect for us, a place we can live for many years, make a good living and raise a family.

We rent a tiny concrete room above a home just out of town. It's ugly but cheap, somewhere to base ourselves while we become established. Strong hooks are cemented into the wall for us to hang up our hammocks and there is a small table with two chairs beside a glass sliding door opening to a small balcony, where we can work. In one corner of the room, we set up a single gas burner where we can cook. We place one saucepan and a few condiments next to it on the white tiled floor. A small bar fridge for milk and beer and a clean bathroom are luxuries we haven't had since leaving Lima.

As the heat of the day dissipates and the air becomes a warm caress of the skin, we stroll into the Quinta Avenida. As we have done in dozens of towns we've visited throughout South and Central America, we lay our manta down and carefully arrange necklaces, bracelets, earrings and hemp jewellery in an attractive display and sit on the ground behind it, awaiting our first customers.

But Playa del Carmen is unlike any other town in Latin America. Within ten minutes, a police officer is moving us on, saying it's illegal to sell in the street here. It's a blow we are not expecting and the usual handshake with a surreptitious exchange of a five-dollar bill doesn't work here. It has worked in every other town we've sold in; but not here. Playa del Carmen is special. It's a town on the verge of great success and everyone is fighting for a piece of it. We are two blow-ins who will have to stand in line.

We pack up and head to the beach, trying to sell directly to tourists, but are once again set upon by local authorities. No selling allowed at the beach, either. We try peddling our wares to local shops, but they're not interested. Most of the jewellery stores here are shining beacons of machine-made, high-polished silver, much of it made with what we suspect are fake stones. Our work is handmade, each piece a one-off. Our work is art, unappreciated and out of place in the stores of Playa del Carmen.

'Mierda,' Gabriel says, slumping against a shady wall in the Quinta Avenida. *Shit*. We've tried all our options and if we can't sell here, we can't stay here.

'We can't give up so soon,' I offer. 'I believe we're meant to be in this town. This is where everything is going to work out for us.'

'I don't know, loca. I don't know. We've paid a month of rent, but if we don't find a way to sell, we will have to leave.' He leans his head on the wall, closing his eyes, defeated.

He's always the more optimistic one and it's not like him to become so despondent, so quickly. He's usually more streetsmart than this. But it gets hard to be the strong one, the one always offering solace, the one always looking on the bright side. The one always propping up his family, his sick brother, his weary mother, his hardworking father. The soul of his house, he said back in Lima. It's too much of a burden to bear. I need to step up, take some of the load.

A man further down the avenue catches my eye. He's sitting between two large tables balanced on milk crates in front of a ramshackle shop different to the others. The shop is called Jimmy's No Problem and the words are painted in uneven purple and red letters above the door. The store isn't lit up with fluorescent lights, like the other stores. Coconut-shell lampshades hang in the window and I can see from where I sit the shop sells amber, ceramics, textiles and leatherwork. Stuff with soul.

'Hey see that guy over there?' I nudge Gabriel and he opens his eyes.
'What about him?'

'He looks cool. Let's go and say hi, ask him if he knows where we can sell.'

'Bueno, vamos.' He doesn't take much convincing; we have run out of options.

'Hola, I'm Gabriel and this is my girlfriend, Leigh,' Gabriel says, extending his hand.

The Mexican man narrows his eyes and takes a long drag on his cigarette, sizing us up. Then he extends his hand.

'Hola, I'm Jimmy.' He shakes Gabriel's hand and in that shake is an immediate rapport. Something in the eyes of one recognises something in the eyes of the other, a fellow artisan, a brother, a compadre.

'Loco, we need somewhere to sell, they won't let us sell in the street.'

'Pinche policia,' Jimmy says, nodding his curly head. *Fucking police.*

'You can put your things on my table. You sell something, I take twenty percent, okay?'

'Sí, sí, buenísimo,' Gabriel says.

'If the police come around, leave the talking to me. It's my work, not yours. I own the shop, they can't do shit to me.'

'Gracias, loco. What are you drinking?'

'Una tequilita, güey.' *Güey* is a colloquial Mexican word that's used in a similar way to 'dude' and it establishes an immediate sense of camaraderie whenever it's spoken. I love it, and I love that Jimmy addresses Gabriel in this way without even knowing him. It's a good sign.

We buy a bottle of good tequila and take it back to the shop. Jimmy hands us each a handmade ceramic cup from his store and we settle in with our drinks.

'Arriba, abajo, al centro, pa' dentro,' Jimmy shouts, raising and lowering his cup as he recites the popular Spanish toast—*above, below, to the centre and inside.*

We sit on milk crates, drinking and getting to know Jimmy No Problem. He's famous for saying 'no problem' in English, with a thick Spanish accent that adds a comical charm to the phrase. He wears a brown leather vest, faded jeans rolled up at the ankles and no shoes. His fingers are laden with enormous turquoise and silver rings which he flashes as he chews his filthy fingernails. He has sparkling green eyes, a bushy moustache and a raucous, pirate laugh. He wears a permanent grin that showcases a glinting gold tooth and his mop of dark curls give him a boyish look. The layers of jade necklaces around his neck would weigh down even a large man, but Jimmy says they are his source of strength. He's the proud father of six children who live with his wife on the nearby island of Cozumel, while he works in the shop and flirts with women of all ages and all shapes and sizes.

We watch Jimmy sell to the passing tourists, laughing his pirate laugh and calling out 'no problem!' at random intervals, like a public announcement. He darts in and out of his shop to get change, the first Mexican I've met who walks quickly and with purpose. He sells three of our pieces and takes his twenty percent. It's a fair deal and as evening descends we see the avenue fill from end to end with tourists from around the world, tanned and relaxed after long days at the beach, hungry for a Mexican feast and ready to party at Capitan Tutix, a thatched roof beach club with a bar shaped like a ship's hull.

The atmosphere is unlike anything we've experienced in any other tourist town in Latin America, bursting with new energy and wealth. These tourists are cashed up and looking for an authentic Mexican experience that's different to the gaudy commercialism of places like Cancun and Acupulco. They want the soulful, the handmade, the artistic, and who better to give it to them than a Peruvian artisan, who can easily pass for Mexican, and a girl from Western Sydney who now speaks fluent Spanish and can act as translator between Jimmy, Gabriel and all the other artisans and musicians who come to hang out at Jimmy's No Problem?

We fall into a routine of lazy beach days, afternoons making jewellery and evenings at Jimmy's shop drinking tequila or *cuba libres* and hanging out with a bohemian crew who congregate every night, drawn to Jimmy's charisma and hospitality.

I make a new friend, Ines, a tiny Argentinian girl with a big toothy smile and long, silky brown hair who makes miniature elves out of polymer clay. Each one has a distinctive personality and she sells her elves while we drink and chat, leaving Gabriel and Jimmy to talk business and booze. I make beaded hemp bracelets while Ines makes her elves and we share our dreams for the future: to make lots of money, to buy land here and build a house. She has left Argentina to see the world and escape a broken heart, but that's all she will say about it. She tells me how she runs on the beach and swims laps in the ocean every day to keep fit and I am envious; I'd love to be fitter, but I do very little exercise. I just don't have the discipline. She's glowing and full of energy and I'd like to look like that, but I can't be bothered pushing myself.

A new girl arrives and we form an instant trio. Sandra is an artist from Mexico City who travels the country alone, stopping wherever it takes her fancy. Tall with a slim, strong body and intelligent eyes, she's the only friend I've made who speaks English, but as everyone else speaks only Spanish, we never use English unless we're talking to tourists. Sandra looks like she's drifting along on a light breeze when she walks, never rushed, never stressed. She exudes the kind of deep contentment and self-acceptance that always fascinates me when I encounter it in someone, especially in someone my age. How do people become happy with themselves like that? It appears easy and effortless, and I watch her the way a child watches an older child; with awe and reverence.

During the day, when it's too hot to sell and all the tourists are at the beach, we spend idyllic hours swimming and snorkelling in the warm sea. Jimmy has an old ute and some days, we all pile into the back and he takes us on adventures into the jungle to swim at *cenotes*, sinkholes of fresh water dotted all over the Yucatán Peninsula. It's the first time since I met Maria in Lima that I've had girlfriends and Playa del Carmen, this lively little party town, is feeling like home.

After a couple of months, Jimmy No Problem invites us to live at Cabañas Doña Rosa, a compound of thatched-roof bungalows overgrown with tropical foliage behind the Quinta Avenida, right near the beach. The compound is surrounded by high stone walls covered in orange and pink bougainvillea and is hidden from the street. Jimmy has taken a lease on the whole place and is renovating the bungalows to rent out, but only to people he knows. He has appointed Sandra as administrator and she's happy for us to move in, too. Jimmy and Sandra are often laughing and talking together and I wonder if they like each other, but Jimmy is married with kids he is devoted to, so I'm sure nothing is going on.

I'm yearning to live in a real home rather than just a basic room. Each morning before it gets too hot, we help Jimmy and Sandra, painting the insides of the cabañas the pastel blue-green that adorns houses all over Mexico. One morning I stroll into town to buy *Por Esto!*, a Yucatán newspaper, and read about the effects of El Niño across Latin America. Sadly, it has hit Peru the hardest. I arrive at the cabañas and find Jimmy, Sandra and Gabriel sitting on the floor sharing a joint, having a break from painting.

'According to this story, prophets are wandering the streets, pronouncing the natural disasters of Peru are the wrath of God,' I announce. 'In Trujillo, floods have washed coffins from the cemeteries and cadavers are floating down the streets. In Piura, the streets are rivers. The Pan-American Highway has been destroyed.'

'Shit! I have to call home,' Gabriel says, startled. 'I have to make sure my family is okay.'

He jumps up and knocks over a tin of paint, which spills all over the chequerboard lino in the kitchen. Sandra springs into action and scoops the paint up with her bare hands, pouring most of it back into the tin. By the time she's finished, she's covered in paint, all over her legs, arms, hands and face. Well stoned by now, Sandra and Jimmy burst into fits of laughter. Jimmy takes her outside and spends an hour removing the paint with turps. She sits on a milk crate and he kneels in the dirt before her, cigarette dangling from his lips, gently wiping her slim legs and arms with paper towels, like a daddy patching up his daughter's grazed knees. They continue to smoke and chat, as if it's no big deal. And it's not. *No pasa nada.* I love this phrase, which translates to 'nothing happens' but really means, there's nothing to worry about, it's no big deal. Most Mexicans I meet have a relaxed vibe that puts me at ease, as if the world could explode and they'd still be eating tacos, drinking tequila and saying, no pasa nada.

Our cabaña is primitive and we love it. A cold shower in one corner, a double mattress sitting on a concrete base connected to the wall in another corner, a kitchen with a sink to wash dishes in, which I haven't had since Lima, stone benchtops where we can set up our cooking gear, and a small lounge area that we furnish with embroidered Mexican cushions. I stick photos to the wall above our bed—the one of Gabriel and me in Buenos Aires and my favourites from Iguazu Falls, the Amazon and the salt flats of Bolivia. I place the little wire mandala Gabriel gave me in Buenos Aires on a small bamboo side table. I still like to play with it, to turn it into the world, the cup, the flower. Fly-screens covered in shocking pink hibiscus flowers have replaced glass in the windows, so security is non-existent. But the stone wall surrounding the compound is overgrown with weeds, so people passing in the street outside don't know it's there and would not think to enter.

We build a communal kitchen area to one side of the compound under a giant thatched roof. Jimmy installs an old double-door fridge that quickly fills with beer, mayonnaise jars housing abandoned half-eaten chips and an assortment of taco remnants. He scatters a few old couches and hammocks around to create a cosy space and that's where we congregate daily. Sometimes there's no water, the power goes off and on and the roof leaks, but it's home.

There are five bungalows in all, occupied by artisans and musicians. The night we all move in, Jimmy strings naked light bulbs across the garden and we have a fiesta awash with tequila and blaring salsa and merengue music. I am in my element with these people; they are my new family. Jimmy is the patriarch and everyone loves him. I watch him holding court, mischievous eyes flashing under his heavy brows. But when he spits a big chunk of mucus onto the ground and puts a cigarette out in it, I almost vomit. He gets up, walks into *our* cabaña, and pisses in *our* toilet without flushing it. Gabriel's totally oblivious, lost in the party as he likes to be, but I see it as a sign of Jimmy marking his territory. I like Jimmy, but I don't trust him. That will take longer.

I'm the only non-Latino living here and cultural differences between us grate on me sometimes, but I'm treated no differently to the Mexicans we live with and I have finally found my place, a place I can blend in. I have a new life here, a home just a few steps from a pristine beach and a steady way to make an income. Gabriel and I are still blissfully in love and nothing could be better.

Creatures of the jungle wander the compound freely. White-nosed coatis—which look like huge racoons—forage around the cabañas looking for food, scorpions inhabit the thatched roofs, and mosquitoes, ants and mice are permanent residents. One morning, I'm stretched out on the bed with a cup of tea, pondering how long I've been out of Australia—over two years now—and a curious little creature wanders into our cabaña. Little legs poke out from underneath a small white shell as it inches along our kitchen floor. I watch its journey with interest. How did it wander so far from the beach? An intrepid, fragile thing, unaware it could be stepped on and squashed in a second. Where is the sand? Where is the sea? I move closer to get a better look and startle it. It turns around and slowly leaves the way it came in, through a big gap underneath the door that lets all the creepy-crawlies in. What is it looking for, this creature so far from home?

CHAPTER TWENTY-ONE

HALCYON DAYS. LAZY mornings sleeping in, eating banana, papaya and mango straight off the tree for breakfast, guacamole and corn chips for lunch, quesadillas or fajitas with Corona for dinner. Days that merge into weeks at shady cenotes making jewellery, and cooling off in the clear water, lying on the powder-white sand of Playa del Carmen's pristine beaches, getting brown, swinging in hammocks with a beer in hand, making mobiles out of driftwood and shells to decorate the cabañas and making enough money each night at Jimmy's shop to continue our laid-back lifestyle.

I buy a second-hand royal blue bike, a Benotto, which I call my Italian boyfriend. I ride it around town, down to the beach or to the market to buy groceries. In Playa del Carmen, whole families travel around by bicycle. They attach a foot stand to the back wheel that can take the weight of a man, so it's common to see someone riding and someone standing on the back, or a whole family crammed onto a motorbike. We attach a foot stand to Benotto and Gabriel rides around town, while I stand on the back, holding onto his shoulders. We sing Argentinian folk songs, Peruvian rock songs and the Rolling Stones out loud while he pedals and I smile at what my life has become.

A few streets back from the Quinta Avenida, a cinema shows new-release films for only a few pesos. When we've been selling well, we treat ourselves to a movie and buy popcorn with chilli sauce on top. To reach the cinema, we pass a primary school. Out the front are food trolleys selling ice-cream topped with chilli and fresh oranges cut up and topped with chilli—a zesty after-school snack. Everyone here eats the stuff; every adult, every child. Jimmy often discusses particularly painful bowel motions he's had after eating too much chilli and laughs his raucous laugh.

One warm afternoon, we're lying around in our hammocks at the cabañas, trying to keep cool. Gabriel is working, Ines is making her elves and I'm reading a book I borrowed from an American woman who owns a café in town—*Jitterbug Perfume*, another Tom Robbins. Sandra glides in through the outside gate and asks us how we are.

'Hola chicos, que tal?'

'Bien chica, y tu?'

'Super-bien. Jimmy has invited us all to go out to a live show tonight. He has free tickets.'

'Órale,' Gabriel answers. *Hell yeah*. It's something out of the ordinary for us. We never go anywhere that charges money to get in, except the occasional movie. The beach and our friends are all the entertainment we need.

'Where is it?' I ask, making room for Sandra to hop onto my hammock.

'There's a warehouse at the end of the Quinta Avenida and some guys from Mexico City have turned it into a theatre. They're having live music and dance performances. Let's get dressed up and go, okay?'

Our version of dressed up is anything that's not our usual clothing—bikini tops or singlets with long skirts, no shoes and lots of handmade jewellery around our necks, in our earlobes, on our fingers, wrists, ankles and toes. I have a halter-neck dress splashed with hot pink hibiscus flowers I bought in town. It's perfect for a night out, but I've had nowhere to wear it. It's fun dressing up for the first time in a long time, brushing my hair and putting on eyeliner, mascara and lipstick. I look at myself in a cane-framed mirror in our cabaña. I've lost a lot of weight since I first left Australia. My collarbones are protruding and I have a deep tan. I think this lifestyle agrees with me.

Gabriel looks handsome in Guatemalan pants, a white shirt and an embroidered vest and I'm proud to be seen on his arm. Ines wears a long blue skirt, a tight blue T-shirt and her long hair in braids. She's tiny and pretty and I can't believe she doesn't have a boyfriend. She says a Peruvian surfer dude travelling through Argentina broke her heart and she escaped here, to this place in the sun. Sandra is wearing a red dress that shows off her fine figure, her long dark hair flowing to her shoulders. She looks gorgeous and I can see by the way Jimmy's eyes light up when we meet him at the theatre that he thinks so too. He's still not wearing any shoes, but he has swapped his leather vest for an embroidered white Mayan shirt, hanging loose over a good pair of jeans. He has combed his wild curls back and he smell faintly of aftershave. He's made an effort. In fact, we've all scrubbed up okay.

Inside the theatre, we sit on long benches and drink beer while we watch the show. A rock band from Mexico City, contemporary dancers, a passionate spoken-word performance and a guy playing flamenco guitar while his girlfriend dances beside him. I look at my group of friends and smile. We're all enjoying this refreshing dose of city culture, way up here in the Yucatán Peninsula.

For the final act, a girl saunters onto the stage completely naked, deep brown skin, slender body, short dark curly hair. A tribal beat echoes through the warehouse and then we see something moving across her body. It's a yellow Burmese python and as she gyrates around the stage to the beat, the enormous snake slithers around her shoulders, across her breasts, curls around her waist and slides between her legs. It's a mesmerising, seductive performance, something so thoroughly unexpected and I am riveted. She is a Mexican goddess, taming a wild creature with her dance, her nudity a natural and integral part of the performance. I forget I'm with the group, entranced, admiring her exotic beauty and how free and confident she is in her body, in her skin.

Weeks and months pass and Gabriel's work is growing more beautiful and complex, fetching admiration and higher prices from tourists. He makes chokers or long necklaces of silver and jade or silver and amber, and I do the selling, reassuring the tourists in English that our stones and silver are genuine. They're nervous, buying off the street, but I am sincere in my insistence that they are not getting ripped off. Not by us. To prove the amber is real, we have a piece set aside to burn in the flame of a lighter. Plastic replicas of amber burn and stink, whereas genuine amber emits a pleasant resin scent and does not burn. I've become a pretty good sales-woman and as Gabriel still doesn't know any English, it makes sense for me to do the talking.

In my mind, it also makes up for my lack of production. I still haven't mastered the art of making jewellery and I've almost given up. I just don't have the gift. I'm a shit artisan, but I'm a good salesperson, which is almost as good as being an artisan. We've struck a good balance, although I don't ask Gabriel what he thinks. I'm sure he'd prefer I spent more time pro-ducing and less time hanging out at the beach with Ines and Sandra, or chilling in my hammock making shell mobiles, or writing in my journal, but he doesn't say anything.

We like to imagine the unseen powers of our little family of stones—the sun energy of amber, the earth energy of jade, the ocean energy of turquoise, the love energy of rose quartz, the feminine energy of rodo-chrosite, the mountain energy of malachite, the forest energy of jasper. Gabriel says the stones speak to him and I lie on the bed and watch him as he begins each new piece of jewellery, holding the stone up to the light, turning it one way then another, waiting for it to speak to him and tell him what it wants to become.

One afternoon he surprises me with a new gift—an amber necklace. He's made the chain in punto peruano-style thick silver, which he knows I love. In the centre is a circular piece of amber that holds an inclusion; a prehistoric leaf. It curves around the centre of the stone and creates one dark half of red amber and one light half of yellow amber, like a natural yin-yang. He sits behind me on the bed, gently pushes my hair over my shoulder and puts it on, then asks me to turn around and show him. The stone sits perfectly at the base of my throat, between my collarbones.

'This stone spoke to me,' he says. 'It told me it belonged to you. It is a perfect representation of us—yin and yang. Light and dark. Male and female. We are different, but we are one.'

We discuss marriage and babies again. We want to have a ceremony with just the two of us at the ruins of Tulum, an ancient Mayan temple that sits high on a hill overlooking the shimmering aqua sea. We'll have two chil-dren before we get too old. We'll do all this one day when we have enough money, when we've had enough partying. We drink rum, tequila, Corona or piña coladas almost every night, first at Jimmy's shop while we sell, then when the tourists hit the bars and clubs and the stores close around eleven, we stroll down to the soft white sand and keep partying in the moonlight.

Our group of friends and passing travellers play hand drums and strum guitars as we sit around on the sand under a clear sky. We're a little family of big drinkers who like to suck the marrow out of each day. We're young and in love, knowing someday, these carefree days and nights will come to an end. Or—maybe they don't have to. Maybe we can live like this forever, never needing to work a nine-to-five job, never needing to sell our souls for money. Staying out of tick-tock. Stuart would be proud.

After one of these boozy beach nights, we're walking back to the cabañas when Gabriel shrieks and doubles over in pain.

'What's wrong?' I ask, pulling his arm over my shoulder for support.

'My stomach. I've been getting pains but not this bad.'

'Why didn't you tell me?'

'I don't know loca, I didn't want to worry you. You always worry so much.'

'Do I?'

'Sí. Every little thing, you worry about.'

'But I love it here, I love our life here.'

'Sí, but you still worry about tiny little things, mi amor. Now you're worrying that you worry too much.'

'Sorry. I'll make you some chamomile tea when we get home.'

He sleeps fitfully, clutching his stomach throughout the night. The next day we decide to visit a doctor Jimmy has told us about: Don Jorge, el brujo de Dzuiche. *The witch doctor of Dzuiche.* Jimmy says he's a miracle worker who lives in the dusty little Yucatán town of Dzuiche, 250 kilometres inland from Playa del Carmen. It does not occur to us to visit a regular doctor at the clinic in Playa del Carmen, the more sensible option.

It will take four hours in 40-degree heat to get there and we share a taxi with a well-groomed man and two children travelling on their own. The kids squash together on the front seat and we take the back. The man tells us how El Doctor cured his daughter of epilepsy. He had taken her to Mexico's best specialists and no one could help. He thought his daughter would die, he says. He stops talking then and gazes out the window.

I settle back and look at the kids. The girl is about sixteen with long black hair tied in a ponytail. She wears tiny diamond earrings and is clean and well-dressed. Her younger brother looks about ten and is crammed in next to the gear stick, leaning his head on his sister's shoulder, eyes closed. Every now and then, the girl looks back at me and smiles. It's a fleeting connection we have, this girl and me. I wonder about her and she wonders about me. She closes her eyes and in the side mirror, I watch her sleeping, imagining how often she dreams of escaping her life, finding a new life away from expectation, away from painful memories that stick like the sweat in this stifling jungle landscape. Does she study hard? Does she make her parents proud? I wonder if her diamonds are real.

I'm taken back to Mother's Day 1978, before Mum had met my step-dad, who I would come to call Dad, because that's what he became, filling the place of the man who brought us into the world, passing the baton to a 'better man'—which he undoubtedly thought was the right thing to do—then starting a family with a new wife and four new kids and vanishing from our lives.

Mum wasn't perfect, as no mother is, but she never gave up on us. She was the one who nursed us when we were sick, celebrated our triumphs at school, taught us to respect our elders and remember our manners. Made sure we were clean. I remember this particular Mother's Day because my brother and I had come home from the cottage and were so happy to see Mum, we decided to buy her a pair of diamond earrings. We had been saving coins, finding them in telephone boxes around the streets of Parramatta. We walked into town on our own and marched proudly into a jewellery store near Happy Granny's pancake restaurant and the slot cars, and my brother dumped a handful of coins on the counter. We picked out the biggest, sparkliest diamond earrings in the cabinet and said we were buying them for our mum, because we hadn't seen her for a long time.

The lady behind the counter smiled and said we didn't have enough, that the earrings were a hundred and something, or a thousand and something. But she took pity on us and gave us a pair of fake diamond earrings that to us, looked just as beautiful as the real thing. Each earring had four little diamonds stuck together in a square. She didn't tell us they weren't real, she just put them in a fancy blue velvet box and wrapped it in pretty paper.

We ran all the way home, me way behind my brother as usual, but determined to keep up. Mum was cleaning the Venetian blinds in the tiny backyard of our red brick units. We ran straight up to her and gave her the present and when she opened it, she cried and cried, which was confusing. But she said she wasn't sad, that sometimes adults cry even when they're happy. We knew she liked them anyway, because she put them straight into her earlobes.

We didn't know until we were older and the porridge cottage was a distant memory that while we lived there, Mum fretted so much that sometimes she would drive across town on school mornings and park in a hidden place, just to watch her babies get on the bus.

I wonder if El Doctor will have feathers on his head. The taxi driver says he used to practice on the island of Cozumel, near Playa del Carmen, until the local doctors ran him out of town for taking too much of their business.

The taxi drops the kids and the man off in a little town along this endless, dirt road and the girl smiles and waves goodbye. I smile and wave back and I know she has someone who cares about her. I can see it in her clean clothes and her polished shoes, in her neat black hair and those little diamonds in her ears.

Finally, we arrive. The driver drops us off at a circular bamboo hut with a thatched roof, no door and a cement floor. A man of about thirty in a white shirt and white pants comes in and stares at us blankly, without speaking.

'Quiero ver al doctor,' Gabriel says.

'Es tu esposa?' he asks, looking at me. *Your wife?*

'Sí.' Gabriel lies, but I like this lie. I like someone thinking I'm his wife. The man in white looks me up and down and I'm too hot and tired to care.

'Well, then, you are lucky,' he tells Gabriel. 'The doctor will diagnose the problem and operate for 80 pesos. Your appointment is tomorrow morning at 5.30am, okay?'

Operate? That doesn't sound good. We're not sure if it's a real operation, a psychic operation or some bizarre, possibly lethal blend of the two. We wander down the dirt road to the surgery, a small pink cement building with an altar housing Mexico's most venerated religious icon, the Virgen de Guadalupe, out the front. There are several benches on the patio and we sit there in the balmy breeze until morning.

Nailed to the wall is a sign advising patients to rest for three hours after the 'operation' and not to drink alcohol or fizzy drinks, eat greasy foods, exercise or have sex for fifteen days, more if possible. Then we read something that shocks both of us: 'Chest and heart operations are performed on the fifteenth of every month.'

How could someone be performing heart surgery in a run-down house in the depths of the jungle? I'm feeling increasingly anxious but Gabriel has no qualms at all. Perhaps it's a Latino thing, trusting your body to a witch doctor. The sign also says patients should arrive clean and with food in the stomach. We doze on the wooden benches, regularly waking to watch the silent curve of a crescent moon, trying to work out what time it is. The smell of cow shit grows stronger as roosters begin to crow and the black silhouettes of palm trees against the moonlit sky lighten.

Patients begin to show up at 5am, chatting quietly amongst themselves. Most are middle-aged or elderly common people, farmers, housewives, truck drivers. For some reason, everyone is holding an egg. We buy hot chocolates from a kiosk across the road and the shopkeeper tells us Gabriel will need to give El Doctor an egg. Man, the guy must love his eggs for breakfast. On the wall of the kiosk is a sign: 'We organise excursions from Toluca to see the angel Jorge Manuel.' So, we're about to meet another angel.

We sit on a rock near a group of campesinos, waiting for the doctor to arrive, and I eavesdrop on their conversation.

'There's no love amongst the young ones these days.'

'They think they know how to love, but it's not true love.'

'Yes,' they agree. 'It's desire.'

They sit in silence, until one of them arrives at a conclusion.

'Television, that's the problem.'

I can't remember the last time I watched television and there's nothing about it I miss. I don't even miss the news, because I catch it all in the entertaining Mexican newspapers, which publish gruesome photos of people with severed body parts on the front page. A never-ending parade of drug-related murders.

Having discussed love, the campesinos move onto death and the approaching Day of the Dead celebrations. They chat about the food their wives are preparing to take to the cemetery, where they will eat and drink with the spirits of their deceased loved ones, who they believe return at this time of year. They discuss *tamales* and sugar skulls and I long to wear a *Dia de los Muertos* mask and attend one of these intriguing celebrations so unique to Mexico, but I know it's not my place. As they chat enthusiastically about their dead relatives, I soak it all up, filled with admiration for how Mexicans approach death: as a natural part of human existence and something to be openly discussed. The Day of the Dead is not a sad day, but a day of celebration. Here in Mexico, there is simply no shying away from death.

A white Nissan van speeds down the road followed by a man on a tricycle. Don Jorge sits in the passenger seat; an older man with piercing blue eyes. He is not wearing feathers on his head. He's wearing a black baseball cap with the word 'boss' printed on it. The tricycle rider unlocks the front door and Jorge walks through the crowd of people with three male helpers.

'Buen dia,' he says as he passes, tipping his cap.

'Buen dia,' the patients reply, their tone steeped in respect.

He looks about seventy and his manner is gruff and serious, that of a man who means business. The town seems to exist around him. His house is close to the clinic, a large, brightly painted building with a Christmas tree on the roof and wire fencing lining its perimeter. It would have taken him two minutes to walk, so the Nissan van seems superfluous, but it does allow for an entrance of sorts.

Don Jorge enters the clinic while the patients wait outside. One of the helpers emerges and reads out names. Gabriel is fifth on the list. The first five walk inside and form a line and I follow. Gabriel holds his hand up to my shoulder, saying I can't come in, but I insist. No way am I missing this. Don Jorge presides over the room at a central desk up the front, like a teacher with no students to teach, only patients to heal. To the side is a larger desk where the three helpers sit, furiously writing as Jorge diagnoses. The first woman sits down.

'What do you have?' Don Jorge asks in a loud voice so everyone can hear.

'I have a pain here in my back,' she answers.

She hands him her egg and he cracks it into a tall beaker of water, then uses a magnifying glass to study the way the egg breaks up in the water. So, this explains the egg situation. After a minute of studying the egg, he begins to recite a list of illnesses, while the other patients in the line lean in and listen intently. No secrets here. The patient is directed to the longer table where she pays eighty pesos for the consultation and is given a paper with her diagnosis and told to come back at 7.30 for her operation. Each consultation takes no longer than five minutes. Gabriel sits down and I pay attention.

'Inflammation of the lower stomach, inflamed ankles, sinusitis, inflamed left shoulder, migraine, gas in the stomach.'

He pauses and looks directly at Gabriel with a haunted look in his eyes.

'And there is very strong envy being directed towards you.'

He's instructed to go to the kiosk and buy a twenty-three-centimetre bandage and alcohol and return for his operation.

The doctor scrawls a list of Gabriel's illnesses on a piece of paper. I wonder how someone can diagnose envy and how he will cure it. We go back to the kiosk and ask the señora who sells eggs and hot chocolate what it means.

'Is the envy something I have, or is it envy directed towards me by others?' he asks.

'No, it's envy towards you,' she answers. 'If it's not happening right now, it will happen in the future. The doctor is psychic. Be wary of people amigo, don't trust them. Don't tell them your secrets.'

'When can the doctor cure me of this?' he asks.

'Fridays,' she answers, without batting an eyelid.

Gabriel's operation takes five minutes. He limps out and a tricycle wheels us to a pharmacy in town where he can buy his medicine. He's given a litre of dark red liquid to drink. It tastes of herbs and bark and we have no idea what it is. On the short tricycle ride to the pharmacy, Gabriel tells me he'd been taken into a room and blindfolded. Then he felt Don Jorge cutting around his left testicle. He says it was quick and there was little pain. As he was being cut, he felt a release of energy. Then it was over. Although he's limping, he feels relief.

When we arrive at the pharmacy, he's taken to see another doctor who asks what operation he's had and prescribes some pills to be taken every six hours. Gabriel asks about his other ailments and he's told he can have another operation if he desires. The second operation is as quick as the first. The doctor cuts a line down the middle of Gabriel's stomach, and this time, it does hurt.

I can't tell whether Don Jorge really is an angel who works magic, or a witch doctor, or a charlatan, but the people who line up to see him every day believe in him and perhaps that's all that matters, because he's the only doctor they have.

Incredibly, Gabriel's pain stops. We go back to our lazy beach days and partying nights sitting out the front of Jimmy's store and all is well again.

One Friday night in late November, I'm sitting next to Ines, watching her crochet a bikini top out of hemp twine, when Gabriel rushes over and whispers into my ear: 'Get away, go!' I don't question him. I drop my things and attempt to fade into the crowd. A mariachi group is busking in the middle of the street and a large crowd has formed, so I stop and pretend I'm just another tourist enjoying the show. If I run, I'm admitting guilt, though I don't know what crime I've committed.

'Miss, excuse me, where are you from?' An immigration official in a grey uniform taps me on the shoulder.

'Australia.'

'Ah Australia… Crocodilo Dundee!'

'Sí,' I respond.

'Kangaroos!'

'Sí,' I sigh.

In his excitement, he momentarily forgets himself, but regains his composure, his voice taking on a stern tone as he clears his throat and smooths his black hair back.

'Passport please.'

'I don't have it on me.'

'What are you doing in Playa del Carmen?'

'Just travelling.'

'How long you been here?'

'A few months.' It has been over a year.

'Are you making jewellery to sell?'

'No.'

'Made out of hemp?'

'No.'

He sizes me up, scribbles something on a notepad.

'Come with me.'

He grips my arm firmly and leads me back past Jimmy's No Problem, where I eyeball Gabriel and he nods, as if to say don't worry, I'll come for you.

I'm taken to an idling coach waiting in a back street and told to get in. It's filled with travellers, many of the friends I've been hanging out with at Jimmy's for months. I spot a German guy I know, looking nervous.

'What's happening?' I ask him.

'Immigration crackdown. They're taking us to Mexico City. Twenty hours away. From there we'll be deported.'

'Fuck! I can't get my bag or anything?'

'No, they won't let us get our stuff. They say we've been working illegally.'

'But they have no proof.'

'They do, unfortunately. They've been watching us.'

'Oh shit.'

I'll never see Gabriel again. They'll send me back to Australia in disgrace and I'll have to save the money to get back and see him. It could take years.

But then he appears, walking up the front steps of the bus in his relaxed way, smiling at me reassuringly.

'Que pasa chica,' he says, casually.

'They're going to take me to Mexico City and send me back to Australia.'

'No pasa nada,' he says. 'Don't worry.'

With the bus now full, an immigration official gets on and asks for passports. Gabriel says he's Mexican, explains I'm with him and my passport is at home. He vouches for me, says I'm just a tourist, and then shakes the official's hand—it's one of *those* handshakes. I catch a glimpse of a US fifty-dollar note pass between them. The official nods and tells me I can go. Just like that.

As we head back towards the Quinta Avenida, hand-in-hand, immensely relieved, Gabriel explains how Jimmy had immediately stepped in to help, told the immigration officials everything on the table was his. He'd also told them to bring their wives and girlfriends to the shop the next day and they could choose something nice for themselves, if they let me go. It's the way things are done in Mexico, where wages are low and an offer like that goes a long way. I'm fortunate to have someone like Jimmy No Problem on my side.

I turn and see the bus leaving for the long trip to Mexico City. The German guy gives me a sad wave through the window and I wave back. His time is up, he has to return home. But my home isn't Australia anymore. I remember my dream, where everyone from my past burnt in a fire and I was damaged, but I survived. I've been burnt and reborn. I am destined to be here with my beautiful artisan and a laughing pirate, a smiling elf girl, a clever artist from the city and a blue-green neon sea.

CHAPTER TWENTY-TWO

BUT THEN, EVERYTHING changes.

Immigration is watching us and if we keep hanging out at Jimmy's shop, they'll discover soon enough Gabriel isn't Mexican. We're both working illegally and we're not safe selling in the street anymore.

'So, what do we do now?' I ask him. He's sitting at his work table in the cabaña, shirtless as usual, making a series of chandelier earrings with beads of amber and turquoise.

'I don't know, loca' he says. 'Go back to Lima?'

'No way.'

I can't stand the thought of that oppressive humidity and polluted air and worse—Gabriel's drug connections.

'My family is there,' he says. 'Mi mamá, she needs me. Mi hermano needs me. Mi papa needs me.' He's been sending money home regularly, but he still feels the weight of obligation. Money is no substitute for his presence.

'Do you really want to go back there and sell salt? Get caught up with cocaine again?'

'No, not really. Lima is too sad for me now. Juan is gone. My best friend, you know, he was an excellent football player.'

'Yes I know, you said you used to play together.'

'In the street, every day. At school, whenever we could. Football, always football. We talked for hours about Maradona. I miss him, loca. Do you know what Maria told me at his cremation that day?

'No, what?'

'She said he thought when we didn't go out with them that weekend, that we were sneaking off on our journey to Mexico.'

His beautiful dark eyes moisten, but still, he doesn't cry.

'Loca—he died thinking I was leaving Lima without saying goodbye. Fuck, life is shit. He was such a good guy. If we go back to Lima, it will only remind me of him, and how he's not there anymore.'

'Where else can we go?'

'We could go back to Buenos Aires and live with Elsa.'

'Maybe. But what will I do there?'

'Find a job as a journalist. Your Spanish is very good now.'

'I could, I guess. But that's my old life, back in Sydney. I don't know if I'm cut out to be a journalist. Anyway, I love this lifestyle in the tropics. It's never cold, we can swim whenever we like, there's no traffic, I can go wherever I need to on Benotto. It's perfect here. I'm not ready to leave yet. It's not time.'

We're quiet for a while. Gabriel picks up a piece of amber, turning it over and over in his fingers.

'Chica?'

'Sí?'

'Will you marry me?'

'Of course, you know I will.'

'But I haven't asked you properly. We could get married here, get Mexican residency, live here in Playa del Carmen, have children. This is a good place for us. We just need to get our FM3 visas, so we can work.'

'How do we do that?'

'I don't know, we have to go to Cancun and apply. It takes three months.'

'Okay, let's do it. But in the meantime, let's go around to all the shops and beg them to put our things in the windows. Or even buy from us; we could wholesale. Then we don't have to sell in the street.'

I am not giving up on Playa del Carmen yet. We will find a way to stay.

Ines and Sandra stop by to see how I am after the incident with Immigration. I invite them in for tea and we sit in our little kitchen area, stretching out on our floor cushions while Gabriel stays at his desk, working. Always working.

'What are you going to do?' Sandra asks. 'Maybe you could find work in Mexico City. You could stay with my family until you find your own place.' Her hospitality, the hospitality of this whole continent, has always comforted me. People invite you in, no matter how rich or poor, and share what they have.

'Gracias amiga,' I say. 'I don't think we want to live in the city. We need to work out a way to make money here, out of sight of Immigration.'

'I'm volunteering at the dive shop so I can learn to be an instructor,' Ines says, her toothy smile beaming at me. 'I can introduce you and you could learn to dive and maybe become an instructor, too. We could do it together.'

'Really?' I consider it for a moment. I love snorkelling and the warm, clear waters of the Mexican Caribbean, teeming with kaleidoscopic tropical fish, are perfect for it. But something stops me. Fear? Lack of confidence? I'm not sure, but I can't see myself as a dive instructor.

'Gracias Ines, it sounds amazing, but I'm not sure I have what it takes to do a job like that. There's so much to learn about tanks and masks and oxygen and stuff.'

'Well, whatever you decide, be careful amiga,' Sandra warns. 'Don't tell anyone what happened to you and what your situation is. You can't trust people around here. Only us and Jimmy. Okay?'

'Okay.' I look at them, both women I have grown fond of, as trustworthy and supportive as any of my Australian friends.

'Ines—do you think you will ever go home?'

'I don't know. This is home for me now. I feel more free, more like myself in Mexico. I have no desire to return to Argentina.'

'What about you, Sandra?'

'Amiga, I go where the wind takes me. I have a good family in Mexico City. My mum, my brother, my aunt and my grandmother. They are always there, waiting for me. They accept me as I am and love me for who I am. That is all I need.'

'When will you go home?'

'I don't know. Things are great for me here right now. I love this lifestyle, the beaches, the slow days, the golden light. It is a beautiful place, Playa del Carmen. No?'

'Sí!' We shout yes in unison and clink our teacups together. We are united in our love for this little village that we hope is not going to grow too fast and will always have a place for us.

The next day, we pack Gabriel's backpack full of jewellery and walk the length of the Quinta Avenida, trying to sell wholesale to the shops. Most of the shopkeepers give us a polite 'no' when they see our work. Some are clearly annoyed at my presence and I begin to realise I am encroaching on their territory. We're about to give up when we meet a German guy who owns his own store and is married to a Mexican woman.

'I can't sell your stuff in my shop, but I have a tip for you. The five-star resorts have artisans' markets one day a week, all on different days. The tourists don't like to leave their all-inclusive resorts because they are too scared of being robbed, but they want to buy handmade crafts from locals. If you can get into one or two of those, you will be set.'

We dress up in our best clothes—me in a white T-shirt and a long white skirt, Gabriel in white pants and an embroidered shirt. People seem to like white around here. We brush all the knots out of our hair and meet with the entertainment staff of three big resorts. They show us their tables—long trundle tables covered in a thick white tablecloth—and ask if we have enough material to fill it. We have enough to fill three tables and they love the quality of Gabriel's work, how unusual it is, different from anything you can buy in the shops. They also like that I can speak English to their guests. They are surprisingly accommodating and we're told we can start the following week. The first to let us in is the Iberostar, a sprawling resort on the beach in the southern end of Playa del Carmen with luxurious lagoon pools, landscaped tropical gardens and good-looking staff in crisp white uniforms.

We exhibit alongside Mexicans selling colourful textiles, striped blankets, sombreros, hammocks, ceramics and souvenir T-shirts. Our gleaming handmade jewellery looks beautiful displayed on the expensive tablecloth, rather than our cheap manta on the ground.

We have a dedicated clientele of tourists confined to the resort and deprived of retail therapy, and they freely hand out US$100 bills. Gabriel sits behind the table making new pieces so the tourists can observe him at work, while I talk to them, tell them stories about who we are, how we met, where we've travelled, the mountains we've scaled to find the stones, where our silver is from and how Gabriel talks to the stones and asks them what they want to become. They trust us, it seems, and it's nothing for Americans, Germans, Swiss and Canadians to buy four or five pieces at $100 a piece. We've hit the jackpot.

On Valentine's Day, we make US$1000 and that night, we get very drunk. We can't believe what we've stumbled into. We no longer have to sit in the street or run from Immigration. They won't find us in these resorts. We do Thursdays at the Robinson Club in Tulum, Saturdays at the Iberostar and Sundays at the Maeva. All of a sudden, we're rolling in cash, stashing it all under our mattress.

Everything is going well until the entertainment manager at the Iberostar, Billie, asks us for a favour one day, a couple of months into our tenure. One of the dancers in the resort's show has a boyfriend who also makes amber jewellery. He needs a place to sell, but all the tables are occupied.

'Could he share your table?' she asks us.

It's not like we have a choice. She could simply ask us to leave if she wants to and give the table to him, but he doesn't have enough material to fill a table. He only has about ten small pieces of amber jewellery, so we make a space for him at the end of our table.

Edson is handsome and softly spoken, with long hair and fine features. His girlfriend Carla is gorgeous, with an incredible body she displays for the tourists during her dance routines. The four of us become friends and we invite them over to the cabañas for dinner.

Jimmy is suspicious of them, but Gabriel assures him they're *buena onda*, which means they have a good vibe. I get the feeling Jimmy is jealous because he doesn't have his buddy to visit cenotes and drink beer with, like he used to. Gabriel doesn't need him anymore, doesn't need his shop. He's still our amigo, the first friend we made here. But he has a nasty side, and he shows it when Edson and Carla are around.

'Don't trust them,' he tells Gabriel, taking off his leather belt and snapping it loudly, as a warning. 'I don't want them coming to the cabañas. Or to my shop.' He spits a thick glob of mucus onto the ground. I'm used to Jimmy's disgusting habits now.

It seems like a harsh reaction and I wonder if he knows something we don't.

'Tranquillo loco,' Gabriel says. 'Just relax, they're cool.'

We come to consider them good friends and confide in them that Gabriel isn't Mexican, but Peruvian. That neither of us has a work visa.

Each week, Edson takes the bus with us to the hotel, lays out his wares, and sells nothing. He watches as tourists hand over hundreds of dollars to us. He can't understand why he doesn't sell anything and the truth is, his jewellery is badly made.

One night, after having shared our table with him for a couple of months, he comes to visit us at the cabañas.

'Hola loco,' Gabriel says, greeting him at the door with a handshake Edson does not return.

'Que pasa?' Edson raises his chin at me, but doesn't smile. Heat rises to my cheeks.

'Wanna beer?' Gabriel asks.

'No,' Edson says coldly, refusing to come in further than the front door. 'I do not want a fucking beer. I want you to leave the hotel. You are making it impossible for me to sell anything. I have sat and watched you, week after week, selling, selling selling. What do I sell? *Nada*. Well fuck you. This is my country, *mi pais*. Tu no eres Mexicano.'

You are not Mexican. The words ring in my ears.

'Loco, loco, tranquillo,' Gabriel says, his hand on Edson's shoulder.

'No me chingues güey,' he says. *Don't fuck with me dude.* 'I want you and your fucking gringa out of this town.'

'Oi loco, it's not my fault if people don't buy your shit.' Gabriel takes a step back.

'You leave the hotel, you leave the town, or I am going to Immigration. I'm sure your gringa would give the police a great suck.'

'Fuck you man,' Gabriel raises his hand and thinks better of it.

'Listen, we will leave Iberostar. It's all yours. But this is our town too, we want to stay here, man. Leave us alone and we won't go back to Iberostar. Okay?'

Edson glares at us for a few seconds, turns and disappears into the darkness.

I throw my arms around Gabriel.

'What the hell are we going to do now? I don't want to get arrested. Maybe we should leave.'

'No way, that arsehole isn't going to run us out of town. We still have the Robinson Club and the Maeva. We'll just keep to ourselves. We'll move to a new apartment so he doesn't know where we live.'

'But I love it here. We helped fix these cabañas up.'

Gabriel is pacing the cabaña, rubbing his forehead.

'We should have listened to Jimmy,' I say. 'We shouldn't have trusted Edson. You can't trust anyone in this fucked-up country.'

He doesn't answer.

'Hey, remember El Doctor?' I say. 'He told us this would happen. He said beware of envy and that lady at the kiosk said be careful, don't trust anyone.'

'You can't trust human beings, loca. Any human beings, from any place. Mexico, Peru, Argentina. Maybe you can't trust people in Australia, either. I trust my stones, I trust my tools, I trust my hands, I trust mi mamá. That's it.'

'Do you trust me?'

'Yes, of course mi amor. I trust you. Do you trust me?'

I hesitate for a moment.

'Yes.'

'Well, that's all that matters.'

We both sleep fitfully, tossing and turning, sweating in the humidity. During the night, I roll over and a searing pain shoots through my thigh, like a thousand bee-stings. I scream and jump out of the bed.

'Que pasa?!' Gabriel shouts.

'Something bit me,' I scream. 'It hurts, it fucking hurts and it's getting worse.'

My leg has a large red welt on it and is burning like hell. Gabriel turns the light on and pulls the sheet back. A scorpion. Big, black and mean. It has dropped from the thatched roof onto the bed. Usually, we check the sheets before we get in, but after the drama with Edson, we'd forgotten.

The pain continues for hours and I become delirious, before falling into a hallucinogenic sleep. Vivid scenes, flashes of being chased by immigration officials, of being locked in a Mexican prison cell, being raped by Mexican police, having all our money stolen. I sweat profusely and beg Gabriel to take me to the doctor, but there are no night surgeries in Playa. I don't know how deadly the scorpion bite is, but there's nothing I can do but wait it out. One of my Mexican friends told me once if you get bitten by a scorpion and you can't get to a doctor, you have to eat the scorpion to nullify the effects of the venom. But the scorpion has disappeared and I think I'd rather die than eat one.

I wake up early the next morning. Still alive. Better than alive. Bursting with energy. A new life force surges through my veins and I get up and go for a run on the beach. I run barefoot along the sand in the early morning light, far north along the beach, past resorts in various stages of construction, until there is just sand and trees. I hear a hiss in the trees and look over to see a construction worker with his pants down, wanking. He doesn't scare me. I laugh at him and keep running. Not jogging, but running, like I'm on speed. The metallic brilliance of the sea is irresistible and I dive in, fully clothed, and float in the calm, crystalline water, gazing up at snakeskin clouds stretched across a pale blue sky. It is a moment of revelation, a turning point. I don't want to numb myself to the world anymore, block it out with alcohol and pot. I'm fearless and I want to soak up every second of this incredible life, head clear, eyes open.

I return to the cabañas to find Gabriel awake and making breakfast, cutting up some papaya from a tree in the yard, adding dollops of yoghurt. Bob Marley is playing, the birds are singing and the morning is fresh with promise.

'Hey, the scorpion injected me with superpowers,' I say, jumping into the cold shower. 'I just ran the whole beach and back.'

'Wow, I couldn't run as far as the front gate,' he jokes. 'Are you okay, my love?'

'Yeah, I'm great. I feel different. Like I want to stop drinking and smoking, get fit and healthy. Get a clear purpose for my life. For *our* lives.'

'Cool,' he says. 'Sounds good.'

But Gabriel keeps drinking every night, smoking pot and partying. I am outgrowing the party lifestyle. I am energised and motivated to move into a new phase of my life. I want to tap into my creativity, do more with my life. I've been gone for almost three years and what have I really achieved? I'm never going to be an artisan, it's not in my blood the way it's in Gabriel's. This blood, this artisan's blood, this Latin blood is not my blood. But I'm yearning to find my thing, the thing I'm good at.

I catch a bus into Cancun and find a large bookstore that stocks books in English, where I buy *The Artist's Way*, a book about tapping into your creativity. I begin to write morning pages, a stream of consciousness writing practice. I treat myself to nice pens, I paint, I draw, I make vision boards with pictures out of magazines, while Gabriel sits for hours making jewellery—our livelihood. One afternoon, he glares at me in frustration.

'Chica, make something. A bracelet, some earrings. You're spending money on these things we don't need. Days and days writing and cutting out pictures. Why?'

'I'm unlocking my creativity.'

'Make jewellery! That will unlock your creativity.'

'I can't. I'm hopeless at it.'

'You haven't tried, loca. You are too impatient.'

'What about my hemp jewellery?'

'It's nice, but it's cheap. I need you making more expensive things, necklaces we can sell for a hundred, two hundred. Not bracelets for a dollar.'

'Well, I do all the selling to tourists. I'm the one who speaks English.'

'Sí, you're good at that. It's just… I thought you wanted to be an artisan.'

'So did I.'

'So do you, or don't you?'

'I don't know anymore. I don't know what I want to do. What I'm *meant* to do.'

'Chica, you are annoying me more and more each day.'

'Oh really, why?'

'Your attitude. You spend all day writing and I'm not allowed to read what you write. I *can't* read it, it's all in English. I don't like there being a distinction between your stuff and my stuff, you and me. I want every part of you, all to myself. I want you to devote every drop of energy you have to me.'

Rage shoots down my arms, reddens my face. Once, that statement would have melted my heart. Now, it just pisses me off.

'I don't know who you think I am, but I'm not some subservient Latina, okay? I don't exist just to make you happy. I am a strong woman, with my own desires, my own talents. I just don't know what they are yet.'

I leave in a huff and walk into town to an internet café. In the years since I first arrived in South America, the internet has become commonplace and I now have a Hotmail account. I can email home whenever I like, though it's expensive to check emails and the connection often drops out.

I have an email from my dear friend Rachel, saying she's coming to visit. She wants to travel Mexico and spend time with me in Playa del Carmen. We've been friends since we were sixteen and she knows just about everything about me. It will be wonderful to have a friend from home, someone who understands me, who can help me figure out what I'm supposed to be doing with my life. I'm also looking forward to a break from Gabriel.

We're fighting more and more. He's impatient with my refusal to learn his craft and I'm annoyed he doesn't want to help me nurture my own talents, whatever they are. When I'm moody or quiet, he jumps to conclusions, assumes he knows what's wrong with me. When I try to explain it to him—that I feel lost and I don't know what my true vocation is—he doesn't want to listen. He doesn't seem interested in the real me, only in the me he wants me to be. He doesn't ask me questions to try and get to know me. As long as we make love every day and I help with the business, he's happy. If I don't feel like making love, he pressures me. He sees it as my duty and tells me what men don't find at home, they find in the street. It's the one time his macho culture clashes with my sense of autonomy as a woman with a right to say no. It's beginning to cause problems, especially when he comes home drunk and insists on it. I despise being pressured.

One morning, we're lying in bed together and a thought occurs to me. The romance has drifted out of our relationship. I think back to when we first met, in San Telmo, and how chivalrous and romantic he was.

'You know what, babe?' I say. 'I'd like you to be more romantic. Give me massages, buy me a rose every now and then. Cook me dinner occasionally.'

His response leaves me speechless.

'If I have to go to all that trouble, I may as well pay a whore.'

He is changing. He's not the same, sweet artisan I met that Sunday in the market in San Telmo. He's been hanging out with Jimmy too much.

Weeks pass and we keep selling at the Robinson Club and Hotel Maeva. We leave the Iberostar to Edson and he leaves us alone. We make friends with an amiable artist called Arturo, who sits at the table beside us at the Maeva. He finger-paints mountain and ocean landscapes on tiny pieces of card slightly smaller than a matchbox and sells them for US$4 to the hotel guests. His wife and children live in the north of the country, but he's here because it's where he can make the most money. He sends money home to support them and is building a house in Tulum, brick by brick, with the profits from his finger-painting. The more pictures he paints with his fingers, the more bricks he buys, the sooner he will be reunited with his family.

I ask him to teach me the technique and he writes me a list of the colours I need, instructing me to buy oil paints and thick white cardboard, which he cuts into the right dimensions. Once a week, I catch a bus to his home in Tulum, an hour south of Playa del Carmen, where he gives me lessons, along with his brother Manuel, and an expat couple, Norman and Monica, from Germany and Italy. We form a new group of friends and I begin to stay with Monica and Norman on the nights of my lessons. Gabriel's not interested in learning to paint and stays home, resenting the time I'm spending away from him, learning this new art form that is so removed from what he loves.

One hot Sunday, I'm sitting in the sun behind our table at the Maeva, gazing out to the sea, as dazzling as the brightest blue of a peacock feather. I'm tying hemp twine into macramé knots, threading ceramic beads through and thinking of nothing in particular. Gabriel has his head down working on a new piece and Arturo has a crowd around him, watching him work.

'You're from Australia, right?' An American man is standing at our table, not looking at the jewellery. Looking directly at me.

'Um, yeah?' I stand up, pulled out of my revelry. Please don't be Immigration.

'I remember you. My name's Marvin.'

I'm taken aback.

'Where do you remember me from?'

'From here. I came here a year ago for my holiday and you sold me a bracelet for my wife. You were very kind to me.'

'Oh, sorry, I don't remember you. We meet so many people.'

'That's okay. I thought of you when I went back to the States and I wanted to bring you a gift when I came back, just in case you were still here.'

He races off to his room and returns with a large plastic bag containing eight children's books. Beautiful, new children's books, some hardcover, with colourful illustrations.

'I thought you could use these,' he says.

I am stunned.

'Thank you,' I say, puzzled by this strange encounter.

'No problem,' he says. 'As I said, you just popped into my mind before I left the States and something told me I should bring you these books.'

It seems this random experience must have greater significance, but I don't know what. I watch him as he wanders off to the bar.

'That was weird,' I say to Gabriel, who doesn't seem to find the interaction as odd as I do.

'Sí, maybe you should use the books to teach some kids English.'

'Hey, that's an idea! I could run little classes in Playa. That would be fun.'

'Might be a good way to earn more cash, loca.'

I go back to my bracelet, gazing out to the sea and picturing myself as a teacher. I think I'd be good at it; I love kids.

Then it hits me: I have to write. It's a sign. I've been increasingly dissatisfied with my life in Playa, yearning to find my true vocation, coming to terms with the fact I'm not an artisan. I don't even enjoy it. In fact, it annoys the crap out of me.

Writing. Writing is my passion. It always has been. As a child, I wrote poetry about war. As a teenager, I poured my heart into page after page of my journals and I still prefer to write in my journal than do almost anything else. I studied to be a journalist at university but never felt like one, even when I was employed as one. I've always felt like an imposter, pretending to know what I'm doing, paralysed by self-doubt. But in the spaces between my self-sabotaging thoughts, I know it's my passion, my true vocation. The thing underneath everything else, the magma of my being.

I suggest to Gabriel that maybe the encounter with the American man means I should become a children's writer. He thinks it's a cute idea, but can't understand how I will ever make money out of it. He wants me to persevere with the jewellery; it's going so well for us. We've saved $US5000, which is a lot of money for us. One day, we might buy land here. Jimmy says we can buy a block of land in Tulum for US$1000 and we'd have money left over to build a house, the way our local Mexican friends do, a little at a time. That's how Gabriel wants to do it. If I learn the craft, he says we'll double production, double our sales. It's a perfect life, he says, sitting around in the sunshine, working with stones, chatting to happy people on holidays.

But I'm not satisfied. There's a gnawing inside me, a lonely little creature desperate for attention. I keep pushing it down, ignoring it. Telling it to go away, leave me alone. I'm not good enough. It's trying to get my attention, to tell me something important, but still, I don't want to hear it.

I continue on my health kick, rising early to run on the beach, eating papaya, mango, banana and lots of fresh vegetables, cutting back on alcohol, writing more and more. My new regime is incompatible with Gabriel and Jimmy's partying, which has resumed with full force now Edson is out of the picture. They go on day trips to cenotes and always take loads of beer and weed. If Ines and Sandra are going, I go along too; I prefer the company of the women to the men.

One day we visit Playa del Carmen's cenote, as clear and blue as an aquamarine stone, and a tourist from a nearby hotel is washing her hair in the water. Shampoo bubbles float in the water and we can't believe it. I tell her she's in a sacred Mayan waterhole, that it's not a place for people to wash their hair, and she merely laughs. I fear it's a sign of things to come.

The town is growing too fast for its own good and I have a terrible feeling this pristine place is going to be ruined. Loved to death.

Jimmy and Gabriel aren't too worried about it, because they're too drunk or too stoned to care. Their intoxicated ramblings are beginning to become boring as they stumble home after hanging out in the Quinta Avenida, laughing and talking shit in the communal lounge area while I hide away in the cabaña, trying to sleep.

Some nights, Gabriel tries to wake me up to make love, breathing beer breath on me. I hate it when he does that. I still love him, but that love is stagnant and not growing because one of us is usually sober and one of us is usually drunk.

CHAPTER TWENTY-THREE

THE SIGN AT the end of the jetty on the island of Caye Caulker in Belize says 'go slow'. It's a tiny island devoid of cars, where scruffy dogs sleep in the sandy streets and reggae echoes through the warm air. It's the escape I need from Playa del Carmen and the darkening energies that are clawing at everyone there, as the town grows and money pours in.

Belize is only four hours by bus from Playa del Carmen and I time my trip there to coincide with Rachel's arrival. I'm tired of the party crowd in Playa and I need a change of scene. Time away to reassess things. I still love Gabriel, but his drinking is worrying me and I know I'm a disappointment to him with my lack of skill as an artisan. He spends more time hanging out with Jimmy than he does me. I know he still loves me, but we're drifting apart.

The island of Caye Caulker is a cheerful canvas of palm trees and calm turquoise sea, with timber homes, stores and restaurants painted in bright pinks, canary yellows and light blues that match the water. Rach and I find a little hostel to rent for a few days and stroll down to the main jetty. There's a thatched roof bar serving cold drinks and a mix of travellers and islanders are hanging out, soaking up the sun and the cruisy vibes. A Rasta guy holding a bike turns to check us out as we stroll up to the bar and drops his bike.

'Man, you girls got some kind of magic? You put a spell on me with your beauty?'

I don't consider myself beautiful. Rachel, on the other hand, with her thick waist-length brown hair and dark, soulful brown eyes, is a goddess.

For the first time in three years, I am missing Australia and this island is a welcome distraction. Mexico is my new home and I'm not giving up on it, but seeing Rachel makes me miss my family, my Australian friends, speaking English, being anonymous.

We strip off to our swimmers and dive into the clear water, cool enough to refresh without being too cold. There's no beach, just a jetty to spread our towels on. A speedboat pulls up and two black guys in white singlets hand out large bottles of rum. They're doing a promotion for Bacardi and have a boatload of the stuff to give away. I decide my health kick can wait until I'm back in Playa del Carmen. This is my tropical paradise holiday away from my tropical paradise home and I'm going to make the most of it.

The guys hand out bottles of Coke and plastic cups and make us rum and Cokes all afternoon while they blast reggae tunes from their boat. A boy of about six approaches us with a basket of warm coconut bread rolls and we buy one each, soft and sweet and fresh out of the oven. It's a blissful first day in this laid-back little corner of the world where a Creole influence infuses everything from the food—which is all about lobster and rum punch—to the music and the easygoing attitude.

'I thought this was going to be just like North Queensland,' Rachel says as the sun sets over the island.

'Ha! And what do you think now?'

'It's nothing like North Queensland!'

The island men with their dreadlocks, muscular bodies and white smiles are irresistibly attractive. The guy with the bike thinks we've put a spell on him, but he has no idea he's had the same effect on me.

This is the first time I've found other men attractive in any real way since I met Gabriel back in the market in San Telmo and I was so smitten I could barely breathe. Am I falling out of love with him? Have we lost our connection, the bond we believed was eternal and born in some other life, long ago? I know I still love him; the deep bond we have is beyond petty arguments. So why am I so easily distracted by these men?

On day two, we go snorkelling on the Belize Barrier Reef, second only in size to the Great Barrier Reef. Down at the jetty, we meet Ras Creek, a local Rasta famous for his ability to summon sea creatures and feed them by hand. He is a fine specimen, with sunbleached dreadlocks, a dazzling smile and a lean, sinewy body. It doesn't take him long to talk us into all-day snorkelling tour, with lunch included.

We step aboard his thatched-roof houseboat, painted the same bright azure as the sea and we know we're in for a fun day. He takes us out to the reef where we dive into beautifully warm water with incredible visibility. He calls placid reef sharks to his side, which he picks up and plonks into our outstretched arms. He holds out a long pole and tells us to hook our feet over it and float on our tummies, as we await the arrival of spotted eagle rays. They glide right past us in a majestic swoop and he shows us how to hand-feed them. He leads us into the murky mangroves, where we snorkel with tiny seahorses. Finally, he leads us to a coral garden where he proceeds to hunt down our lunch: rainbow-hued tropical fish, timid rock lobsters and the luscious Queen conch. We watch through our masks as he catches the poor creatures by hand.

Back on his houseboat, Ras Creek cooks up a seafood lunch on a small gas stove. As he slides the conch meat out of its sexy pink shell, he teases us with tales of its powers as an aphrodisiac. With the white conch meat cubed and set aside to cure in freshly squeezed lime juice, he tempts us with the scent of fresh fish and lobster, cooking in a coconut curry sauce. He adds chopped coriander, onion, garlic and bright green peppers to the conch meat to make an aromatic ceviche. He serves us cold jugs of sweet rum punch and I momentarily forget I'm vegetarian, as I savour every bite.

Surrounded by the blinding blue Caribbean Sea, guilt at eating sea creatures that were alive only moments before, is replaced with gratitude and we eat with great respect. Sitting barefoot in our swimmers, sunburnt and totally satisfied, this little houseboat is the finest restaurant in the world.

That night, Ras Creek comes looking for us in town and invites us back to his houseboat. We don't even need to discuss it. We just silently follow his lead, hypnotised like the marine life he holds under his command. I tell myself it's innocent, that nothing is going to happen. But when he heaves us by our bums up onto the roof of his boat and the three of us lie together, arms entwined, watching for shooting stars, reason disappears and I am possessed by a primal urge too strong to ignore.

Fecund sea smells and the sound of the water lapping against the shore lull me into a state of openness, receptive to the gifts this island wants to give. He kisses both of us alternately and strokes our skin, which glows in the moonlight against his black skin.

It's a night of sensuality and affection, something separate from my relationship with Gabriel. A night I will look back on when I'm an old woman with wrinkled skin and smile. When my grandchildren ask me what I'm smiling about, I'll remember the scent of coconut on the breeze and the taste of salty skin and I'll say, once I had a whole day and night of pure pleasure, on a little island in the sun covered in palm trees, with streets filled with music instead of cars.

CHAPTER TWENTY-FOUR

I RETURN TO Playa del Carmen with trepidation. I'm excited to see Gabriel, but I'm unsure of our future. I should feel guilty about my infidelity, but I don't. I know we are coming to a crossroads and something needs to change. If we don't make the change, it will be made for us.

Rachel and I dump our bags at the cabañas. One of the older artisans is sitting in the communal kitchen area and says everyone is down at the shop. No one else is around and nothing is locked. That's what I love about this place. I'm happy to be back.

We walk down to Jimmy's shop and see the usual crew hanging around out the front, playing music, dancing, chatting. Ines and Sandra are there and we greet each other with a big hug. I introduce them to Rachel and they warmly embrace her. Gabriel's sitting on a crate, deep in conversation with Jimmy. He jumps up when he sees me.

'Look who it is,' he says to Jimmy, grabbing me. He's so familiar; part of me. He's still my soul mate and it only takes one embrace to realise it.

'Hola chicas,' Jimmy shouts. 'Come and have a drink.'

'Thanks Jimmy, we just got back and we're hungry. We might go and get some dinner and then we'll come back and have a drink.'

He laughs his pirate laugh, bares his bad teeth, smiles his crazed smile and winks at Rachel.

'No problem!' he says in his thick Mexican accent.

Jimmy's been good to us. He's led Gabriel astray a little, but he was happy to go along for the ride. We would not have been able to stay here as long as we have without him. We've been living in Playa for over two years and it feels good to be home. My few days in Belize have made me realise that.

Rachel only has a couple of days left before she returns to Australia and has enough money left to pay for dinner in a nice restaurant; a rare indulgence for me. I've become used to living frugally so we can save as much money as possible. I eat only once or twice a day and with all my running on the beach, I've lost ten kilos. People don't call me gordita anymore and my old clothes hang off me.

We order tacos and Coronas in one of the tourist restaurants in the Quinta Avenida, snacking on a bowl of corn chips and guacamole brought to the table as soon as we sit down, one of the welcoming touches I love about this place and perhaps a ploy to stop customers going anywhere else. The evening atmosphere is festive, all the restaurants full. Men in white shirts and pants stand out the front, enticing customers in with promises of the best margaritas in town. The warm night air is scented with frying meat, lime, chilli and garlic and mariachi music, salsa and merengue is blasting out of every restaurant, bar and club.

But in our restaurant, the music changes suddenly, from exuberant salsa to a slow panpipe tune. It immediately transports me back to the Andes, to the crisp air infused with woodsmoke, to the cholitas with their black braids, the llamas, the condors, the dramatic landscapes. It touches me in a deep and timeless place and I know I have a karmic connection with the Andes that goes a long way back. Those roots are deeper than anything I have in this life and are intertwined with Gabriel. Playa del Carmen is paradise—the coconut palms, the turquoise sea, the party days and nights, the shining brown skin everywhere you look. But even now, in this place of tropical beauty, I long to be somewhere else.

I begin to weep.

'What's the matter, hon?' Rachel moves her chair closer.

'This music,' I say, wiping my eyes on my napkin. 'Bloody panpipes. They get me every time.'

'Really?'

'Yeah, I hear a panpipe and it's like my soul is back in the Andes and my physical body is here and the world is upside down. I'm sitting at the

Colca Canyon watching condors soaring through the valley. The music captures the soul of that place so perfectly.'

I pause, take a sip of beer.

'You know, if I said to Gabriel, let's just go and live in Cusco, I bet he would. But what would I do with my life? Get married and have Peruvian babies?'

'I don't know, what do you want?'

'Who knows, Rach. I want to be with Gabriel. I love him, I can't imagine my life without him. But this place is becoming crazier the more popular it gets. The partying is relentless. I want a normal life, away from temptation. I want to work hard. I want to write. I just never feel good enough.'

'Do you want to go home?'

'No... not yet. I've only been gone three and a half years.'

'That's a long time.'

'I don't know where home is anymore.'

'Is it here?'

'I thought it was. Once.'

'Is it Peru?'

'I'm not sure.'

'Argentina?'

'Maybe.'

'Why don't you and Gabriel go and live in Australia together? He could sell his work at the markets.'

'Maybe, one day. It's difficult for him to get residency on a Peruvian passport. It seems easier just to stay here, get married and live together so if we do decide to live in Australia, he'll get in without any problems.'

'Does Gabriel want to go to Australia?'

'Not really. He's Latino through and through. This is his land, his people. His culture. He wouldn't have the brotherhood of artisans and musicians he has here. They're his lifeblood.'

'Do you feel like it could become your culture?'

'No. I wanted it to be. I so wanted it to be. I thought if I stayed here long enough, if I became an artisan, if I loved Gabriel enough, I could adopt this culture; be adopted by it. That the mask I wear would no longer be a mask and I could belong. Just belong.'

'You don't feel you belong here?'

We pause while the waiter brings our meals, vegetarian fajitas, still sizzling in their pans. I look around the restaurant at the tanned and relaxed tourists, the cheerful striped tablecloths, the bright yellow walls draped in Mexican flags and sombreros. I take in the smell of chilli and melted cheese and tacos and tequila.

'I did, but then people started getting pissed off at me for taking away their business, telling me I'm not Mexican. I have no right to be working here and making money. And they're right, Rach. I'm encroaching on their territory. It's hard enough for them to make a living as it is. What the fuck am I doing, taking their livelihood away?'

We sit quietly sipping our beer, listening to the last refrains of the sad panpipe song.

'To be honest, I have no idea where I belong. After all this time travelling, I'm still no closer to knowing.'

The panpipe song ends and a happy mariachi song almost bursts our eardrums, all horns and guitars and soaring vocals. It lifts my spirits.

'I don't know, maybe I do belong here. I'll always be a gringa, but who cares?'

We clink beer bottles and say salud!

'It will work itself out, hon. One way or another.'

I have a tearful goodbye with Rachel when it's time for her to leave and feel a tiny twinge of envy that she's going back to Australia. I'm not homesick, no way. But there are things I yearn for. I miss walking down the street without being a target, I miss my family, I miss my friends. I miss Vegemite.

After Rachel leaves, things go back to the way they were. I'm up early to run on the beach and write my morning pages. Gabriel sleeps off a hangover, then hassles me to make love or make some jewellery, add to our production. I continue to avoid it. Twice a week, we sell at the hotels and make good money.

I hang out with Sandra and Ines, swimming and snorkelling, visiting the local cenote, or just swinging in our hammocks at the cabañas, keeping cool in the shade.

'I'm fucking pissed off,' Sandra says one afternoon, when all the guys are at Jimmy's shop.

'Why?' I ask. It's not like her. She's usually such an upbeat girl.

'I have colitis and I'm in a lot of pain. And I'm sick of these pigs leaving their shit lying around. I'm always tidying up, cleaning out the disgusting fridge.'

'They definitely like women to do the dirty work, don't they?' Ines says.

We've all experienced it—the sexist Latinos who believe women are for fucking and cleaning up after them. We love them, but we love our time with our girlfriends—no farting, burping, spitting men.

Sandra swings silently in her hammock, looking up at the trees. She looks like she's fighting back tears.

'Is that all that's wrong Sandra,' I ask.

'No. It's Jimmy. He told me not to fall in love with him because he's married.'

'Oh.' So they are an item. Finally, it's out in the open. 'What did you say to him?'

'I said, it's my problem if I fall in love with him.'

She tells us about Jimmy and his many lovers, that he and his brothers sleep around and visit prostitutes. It's the done thing in Mexico, she says. But their wives are sacred, the mothers of their children. Jimmy will never leave his wife for Sandra. Later, I ask Gabriel if that's how he'll be with me one day after we're married, sleeping with prostitutes and pretty young girls who come to town. He swears he won't.

Sandra goes back to Mexico City and we promise to stay in touch. She leaves a cabaña vacant at the compound, and a creepy guy called Domingo moves in. Jimmy says he's the owner of the cabañas, but to me, Domingo looks like the kind of person who wouldn't own anything but a drug habit. He's a skinny Spanish man with missing teeth and straggly hair. I am instantly uncomfortable around him. Gabriel thinks he's hilarious and entertaining, the kind of guy you can party with all night, every night.

They form a trio, sitting in the communal kitchen area at the cabañas till all hours, drinking tequila, rum, beer and smoking pot.

And, taking cocaine.

Domingo is the person who brings it back into Gabriel's life, as I suspected someone would eventually. I am powerless against these three men, who live like there's no tomorrow and don't see a problem with it. There is no talk of addiction and how it can ruin lives. No enquiring as to its causes. Life's one big party. *Pura vida. No pasa nada.*

No problem.

I begin to spend more time alone in my cabaña, rather than joining everyone at the shop. Ines stays in too. She's still volunteering at the local scuba diving shop, trying to get the hours up to get her dive ticket. She's moving ahead in the world, still selling her little elves but with an eye on a new career. I spend hours lying on the bed, writing in my journal, sorting through conflicted emotion. Loneliness. Confusion. Fear. Sadness. Stagnation. I feel like an insect trapped inside a piece of prehistoric amber.

I'm lying alone on the bed one Friday night while everyone is at Jimmy's shop and I hear footsteps. The front door opens and Domingo walks in, all missing teeth, gaunt cheeks, hollow eyes. He looks like he's off his face.

'Hola preciosa, que tal?' *Hello my precious, how are you?*

I freeze.

'What are you doing here?'

'Tranquilla, tranquilla. It's okay baby, I just thought you might want some company.'

'No, gracias.'

'Aren't you lonely with Gabriel always hanging out with Jimmy?'

'No, I'm fine. Can you go please?'

He smiles his disgusting smile and sits on the edge of the bed. He stinks of cigarettes, piss and something putrid I can't put my finger on.

'You're such a pretty girl. Gabriel is lucky to have you.'

I edge away from him, move back on the bed towards the wall.

'Oh princesa, don't be scared. I just want to let you know I am here for you, if you are ever lonely.'

He runs his hand up my bare leg, from my ankle to the inside of my thigh.

The door.

The windows.

Heavy objects.

My mind scrambles for escape routes, searching for weapons, straight into survival mode.

'Hola chica, I'm home!' Gabriel's voice rings out across the garden. He's making lots of noise putting bottles of something or other in the fridge out in the communal lounge area.

Domingo drops his hand, licks his lips and makes a kissing sound.

'Hasta la proxima,' he says. *Until next time.*

I'm shaking as he slips unseen out the front door and joins Gabriel and Jimmy in the garden. I switch off the light and stare at the wall until I fall asleep. I dream of voices, whispering. It sounds like Domingo and Gabriel. I feel the mattress move. Just a dream.

Gabriel is in a chirpy mood the next morning, cutting up fruit and making coffee, up even before me. Then I realise he hasn't gone to bed. He's still high and has some great news for me.

'I made a wonderful decision for us, mi amor,' he says.

'What?'

'A business decision.' He's beaming, ecstatic with his decision.

'What sort of business decision?'

'I invested our money!'

'You what?'

'We're going to double it very soon, so our $5000 is going to be $10,000. Then we can go anywhere in the world, live wherever we want. Buy land, start building a house. It will be a new life for us.'

Nausea rising in my gut, fire shooting down my arms, bile in my throat. I can't speak, so I simply stare at him, dumbfounded. Hoping it's not what I think it is. Hoping I'm still dreaming.

'I gave the money to Domingo to go to Guatemala and buy a mountain of cocaine. He has a connection there. He's going to sell it for us and we will double our investment. We might keep a few grams for ourselves, but we will sell most of it and make more money than we've ever had.'

The words come from far away, as if Gabriel has melted into the wall. All that's left of him are these disembodied words and they kick me so hard, I collapse.

I cave in on myself, flop to the floor like a gutted fish. Words will not form in my mouth. I am mute. Deaf. Dead. Finally, this place has defeated me.

'Que pasa, esta todo bien,' he says. *It's fine.* He sings along to Bob Marley as he continues to make breakfast, as if giving all our money to a Spanish drug dealer was a brilliant idea. No problem, as Jimmy would say.

Finally, I find my voice. It comes out as a roar that reverberates across the compound.

'WHAT THE FUCK HAVE YOU DONE?'

He turns, shocked.

'It's okay, loca. We can trust Domingo. Es un amigo.'

'No,' I cry, shaking my head. 'No no no no no! We have lost all our money, everything we've worked for. He will never be back. He is gone. Fucking gone. Our money is GONE!'

I'm sobbing as I pull all my jewellery off and throw it at Gabriel. First I pull the carnelian earrings out of my ears. Then I rip off the bracelet he made with our plaited hair. Then I undo my amber necklace and fling it as hard as I can at his face, crying the ugliest cry of my life.

Gabriel tries to comfort me and I push him away, even angrier than the day I pelted rocks at him on the beach in Callao. I wish I had those rocks now.

'Fuck off! Leave me the fuck alone. I can't do this anymore. I'm done. I can't fucking do this anymore. It's too much. It's all too much.' I'm sobbing so much my body is almost convulsing.

The realisation of what he's done dawns on him as he begins to come off his high. He crumples onto the floor next to me.

'Loca,' he says, his voice trembling. 'You don't think he'll be back?'

'What do *you* think you fucking idiot? Of *course* he won't be back! Not with our money, anyway.'

Gabriel is stricken. My heart softens. I gently place my hand on his thigh, a sliver of compassion stirring for him, this brittle, broken man. My love, this hopeless love of mine. He has made a monumental mistake.

'When did he say he'd be back?'

'In a week.'

We sit together, silently. What is there to say? I stare at the pink hibiscus flowers covering the window, my eyes sore and puffy. I stare at the mobiles I've made out of shells and driftwood, dangling from the thatched roof. I stare at the chequerboard lino on the kitchen floor, where I once saw a little shell walking, far from home.

Fuck it. I'm not ready to leave. Not ready to give up my dream of this lifestyle, this tropical heaven with my beautiful, but messed up, man. I turn to him, grab his hand.

'If he's not back in a week with our money, we are leaving this town and we are never coming back. We're going to start a new life, somewhere far from here. Okay?'

'Okay my love.'

Finally, he begins to cry and every cut and break and burn he has been burying beneath his happy-go-lucky party guy persona comes tumbling out of him—his grief at losing Juan, who died thinking we had left without saying goodbye. His despair at Jorge's brain damage. His concern for his mother and the children. His guilt at leaving his family behind, his obligation to his father, his shame at getting back into cocaine. He clutches onto me, like I'm the only one who can save him from plummeting over the edge of the tallest Andean mountain. He apologises profusely, tells me he loves me over and over, pleads for my forgiveness. This flood of tears is a long time coming. I hold him and say it's okay, but it's not. It's far from okay.

A week later, Domingo returns.

'Sorry amigos, they robbed me,' he says, smiling, licking his rotting teeth. 'I didn't even get a chance to do the deal, they just held a gun to my head and took all the money. Fucking Guatemalan bastards.'

It's the biggest load of shit I've ever heard. We're not getting our money back, that much is clear. He says he's back to stay at Cabañas Doña Rosa and gives me a little wink. Domingo will never leave this place. His fetid energy will linger; he will continue to lurk in the shadows.

The next day, Gabriel and I place all of our stones back into their compartments—all the blue in one, the brown in another, the pink, black, white, orange, green and amber—all tucked away safely inside sturdy plastic boxes. Gabriel rolls up all the wire and layers it at the bottom of his backpack. I roll up all the hemp and leather and place it in a zipped compartment in my backpack. I pack my mandala, which has accompanied me across South and Central America, into my little brown suede pouch. I take the photo of us in Buenos Aires three years earlier off the wall and place it carefully inside the pages of my journal. We wrap our tools in a bright embroidered Mexican cloth, roll up our hammocks and tie them to our backpacks. I put my mangled passport back inside the sole of my boot. I put my earrings, necklace and bracelet back on. We take one last look at Cabañas Doña Rosa, walk to Jimmy's No Problem, hug Jimmy and Ines goodbye and take the last bus out of Playa del Carmen.

CHAPTER TWENTY-FIVE

PEYOTE WILL GIVE us the answers we seek. The hallucinogenic cactus, sacred to the Huichol Indians, is found in the deserts of Real de Catorce in the mountainous state of San Luis Potosí. We need to expand our consciousness, cleanse our souls of the dark energies of Playa del Carmen. Find out who we are, where we belong, what our true life's purpose is.

We take an overnight bus for twenty hours from Playa del Carmen to Mexico City. From there, it's another nine hours to the north. We meet a Brazilian artisan, Jorge. He's returning home to Real de Catorce, where he lives with his Chilean girlfriend. They've just had a baby and he's been in Mexico City buying materials.

More than 2000 kilometres away from Playa del Carmen, we reach the old silver mining town and follow Jorge up rocky laneways to his home, an old stone house with one bedroom and an outdoor kitchen. Not really a kitchen, more a slab of concrete where his girlfriend cooks over an open fire.

Elena is fair-skinned, Jorge is black and their baby is caramel. Elena is strong, stronger than I could ever imagine, building fires to boil water for her newborn baby and herself, all alone while Jorge has been away.

She is quiet and calm, thrilled to see her man return, but apparently coping well on her own. The baby looks healthy and they live a primitive lifestyle, but seem happy. I am intrigued as to why this girl from an affluent South American country is raising a child under these conditions, far away from the support of family and friends, in an isolated mountain town in the north of Mexico.

We leave what we know in search of something and sometimes, we find it. Ines has left Argentina to see the world and find love again. What she has found is peace, in the warm waters of the Caribbean, in the realm of fish and coral. Sandra has left home to roam her great country, allow its diverse landscapes to seep into her artist's soul. Or, maybe she's just drifting, happy to inhabit life's fringes, comfortable with herself and safe in the knowledge she belongs to this place and it belongs to her. Gabriel has left a family that needs him too much, to become who he really is: an artisan. With that, he has found success. But he has tried to outrun his shadow and with that, he has found failure.

Some of us, the lost ones, leave in search of ourselves. We leave in search of love. We leave in search of healing. We leave in search of redemption. We leave in search of truth, in scarch of a place to belong when we don't feel we belong in our own skin.

I don't want to admit to myself how much Gabriel has broken my heart. When he gave our money away, when he started back on cocaine, our bond, the bond I thought was eternal, suffered a devastating blow. I am not sure we can heal from the damage it caused. We could give it one more chance, in a place where there are no temptations, but first we need to seek a higher truth by ingesting peyote. We need its guidance.

Late one afternoon, Jorge takes us walking through the sweeping arid mountain landscape, up to a high escarpment, and points to the valley below. A big blue sky stretches above a vast desert, sparsely vegetated with small scrubby plants. He tells us to simply walk into the desert until we find the peyote. It will appear to us when the time is right, and once we see one button, we'll see many more. Like magic.

We set off the next morning, unprepared, with not enough water or food, one tent and a couple of sleeping bags. We walk in the direction Jorge showed us and after half an hour, notice four men following us. They're in the distance, but as the landscape is flat and they can track our movements, they don't need to hurry.

So now, we can't turn back, even if we want to. Each time we change direction, they change direction too. But we keep walking, eyes on the ground, looking for the little green buttons growing under bushes on the desert floor.

We've been walking for what must be hours, without a map or any way of knowing where we are, when we come upon a tiny town. Not exactly a town, more like a hut with a water tank outside. We make a beeline for it and find an ancient woman sitting inside, in a dark room, alone. She's selling bottles of water and homemade popcorn, sprinkled with chilli. We feel safe knowing she's there. If the men keep following us, at least we have a little old lady to protect us.

We walk on, keeping the señora's hut in sight, and notice the men have turned and are heading back the way they'd come. Perhaps they know something about her we don't. Now we can relax and as we walk on, I'm the first to spot a peyote plant.

'Look, look!' I shout to Gabriel. 'I found one!'

'Bueno, chica!'

Jorge said it's important to conduct a ceremony of respect by eating the peyote straight out of the ground, without washing it down with water. I follow the ceremony with reverence, kneeling on the hot, dry earth, as if it's a church pew. Unlike other cacti, peyote doesn't have spines. It grows out of the ground in clumps and looks like a squashed bread roll that has been sliced into triangular segments that begin in the centre and radiate outwards. Its colour is a dusty green, as if the bread rolls are covered in thick mould. I lean down and bite into the horrifically bitter cactus and quickly swallow it.

As we walk, more peyote appears, as Jorge said it would. We cut the buttons out of the ground and fill my brown suede pouch. We set up our tent within sight of the little old lady, and set about making a fire and chopping the peyote into pieces we can wash down with water.

Nausea grips us quickly, but we know we have to keep it down as long as possible for the hallucinogen to be absorbed into our bloodstreams. After about half an hour, we vomit green slime all over the ground and both begin to hallucinate.

I hear a bird's call as if it's in my own ear. I look at the sky and see it far overhead, but it's also right beside me. Inside me. I look at the ants and insects on the ground and watch them on their journeys. I know each one of them. I love each one of them. I look at the rocks and they are alive, they're sentient beings, with feelings. I trace bright red wiggly lines with my fingers, as if the rocks contain veins filled with blood.

I become one with the entire landscape and everything in it as I did at the Colca Canyon—the animals, the birds, the insects, the snakes. I am warm, safe, content, wrapped up in universal love and at one with the present moment.

But Gabriel isn't having a great time. He's lying in the tent sick, tripping and imagining snakes and demons burrowing up through the ground and into the tent.

'Fuera, fuera!' he shouts. '*Get away, get away!*' He kicks at imaginary monsters, his eyes wild with fear.

I try to calm him, tell him there are no snakes, the demons are only in his mind, but he's in another reality and can't hear me. While I am experiencing all-consuming love and connection, he is experiencing fear, anger and disconnection. I go light, he goes dark. I don't think he's ready for the light.

Gabriel stays cowering in the tent and I sit alone beside the fire and watch the sky blacken. Shadows move in the distance and I think it's a trick of the firelight. But then I hear howling. Coyotes. I'm not afraid, as one by one they wander into our camp, a pack of six, sniffing around for food. Instinctively, I know they're not a threat, their body language is curious rather than threatening. One coyote with extra thick grey fur stands closest to me, about a metre away, and holds my gaze with its luminescent yellow eyes. Perhaps I should be afraid, but I'm not. I'm never afraid of things I should be afraid of; always afraid of things I shouldn't be.

I stare into the fire and see skulls and distorted faces, curvaceous shapes, melting letters and psychedelic colours dancing in the flames, as the coyote stands and watches me, silently. I return its gaze and smile, the crackling fire the only sound in a landscape of silence and space. I don't know how long we stay like that, but I'm happy for it to last all night. This coyote has a message for me, but I can't work it out and as its pack moves away, it calmly follows and disappears into the dark desert night.

We sleep deeply that night and wake early, pack our things and begin the walk back to town.

'I know where we should go,' Gabriel says, walking his jaunty walk, back to his cheerful self.

'Where?'

'Taxco. A town near Mexico City. They mine silver there. We can buy silver and stones, we can rent an apartment, keep producing, sell to the tourists. We'll have a normal life. We won't hang out with the party crowd. It will just be you and me, mi amor.' He's happy his demonic peyote trip is over.

'Okay. But it's our last chance. No more drugs, no more partying.'

He agrees and with our spirits cleansed by the peyote, I feel it's going to be a fresh start for us. We spend a few days in Mexico City with Sandra on the way to Taxco. She lives with her mother, brother, aunt and grandmother in a middle-class part of the city in a large four-bedroom apartment filled with art. Her grandmother's name is Pepa and she's a spritely ninety-three. Mama Pepa likes Sandra's brother to play techno music on the stereo so she can dance in the living room and he paints her nails bright red because she can't see.

Sandra takes us to the Zocalo, Mexico City's main square, buzzing with tourists and colourful Aztec dancers, and teeming with taxis in the fun form of bright green VW Beetles. We also visit the markets at Coyoacán, where two kind souls invite us to share their stall so we can make some cash. We wander the stalls and I buy a pair of hand-tooled brown leather sandals painted with bright flowers. They're one of the few purchases I've made in the entire three and a half years I've spent in Latin America.

Also in Coyoacán is Frida Kahlo's house, which has been turned into a museum. She is one of my idols, a woman of creativity and integrity, strong in her sense of self. I'm intrigued by her surreal self-portraits and her devotion to her soul mate, the toad-faced Diego Rivera. Visiting her home renews my love for Mexico, for Latin America and for Gabriel. My original dream is still alive. The desire to live an extraordinary life in an extraordinary place. To be anything but normal. To live like a butterfly, beautiful, fast and free.

We arrive in Taxco, renewed and refreshed. It's a charming pueblo with whitewashed buildings and red-tiled roofs, surrounded by mountains, with the colonial ambience I loved about Cusco, Quito and Antigua. Best of all, it's only two hours from Mexico City and is not a party town like Playa del Carmen. It's a place to call home, a place where we can settle down. Start again.

We find a two-bedroom apartment for rent right in the centre of town, with a decent kitchen, a clean bathroom and a lounge room. It's the first proper home we've had on our own; a good space to be productive. Gabriel wants to learn to solder, and there are classes in town. He buys the tools and materials and we both try it out. I'm terrible of course, cutting a jagged piece of silver and sticking a piece of rose quartz to it with the soldering iron so badly the stone simply falls out. But Gabriel takes to it immediately like the true artisan he is, creating even more beautiful pieces of amber and turquoise and jade jewellery than I've ever seen him make. Immediately he makes me a new necklace, a solid silver triangle with a large circular piece of turquoise in the centre and a smaller piece of round amber above it, with a fringing of silver arrows dangling beneath it. Another gift to add to my collection.

In a place like this, without the distraction of beach life, I can get serious about writing. I can write a children's book. I can write about my travels. I can just write. I've run from it for too long. It has been a need in me, an impulse as natural as breathing, and fear has forced me to abandon it. Not good enough. Not good enough. Not good enough.

But I'm ready now. Ready to establish my identity separate from Gabriel. Ready to be me. Ready to accept myself as I am, or at least to try. I don't have to bend and twist myself into exotic shapes to live an extraordinary life.

Something has dawned on me, a thought that didn't strike out of the blue but crept up on me like a jungle vine, squeezing until I paid attention. My father cared about me. Yes, he abandoned me as a young child, but maybe he thought I was better off without him. He wrote to me in London after Grandma died, the first letter I'd ever received from him. It was disarming to see his neat cursive writing curling across the page. It wasn't what I'd expected. He told me about his heroin addiction, said he was sorry. He said after everything, I'm still his daughter, that my photo is on his mantelpiece. When I return to Australia, maybe we can get to know each other, he wrote. I sobbed a waterfall of tears.

A small part of me liked what he wrote and for an instant, contemplated getting to know him. Almost immediately, a stronger voice smothered it, a voice that refuses to forgive. A fierce part of me that says no, he does not deserve to know me. I don't know which of these two voices is dark and which is light. Which voice to listen to and which voice to ignore. But for now, I know one thing: he has always believed he loved me and perhaps that was the best he could do.

Settled and content with our new home in the mountains, Gabriel and I fall into a productive, happy phase. It lasts four weeks. Early one afternoon, I'm strolling home from the market with a basket of groceries, when the familiar smell of pot wafts down the steep cobblestone lane. I hear people laughing. Loud music playing.

My heart sinks lower with each step I take towards the apartment and the sight of a ragged bunch of people partying inside is the final blow. I don't know where Gabriel has found them all—probably at the silverwork classes he's been going to—but they're drinking and telling tales of their exploits around the continent, of where they bought the cheapest stones, who they ripped off, what scams they pulled.

I float into the bathroom and find the waste paper bin on fire. Someone has dropped a cigarette into it and the soiled toilet paper is in flames, steadily growing higher and licking the stone wall, rising dangerously close to the curtain. No one has noticed. I calmly walk out to the kitchen, grab a saucepan and fill it with water, walk back into the bathroom and put the fire out.

Smoke rises around me as I look into the bathroom mirror. For a long time, I stare at my face and see how three and a half years in Latin America has etched new lines around my eyes, changed my gaze, darkened my skin. My bones begin to shift and I see a grey coyote staring back at me. Its yellow eyes are saying: you found what you came for. Time to go. Go now, or you will be consumed.

I leave the apartment, find a phone box and call home reverse charges.

'Hi, Mum.'

'Hi, love. I'm glad you rang. Where are you?'

It's so good to hear her voice.

'In a little town called Taxco. It's pretty.'

'Love...'

'Yes?'

'Granky is very sick. They say she has about three months. I don't want you to cut your trip short, but I just wanted to let you know. I know how upset you were when Grandma died and you didn't have a chance to come back.'

'Mum—I'm coming home.'

I hang up, call Qantas and using my emergency credit card, book a return ticket to Australia for the next day. Then, not wanting to return to the revellers, I wander the winding old laneways of Taxco for hours. Finally, as it's getting dark, I return to find everyone passed out. I step over the bodies in the living room, walk into the bedroom and begin to pack my bag.

'Chica, que haces?' Gabriel stumbles into the bedroom, rubbing his eyes.

'I'm going home, just for a little while. My grandma is dying. I have to go home and say goodbye.'

'You're not coming back, are you?' The thought seems to hit him like a hurricane and he falls onto the bed.

'Yes, of course I am. I've booked a ticket with a return date in three months. I'll leave all my stuff here. I'm coming back, I just have to go and see her.'

I tell myself I will come back, because I can't bear the thought of a single day without him. To reassure myself and Gabriel I'm not really leaving for good, I leave behind my books, my CDs, my jewellery and most of my clothes.

'Loca, I'm sorry about the party. It's the last one. I promise.'

'It's okay, you can party as much as you want when I'm gone.'

'But I don't want you to go. I love you so much. You are my soul. When you smile, you have a mixture of happiness, tenderness and sadness in your face. You are the key to my freedom. To my happiness. To my new life. I waited a long time for you. You are my light, my love.'

He grabs me and pulls me onto the bed, holding me tight.

'I love you too,' I say. 'I have always loved you and I will always love you.'

We lie down together, our arms and legs entangled, and cry ourselves to sleep.

The next morning, he walks me to the bus. We're silent as the driver puts my backpack underneath. We fall into each other, as if the space between us simply ceases to exist. He smells like he always has: like home. His dark eyes are on me, willing me to stay.

'No te vayas. *Don't go.*' His voice is barely a whisper. His hands, those beautiful artisan's hands I noticed the first day I met him in Buenos Aires, are trembling.

'It's going to be okay,' I tell him. 'You'll be okay.'

'You're not coming back. Are you?'

'I don't know.'

This is the most honest answer I can give.

'Mi amor, you are my light, my soul, my world,' he says. 'All I want is for you to be happy. So travel well and know you always have my love and my deepest blessings.'

His final gift requires no tools, no silver, no stones. His final gift is to let me go.

We share one last, gentle kiss before I pull away, make myself get on the bus. He stays rooted to the spot, hands in his pockets, jade and amber around his neck, still beautiful. Still the sweet, soulful artisan I fell in love with the second I saw him in a market in San Telmo. He looks fragile standing there, like he's about to shatter. I want to jump off the bus and save him from breaking. I can come back. I will find him, wherever he is, and save him from himself. Help him face his shadow.

Our eyes stay locked until the bus turns a corner and he's gone. I'm tearing, ripping myself in half, but a new strength is rising. I feel it already. My blood is rearranging itself once again.

As the bus nears Mexico City, I see a group of people gathered on the side of a busy road and as the crowd parts, I'm not at all shocked to see a body on the ground. A woman is lying in the street dead and it's the second corpse I've seen here. I think of Juan lying in his open coffin, a peaceful look on his patched-up face, his life over at such a young age.

Time seems to speed up now and I feel a momentum beneath me, propelling me forward. I arrive at the airport, take my passport out of my boot, and tentatively hand the stinking, crumpled blue booklet over to the airline attendant.

'Where are you going today, Miss?'

'Sydney.' I smile at the sound of it.

'You've had quite a journey', she says, flicking through my passport's pages filled with stamps from Argentina to Brazil and Bolivia to Peru, Ecuador, Colombia and all the way up to Mexico. I board the plane, lean my head against the window and close my eyes. Time to rest.

Twenty-one hours later, we are gliding slowly over the Blue Mountains, early in the morning. We are entering Sydney from the west, where I grew up. Small plumes of smoke rise from the eucalypt haze of the mountains and once again, my face is plastered to the plane window. I'm not fascinated, the way I was when I flew into South America over Patagonia. This is different—the profound relief of homecoming. This is a landscape I know intimately, the dry, olive bushland, the tall white eucalypts, the rolling mists. Then we're above the red-tiled roofs of Western Sydney, where I spent the hot summers of my youth dreaming of great adventures.

It's so long since I've been home.

The plane lands and we are instructed to disembark onto the tarmac, so instead of walking directly into the airport, I walk out of the plane and into the morning light. As my feet touch the tarmac, I know I'm not going back. It's as clear to me as the deep blue sky on this bright Sydney morning and any doubts I've had about leaving my love behind, my dreams behind, evaporate. I can feel new dreams bubbling up and the familiar clarity of light comforts me and confirms my decision.

I am in my true home. I am anonymous, unremarkable. Nothing out of the ordinary. Normal.

But for three and a half years, I had another home. It gave me days of silver and stone, nights of music and passion, memories of human kindness and a gushing cascade of creativity. It left new lines in my skin, carved a place so far into my psyche, I'm certain it will never entirely let me go. I dream in Spanish now, and it will take a long time for me to dream in English again.

These memories are part of me, mixed into my blood like emeralds and jade dropped into a crimson lake, sinking deep down to an unreachable place. This is what I will remember. A market in San Telmo, where it all began. The roar of Iguazu Falls, powerful enough to cleanse a million sins. The kaleidoscopic sounds and colours of the Amazon jungle, where everything is moist and moving and alive. The sun-worshippers of Rio, bronzed and beautiful under the watchful eye of Christ the Redeemer. The astounding star-splashed sky of the Bolivian desert. The breathtaking beauty of the Andes that rise up around you and hold you in place, a monumental family of mothers and fathers, grandmothers and grandfathers, all there to make you feel safe, because next to them, you are so small.

And Mexico, the place I called home. The place where I left my first great love behind.

In Frida Kahlo's bedroom is a four-poster bed. Its roof holds a display of butterflies encased in glass. Lying there in agony, she could drift off to sleep gazing at butterflies and maybe, forget her pain. Dream of them with their pretty, fleeting lives that bring joy and lightness of being to the world for a brief time.

The thing about butterflies is they retain their beauty after they die. What we loved about them is still here, in the same way the scent of my grandmother remains in her sheets after she dies. The best parts of the people you once loved stay with you, never fully fading away.

The Caribbean Sea reminds me of the silvery turquoise wings of a butterfly. When I think about my last days in Playa del Carmen, I remember the gentle sunlit sea. I remember colour and light and salt and heat and sweat and sex. I remember sand and salsa, corn chips and Corona, lime and avocado and a beautiful woman dancing naked with a yellow python draped around her shoulders.

And I remember a smooth-skinned artisan who made beautiful things with his hands. He invited me into his world, shared what little he had with me, and showed me how worthy I was of love. All he asked of me was that I love him back.

And for a time, I did.

ACKNOWLEDGEMENTS

Thank you to Rose Allan who mentored me during the writing of this book. I will always be grateful for your expert guidance and encouragement.

To Mary Garden for being such an enthusiastic supporter of my work, my sounding board, my adviser and my coffee buddy. You are a gem.

Thanks to my colleagues at *My Weekly Preview* and *SALT*, particularly Jemma Pearson, Kath Hawkins, Candice Holznagel and Roxanne McCarty-O'Kane for cheering me on.

To my talented friend Carly Head of design house Carly. Co for your creative eye – I can always rely on you for exceptional photography and design work.

To Constance Hall, Denim Cooke and Caitlin O'Reardon for caring about my book and sharing your invaluable feedback.

To Leon Nacson and the late Stuart Wilde— thank you for taking me under your wings, teaching me to take a lighter approach to life, aim high and not take any shit.

Others who believed in me and my writing and encouraged me to keep going: Steven Lang, Faith Baigent and the late Michael Berry. I have great respect for you all.

To Renée Johnson, Ines Vicentin Fraile, Sandra Pablos, my first best friend Jo Clancy (who kept every letter I wrote to her while I lived in South America) and all my friends who have patiently listened to me tell this story.

To my family—Mum, Dad, Romaine, Danny, my cousin Melinda and my mother-in-law, Faye Larkan for your love and support.

Finally, to my late husband Herrin Larkan, who died in May 2020. I am eternally grateful for his unwavering support, encouragement and for understanding why I needed to write this book.

About the Author

Leigh Robshaw is a journalist, freelance writer and editor. Her features and news stories have been published by magazines and newspapers across Australia and internationally. She also contributes to a number of business and lifestyles websites.

She lives in the subtropical hills of Maleny on Australia's east coast with her sons, Jasper and Cohen. This is her first book.

Visit leighrobshaw.net for news and blog updates.

Lightning Source UK Ltd.
Milton Keynes UK
UKHW011826061021
391777UK00001B/169